Table of

~ Welcome & What You'll Learn

Section I: Getting Started with Go — Page No. 4-30

- **Chapter 1:** Introduction to Go: A Quick Overview
- **Chapter 2:** Setting Up Your Go Development Environment
- **Chapter 3:** Go Fundamentals: Syntax, Data Types, and Operators

Section II: Building Blocks of Go Programs — Page No. 31-85

- **Chapter 4:** Working with Variables, Constants, and Control Flow
- **Chapter 5:** Functions: The Backbone of Go Code
- **Chapter 6:** Mastering Go Data Structures: Arrays, Slices, and Maps
- **Chapter 7:** Understanding Structs and Custom Types in Go

Section III: Intermediate Go Concepts — Page No. 86-136

- **Chapter 8:** Pointers and Memory Management in Go
- **Chapter 9:** Error Handling: Gracefully Handling Errors in Go
- **Chapter 10:** Packages: Organizing and Reusing Go Code
- **Chapter 11:** Interfaces: Achieving Polymorphism and Code Flexibility

Section IV: Concurrency in Go — Page No. 137-171

- **Chapter 12:** Introduction to Concurrency and Goroutines
- **Chapter 13:** Synchronization: Channels and Select Statements
- **Chapter 14:** Advanced Concurrency Patterns: Worker Pools, WaitGroups, and Mutexes

Section V: Working with Files and the Web — Page No. 172-218

- **Chapter 15:** File I/O in Go: Reading and Writing to Files
- **Chapter 16:** Building Web Applications with Go's net/http Package
- **Chapter 17:** Web APIs and JSON Handling in Go

Section VI: Advanced Go Techniques — Page No. 219-251

- **Chapter 18:** Generics in Go: Writing Reusable Code
- **Chapter 19:** Testing and Benchmarking in Go
- **Chapter 20:** Best Practices and Optimization Tips for Go Code

Section VII: Building Real-World Applications — Page No. 252-285

- **Chapter 21:** Building a CLI Tool with Go
- **Chapter 22:** Creating a Simple Web Server in Go
- **Chapter 23:** Building a Chat Application with Go

Appendices   Page No. 286-292

- **Appendix A:** Go Syntax Quick Reference
- **Appendix B:** Go Toolchain Reference
- **Appendix C:** Further Learning Resources

~ Conclusion

Welcome & What You'll Learn

Welcome to "Go Programming Mastery: A Deep Dive into Golang!" In the dynamic landscape of programming languages, Go, often referred to as Golang, has emerged as a powerful and efficient contender. Created by Google, Go offers a unique blend of simplicity, performance, and concurrency that has made it a favorite among developers building everything from web servers to cloud infrastructure and distributed systems.

Why Go?

Go's popularity is driven by several key factors:

- **Simplicity:** Go's syntax is clean and easy to learn, even for those new to programming. This allows developers to quickly grasp the language's fundamentals and focus on building applications.
- **Performance:** Go is compiled to machine code, making it incredibly fast. It's designed for modern hardware and can handle heavy workloads with ease.
- **Concurrency:** Go's built-in concurrency model, based on goroutines and channels, makes it remarkably efficient at handling concurrent tasks. This is crucial in today's world of multi-core processors and networked applications.
- **Strong Standard Library:** Go comes with a comprehensive standard library that provides tools for a wide range of tasks, from networking and web development to cryptography and testing.

What You'll Learn

This book is your comprehensive guide to mastering Go programming. It will take you from the basics to advanced techniques, equipping you to build robust and efficient applications. Here's a glimpse of what you'll learn:

- **Section I: Getting Started with Go** You'll get a quick overview of Go and set up your development environment. You'll then dive into the fundamentals of Go syntax, data types, and operators.
- **Section II: Building Blocks of Go Programs** You'll learn how to work with variables, constants, control flow, functions, and the essential data structures (arrays, slices, maps, and structs) that form the foundation of Go programs.
- **Section III: Intermediate Go Concepts** You'll explore intermediate-level topics like pointers, error handling, packages, and interfaces. These concepts are crucial for writing well-structured and maintainable Go code.
- **Section IV: Concurrency in Go** You'll unlock Go's superpower: concurrency. You'll understand goroutines, channels, and synchronization techniques that enable you to write highly concurrent programs.
- **Section V: Working with Files and the Web** You'll discover how to work with files, build web applications using Go's `net/http` package, interact with web APIs, and handle JSON data.
- **Section VI: Advanced Go Techniques** You'll delve into advanced topics like generics, testing, benchmarking, and best practices to elevate your Go skills.
- **Section VII: Building Real-World Applications** You'll apply your knowledge to build real-world projects like a command-line tool, a web server, and a chat application.

By the end of this book, you'll have a solid understanding of Go's core concepts and be well-prepared to tackle a wide range of projects. Whether you're interested in web development, cloud computing, DevOps, or simply want to add a powerful tool to your programming arsenal, Go is a language worth learning. So, let's dive in and embark on this exciting journey into the world of Go programming!

Section I:
Getting Started with Go

Introduction to Go: A Quick Overview

Outline

- What is Go?
- Why Go?
- Go's Key Features
- Go's Use Cases
- Chapter Summary

What is Go?

Go, often referred to as Golang, is a modern, open-source programming language developed at Google in 2007 by Robert Griesemer, Rob Pike, and Ken Thompson. It was officially released in 2009 and has since gained immense popularity for its simplicity, performance, and concurrency capabilities.

Go was born out of frustration with the complexities and limitations of existing languages for building large-scale software systems at Google. The creators sought a language that could combine the ease of use and productivity of languages like Python with the performance and efficiency of languages like C++. The result was Go, a language designed to tackle the challenges of modern software development:

- **Scalability:** Go's lightweight concurrency model, based on goroutines and channels, makes it well-suited for building scalable applications that can handle massive workloads and concurrent operations.
- **Efficiency:** Go is compiled to machine code, resulting in fast and efficient execution. Its efficient memory management and garbage collection further contribute to its performance.
- **Simplicity:** Go's syntax is clean and minimalistic, making it easy to learn and understand. It prioritizes readability and maintainability, leading to more productive development cycles.
- **Modern Tooling:** Go comes with a comprehensive set of tools for building, testing, and debugging applications. These tools streamline the development process and promote best practices.
- **Strong Standard Library:** Go's standard library offers a wide range of packages for common tasks like networking, file I/O, cryptography, and web development, reducing the need for external dependencies.
- **Cross-Platform Compatibility:** Go programs can be compiled to run on various operating systems and architectures, making them portable and easy to deploy.

By addressing these challenges, Go empowers developers to build robust, high-performance applications that can scale to meet the demands of modern software systems. Whether you're building web servers, cloud infrastructure, network services, or distributed systems, Go provides the tools and features to simplify the process and deliver efficient solutions.

Why Go?

Go's rapid ascent in popularity among developers can be attributed to a combination of compelling strengths that address the needs of modern software development:

1. **Simplicity and Readability:**
    - Go's syntax is intentionally designed to be clean, concise, and easy to grasp. This reduces the learning curve, allowing developers to become productive quickly.
    - The language emphasizes readability and avoids unnecessary complexity, making code easier to understand and maintain, even in large projects.
2. **Performance and Efficiency:**
    - Go is a compiled language, meaning it translates source code directly into machine code. This results in highly performant applications that can rival languages like C and C++ in terms of speed.
    - Go's efficient memory management and garbage collection further enhance its performance by automatically handling memory allocation and deallocation, reducing the risk of memory leaks and improving runtime efficiency.
3. **Concurrency:**
    - Go's built-in concurrency model, based on goroutines and channels, is a standout feature. Goroutines are lightweight threads that enable concurrent execution of tasks, while channels provide a safe and efficient way for goroutines to communicate and synchronize.
    - This concurrency model simplifies the development of highly concurrent and scalable applications, making Go well-suited for tasks like network programming, web servers, and distributed systems.
4. **Strong Standard Library:**
    - Go boasts a comprehensive standard library that offers a rich set of packages for various functionalities, including networking, file I/O, cryptography, testing, and more.
    - This robust standard library minimizes the need for external dependencies, making Go applications more self-contained and easier to deploy.
5. **Garbage Collection:**
    - Go's automatic garbage collection relieves developers from manual memory management. This simplifies development and reduces the risk of memory-related errors, leading to more reliable software.
    - While garbage collection introduces some overhead, Go's implementation is efficient and has minimal impact on overall performance.
6. **Cross-Platform Compatibility:**
    - Go's compiler generates native executables for a wide range of operating systems and architectures. This means you can write Go code once and easily deploy it on different platforms, from Windows and macOS to Linux and various cloud environments.
    - Cross-platform compatibility simplifies the deployment process and broadens the reach of Go applications.
7. **Growing Community and Ecosystem:**
    - Go has a vibrant and growing community of developers who contribute to its ecosystem by creating libraries, frameworks, and tools.
    - This active community provides valuable resources for learning, troubleshooting, and staying up-to-date with the latest developments in the Go world.

These strengths collectively make Go a versatile language suitable for a wide range of applications. Its simplicity and performance make it ideal for beginners and experienced developers alike. Its concurrency model and strong standard library make it a top choice for building scalable network services, web applications, and cloud infrastructure. Additionally, its cross-platform compatibility and growing community ensure that Go remains a relevant and adaptable language for the future of software development.

Go's Key Features

Simplicity and Readability

Go's syntax is intentionally designed to be clean, minimalistic, and easy to grasp. This simplicity is a deliberate choice made by its creators to prioritize readability and maintainability. Unlike some languages with complex syntax and verbose code structures, Go opts for a more straightforward approach.

Here's how Go's simplicity contributes to its readability and ease of learning:

1. **Minimalistic Syntax:** Go has a relatively small set of keywords and built-in constructs. This means there are fewer concepts to learn, and the language avoids unnecessary features that might lead to confusion.
2. **Explicitness:** Go favors explicitness over implicitness. This means that code is more straightforward and easier to understand because it doesn't rely on hidden behaviors or magic.
3. **Consistent Formatting:** Go enforces a standard code formatting style using the gofmt tool. This eliminates debates about code style and ensures that all Go code looks consistent, making it easier to read and navigate.
4. **Reduced Boilerplate:** Go avoids excessive boilerplate code, which is repetitive code that doesn't add much value. This allows developers to express their ideas more concisely and focus on the core logic of their programs.
5. **Opinionated Design:** Go has a strong opinion on how code should be structured and organized. This opinionated approach reduces the number of choices developers need to make, leading to more consistent codebases.

By prioritizing simplicity and readability, Go reduces the cognitive load on developers. This makes it easier for newcomers to learn the language and for experienced developers to understand and maintain codebases. Instead of wrestling with complex syntax and obscure features, developers can focus on solving problems and building applications.

Go's simplicity doesn't mean it's lacking in expressive power. It strikes a balance between simplicity and functionality, providing the necessary tools to build complex software systems while maintaining a clean and readable codebase. This approach has made Go a popular choice for projects where code maintainability and developer productivity are paramount.

Performance and Efficiency

Go's performance and efficiency are among its most compelling features, making it a preferred choice for applications where speed and resource utilization are critical. This performance advantage is achieved through a combination of factors:

1. **Compilation to Machine Code:**
   - Unlike interpreted languages that execute code line by line at runtime, Go is compiled directly into machine code. This means that the Go compiler translates the source code into instructions that the computer's processor can understand and execute directly.
   - Compilation to machine code eliminates the overhead of interpretation, resulting in faster execution speeds. Go programs typically perform on par with those written in languages like C and C++, known for their performance.
2. **Efficient Memory Management:**
   - Go employs a sophisticated memory management system that minimizes memory usage and reduces the likelihood of memory-related errors.
   - Go's memory allocator is designed to be fast and efficient, minimizing the time spent allocating and deallocating memory, which is a common bottleneck in many applications.
3. **Garbage Collection:**
   - Go features automatic garbage collection (GC), a mechanism that automatically identifies and reclaims memory that is no longer in use by the program.
   - This relieves developers from the burden of manual memory management, reducing the risk of memory leaks and improving developer productivity.

- Go's garbage collector is designed to be concurrent and efficient, minimizing the impact on application performance. It operates in the background, periodically cleaning up unused memory without causing significant pauses in the program's execution.

The combination of compilation to machine code, efficient memory management, and garbage collection makes Go an excellent choice for building high-performance applications that need to handle heavy workloads and utilize system resources effectively. Whether you're building web servers, data processing pipelines, or real-time applications, Go's performance characteristics can significantly enhance the responsiveness and scalability of your software.

Concurrency

Concurrency is a hallmark of Go, setting it apart from many other programming languages. It's a core feature that allows Go programs to efficiently execute multiple tasks simultaneously, making it well-suited for modern multi-core processors and networked environments. Go's concurrency model is built upon two fundamental concepts: goroutines and channels.

Goroutines: Lightweight Threads

- At the heart of Go's concurrency lies the concept of goroutines. Goroutines are lightweight threads managed by the Go runtime. Unlike traditional operating system threads, which are relatively heavyweight and resource-intensive, goroutines are inexpensive to create and manage.
- You can think of goroutines as functions or methods that run concurrently with other goroutines. Spawning a goroutine is as simple as prefixing a function call with the go keyword. For example:

```
go myFunction() // Starts myFunction as a goroutine
```

- The Go runtime efficiently schedules goroutines across available processor cores, enabling true parallelism. This means that multiple goroutines can execute simultaneously on different cores, maximizing the utilization of your hardware.
- The lightweight nature of goroutines allows you to create thousands or even millions of them within a single Go program, making it possible to handle massive workloads and concurrent operations without overwhelming system resources.

Channels: Communication and Synchronization

- While goroutines provide the means to execute tasks concurrently, channels provide the mechanism for goroutines to communicate and synchronize with each other.
- A channel is a typed conduit through which goroutines can send and receive values. You can create a channel using the make function, specifying the type of data it will carry. For example:

```
ch := make(chan int) // Creates a channel for integers
```

- Goroutines can send values to a channel using the ch <- value syntax, and receive values from a channel using the value := <- ch syntax.
- Channels are inherently blocking. This means that if a goroutine tries to send a value to a channel that is already full, it will block until space becomes available. Similarly, if a goroutine tries to receive a value from an empty channel, it will block until a value is sent.
- This blocking behavior provides a powerful mechanism for synchronization. Goroutines can coordinate their activities by waiting for specific signals or data to become available through channels.

The Power of Goroutines and Channels

The combination of goroutines and channels allows you to build highly concurrent and scalable applications in Go. You can break down complex tasks into smaller, independent units of work (goroutines) that can execute concurrently. Channels enable these goroutines to communicate results, exchange data, and synchronize their actions, ensuring the correct flow of information and preventing race conditions.

Go's concurrency model is not only powerful but also relatively easy to use. The language handles much of the complexity of thread management and synchronization, allowing developers to focus on the logic of their programs. This makes Go an excellent choice for building concurrent applications, from network servers and web crawlers to parallel data processing pipelines and real-time systems.

Strong Standard Library

One of Go's standout strengths is its comprehensive and well-designed standard library. This library is a treasure trove of packages that provide ready-to-use functionalities for a wide range of tasks, making it a valuable asset for developers.

Key Features of Go's Standard Library:

1. **Comprehensive Coverage:** The standard library covers a vast array of domains, including:
    - **Networking:** Packages like `net` and `net/http` provide tools for building network applications, handling TCP/UDP connections, creating web servers, and interacting with APIs.
    - **File I/O:** Packages like `os` and `io` offer functionalities for reading from and writing to files, working with directories, and handling file paths.
    - **Cryptography:** Packages like `crypto` and `crypto/tls` provide secure communication protocols and cryptographic algorithms for data encryption and security.
    - **Testing:** Packages like `testing` and `testing/quick` enable unit testing, benchmarking, and code coverage analysis to ensure the quality and correctness of Go programs.
    - **Data Structures and Algorithms:** Packages like `container` and `sort` provide implementations of common data structures like lists, stacks, queues, and sorting algorithms.
    - **Text Processing:** Packages like `strings`, `regexp`, and `encoding/json` offer tools for manipulating strings, working with regular expressions, and handling JSON data.
    - **And much more:** The standard library also includes packages for image manipulation, time and date handling, compression, archiving, and many other tasks.
2. **High Quality and Reliability:** The packages in the standard library are meticulously crafted, well-documented, and thoroughly tested. They adhere to Go's idiomatic style and best practices, making them reliable and easy to integrate into your projects.
3. **Promotes Code Reusability:** The standard library encourages code reusability by providing pre-built solutions for common tasks. This means you don't have to reinvent the wheel for every project. You can simply import the relevant packages and leverage their functionalities.
4. **Reduces External Dependencies:** By relying on the standard library, you can minimize your project's dependence on external third-party libraries. This reduces the risk of compatibility issues and simplifies the management of your project's dependencies.

Benefits of a Strong Standard Library:

- **Faster Development:** The availability of pre-built solutions in the standard library accelerates development cycles. You can quickly prototype and build applications without having to write everything from scratch.
- **Improved Maintainability:** Using standard library packages enhances code maintainability. These packages are well-tested and maintained, reducing the risk of bugs and security vulnerabilities.
- **Easier Collaboration:** When working in teams, using standard library packages ensures a common foundation and understanding among developers. This simplifies collaboration and code review processes.

- **Consistency and Idiomatic Style:** The standard library reinforces Go's idiomatic style and best practices. This leads to more consistent and readable codebases, making it easier for developers to understand and contribute to projects.

Go's strong standard library is a testament to its philosophy of simplicity and practicality. It empowers developers with a rich set of tools and functionalities, enabling them to build robust and efficient applications without the need to rely heavily on external libraries. This contributes to Go's appeal as a language for building large-scale, reliable, and maintainable software systems.

Garbage Collection

Go's automatic memory management through garbage collection (GC) is a significant feature that simplifies development and enhances the reliability of Go programs. It relieves developers of the burden of manual memory management, a task that can be error-prone and time-consuming.

How Go's Garbage Collection Works:

1. **Memory Allocation:** When a Go program needs to store data in memory, it requests memory from the Go runtime. The runtime allocates a block of memory to hold the data.
2. **Object Tracking:** The Go runtime keeps track of all the objects (variables, data structures, etc.) that are currently in use by the program. It maintains a set of references to these objects.
3. **Garbage Collection Cycle:** Periodically, the garbage collector initiates a cycle to identify and reclaim memory that is no longer in use.
   - The garbage collector starts by identifying the root objects, which are objects directly referenced by the program's main execution context (e.g., global variables, function parameters, and local variables on the call stack).
   - From the root objects, the garbage collector follows references to other objects, marking them as reachable. This process continues recursively, creating a graph of reachable objects.
   - Any objects that are not reachable from the root objects are considered garbage, as they are no longer in use by the program.
4. **Memory Reclamation:** Once the garbage collector has identified all the garbage objects, it reclaims the memory occupied by these objects. The reclaimed memory is then made available for future allocations.

Benefits of Garbage Collection in Go:

- **Simplified Memory Management:** Developers don't need to explicitly allocate and deallocate memory for every object they create. The garbage collector takes care of this automatically, reducing the risk of memory leaks and dangling pointers.
- **Improved Developer Productivity:** Developers can focus on writing the core logic of their programs without worrying about the intricacies of memory management. This leads to faster development cycles and more productive development experiences.
- **Enhanced Reliability:** Garbage collection helps prevent memory-related errors like double frees and use-after-free bugs. This results in more reliable and stable software.
- **Concurrent and Efficient:** Go's garbage collector is designed to be concurrent, meaning it runs in parallel with the main program, minimizing the impact on application performance. It also employs efficient algorithms to identify and reclaim unused memory quickly.

Considerations with Garbage Collection:

- **Overhead:** Garbage collection does introduce some runtime overhead. However, Go's garbage collector is highly optimized and its impact on performance is usually minimal.
- **Pause Times:** During a garbage collection cycle, the program might experience a brief pause while the collector does its work. Go's garbage collector is designed to minimize these pause times, but they can still be a factor in real-time applications.

- **Tuning:** Go provides options for tuning the garbage collector's behavior to optimize it for specific workloads. This can help fine-tune performance in scenarios where garbage collection overhead is a concern.

In summary, Go's garbage collection is a powerful feature that simplifies memory management, improves developer productivity, and enhances the reliability of Go programs. By automating memory allocation and deallocation, it frees developers to focus on solving problems and building robust applications. While garbage collection does introduce some overhead, its benefits often outweigh the costs, making it a valuable tool in the Go developer's arsenal.

Cross-Platform Compatibility

Go's cross-platform compatibility is a significant advantage that simplifies the deployment and distribution of Go applications. It enables you to write code once and run it on a wide range of operating systems and computer architectures without major modifications.

How Go Achieves Cross-Platform Compatibility:

1. **Compilation to Machine Code:** Unlike interpreted languages that require an interpreter to execute code on each platform, Go is compiled directly into machine code. This means that the Go compiler translates your source code into instructions that are specific to the target operating system and architecture.
2. **Standardized Build Process:** Go has a standardized build process that produces executable binaries for different platforms. You can use the `go build` command to create executables for Windows, macOS, Linux, and various other operating systems, as well as different processor architectures like x86, ARM, and others.
3. **Go Toolchain:** The Go toolchain, which includes the compiler, linker, and other tools, is designed to be portable. This means that you can install and use the Go toolchain on different operating systems, allowing you to build Go applications on your preferred development environment.
4. **Standard Library:** Go's standard library is designed to be platform-agnostic, meaning that most of its packages work seamlessly across different operating systems. This ensures that the core functionalities of your Go applications are consistent regardless of the platform they run on.

Benefits of Cross-Platform Compatibility:

- **Simplified Deployment:** Cross-platform compatibility eliminates the need to maintain separate codebases for different platforms. You can build a single Go application and deploy it on multiple operating systems, reducing development and maintenance efforts.
- **Wider Reach:** By supporting multiple platforms, Go applications can reach a broader audience. You can distribute your software to users on different operating systems without having to rewrite or adapt your code.
- **Easier Testing:** You can test your Go applications on various platforms during development, ensuring that they behave consistently across different environments.
- **Cloud-Native Development:** Go's cross-platform nature aligns well with cloud-native development principles, where applications are often deployed in containerized environments that can run on diverse infrastructures.

Example:

Let's say you've developed a Go application for data processing. You can use the `go build` command to create executable binaries for Windows, macOS, and Linux. You can then distribute these binaries to users on those platforms, and they can run the application directly without needing to install Go or any additional dependencies.

Go's cross-platform compatibility is a powerful feature that simplifies development, deployment, and distribution of applications. It allows you to reach a wider audience and focus on building software that works seamlessly across different environments.

Growing Community and Ecosystem

Go boasts a vibrant and expanding community of developers who are passionate about the language and actively contribute to its growth. This community plays a crucial role in Go's success and provides numerous benefits to developers:

Active and Supportive Community:

- Go's community is known for its friendliness, inclusivity, and willingness to help newcomers. Online forums, discussion groups, and social media platforms provide avenues for developers to ask questions, share knowledge, and collaborate on projects.
- The Go team at Google actively engages with the community, listens to feedback, and incorporates suggestions into the language's development. This open communication fosters a sense of collaboration and ensures that Go evolves to meet the needs of its users.

Thriving Ecosystem of Libraries and Frameworks:

- The Go ecosystem has seen a significant increase in the number of libraries and frameworks available for various purposes. These libraries and frameworks simplify development by providing pre-built solutions for common tasks, such as web development, database access, logging, testing, and more.
- Popular Go libraries include:
    - **Gin:** A high-performance web framework known for its simplicity and speed.
    - **GORM:** An ORM (Object-Relational Mapping) library that simplifies database interactions.
    - **Gorilla WebSocket:** A library for building real-time applications with WebSockets.
    - **logrus:** A structured logging library that makes it easier to manage logs.
- This rich ecosystem of libraries and frameworks accelerates development, reduces the need to reinvent the wheel, and allows developers to focus on the unique aspects of their applications.

Contributions to Go's Evolution:

- The community actively contributes to Go's evolution through:
    - **Proposals and Discussions:** Community members propose new language features, improvements, and changes through the Go proposal process. These proposals are thoroughly discussed and evaluated by the Go team and the community.
    - **Open-Source Contributions:** Developers contribute to Go's core development by submitting bug fixes, performance enhancements, and new features.
    - **Tool and Library Development:** The community creates and maintains a wide range of tools and libraries that complement the standard library and extend Go's capabilities.

The growing community and ecosystem surrounding Go are a testament to its popularity and potential. This active community not only contributes to the language's development but also provides a wealth of resources and support for developers at all levels. Whether you're a beginner just starting with Go or an experienced developer tackling complex projects, the Go community is there to help you succeed.

Go's Use Cases

Go's unique blend of simplicity, performance, concurrency, and strong standard library makes it a versatile language well-suited for a wide array of real-world applications across various domains:

1. **Web Servers and APIs:**

- Go's `net/http` package and its ecosystem of web frameworks (like Gin, Echo, and Beego) enable the rapid development of high-performance web servers and APIs.
- **Examples:**
  - **Google:** Uses Go extensively for various backend services and APIs.
  - **Dropbox:** Migrated some of its performance-critical backend services to Go.
  - **Netflix:** Employs Go in its server architecture for content delivery.

2. **Cloud Infrastructure and Microservices:**
   - Go's lightweight concurrency and efficient resource utilization make it ideal for building scalable cloud infrastructure and microservices.
   - **Examples:**
     - **Docker:** The core of the Docker containerization platform is written in Go.
     - **Kubernetes:** The popular container orchestration system relies heavily on Go.
     - **Hashicorp:** The company behind tools like Terraform and Vault uses Go extensively.

3. **DevOps Tools:**
   - Go's speed, cross-platform compatibility, and strong standard library make it a great choice for creating DevOps tools for automation, monitoring, and infrastructure management.
   - **Examples:**
     - **InfluxDB:** A time-series database used for monitoring and observability.
     - **Prometheus:** A popular open-source monitoring and alerting toolkit.
     - **Grafana:** A widely used observability platform for visualizing metrics and logs.

4. **Network Services:**
   - Go's networking capabilities and concurrency model make it ideal for building network services like proxies, load balancers, API gateways, and messaging systems.
   - **Examples:**
     - **Etcd:** A distributed key-value store used for configuration management and service discovery.
     - **Consul:** A service mesh solution providing service discovery, configuration, and segmentation.
     - **Traefik:** A modern reverse proxy and load balancer designed for microservices.

5. **Distributed Systems:**
   - Go's concurrency primitives and support for distributed communication protocols like gRPC make it well-suited for building distributed systems that can scale across multiple machines.
   - **Examples:**
     - **CockroachDB:** A distributed SQL database designed for scalability and resilience.
     - **TiDB:** A distributed NewSQL database that offers high scalability and availability.
     - **Dapr:** A distributed application runtime that simplifies building microservices.

6. **Command-Line Tools:**
   - Go's simplicity and cross-platform compatibility make it an excellent choice for developing command-line tools for various purposes.
   - **Examples:**
     - **Hugo:** A static site generator used for building websites and blogs.
     - **Cobra:** A library for creating powerful command-line interfaces (CLIs).
     - **GoFmt:** The official Go code formatter, used to maintain consistent code style.

7. **Data Pipelines and Processing:**
   - Go's performance and concurrency make it suitable for building data pipelines and processing systems that need to handle large volumes of data in real time.
   - **Examples:**
     - **Kafka:** A distributed streaming platform used for building real-time data pipelines.
     - **NATS:** A simple and high-performance messaging system.
     - **BigQuery:** Google's serverless data warehouse utilizes Go for some of its components.

This is just a glimpse of Go's diverse use cases. Its versatility and ability to address modern software development challenges have led to its adoption by a wide range of companies and projects, including startups, tech giants, and open-source initiatives. As Go continues to evolve and its ecosystem expands, its potential applications are only expected to grow, solidifying its position as a powerful and relevant language for the future.

Chapter Summary

In this chapter, we've taken a whirlwind tour of Go, exploring its origins, motivations, and key features. We've seen how Go's simplicity, performance, concurrency, and strong standard library make it a compelling choice for a wide range of applications. We've also discussed its growing community and ecosystem, which contribute to its evolution and provide valuable resources for developers.

As you embark on your journey to master Go programming, remember that this chapter is just the beginning. The following chapters will delve deeper into the language's syntax, data types, control flow, functions, data structures, and more. You'll learn how to harness Go's concurrency model, build web applications, work with files and networks, and apply advanced techniques to create robust and efficient software.

With its unique blend of simplicity, power, and versatility, Go is a language that empowers developers to build the next generation of software systems. Whether you're a beginner or an experienced programmer, Go has something to offer. So, let's dive in and explore the exciting world of Go programming!

Setting Up Your Go Development Environment

Outline

- Installing Go
- Choosing a Code Editor or IDE
- Understanding the Go Workspace
- Exploring Go Tools
- Hello, World! Your First Go Program
- Chapter Summary

Installing Go

To embark on your Go programming journey, the first step is to install Go on your system. Fortunately, Go is available for a wide range of operating systems, including Windows, macOS, and Linux. This section provides step-by-step instructions on how to download and install Go on each of these platforms.

1. Downloading Go

The official Go website (https://golang.org/dl/) is the best place to obtain the latest Go installation package. Head over to the website and select the appropriate installer for your operating system.

- **Windows:** Download the MSI installer (e.g., `go1.20.windows-amd64.msi`).
- **macOS:** Download the PKG installer (e.g., `go1.20.darwin-amd64.pkg`).
- **Linux:** Download the TAR.GZ archive (e.g., `go1.20.linux-amd64.tar.gz`).

2. Installing Go on Windows

- Double-click the downloaded MSI installer.
- Follow the on-screen instructions, accepting the default settings.
- The installer will typically place Go in the `C:\Go` directory.

3. Installing Go on macOS

- Double-click the downloaded PKG installer.
- Follow the on-screen instructions, accepting the default settings.
- The installer will typically place Go in the `/usr/local/go` directory.

4. Installing Go on Linux

- Open a terminal.
- Extract the TAR.GZ archive to the `/usr/local` directory using the following command:

    ```
    sudo tar -C /usr/local -xzf go1.20.linux-amd64.tar.gz
    ```

- This will create a go directory inside `/usr/local`.

5. Setting Environment Variables (All Platforms)

After installing Go, you need to set two environment variables:

- **GOROOT:** This variable points to the location where Go is installed (e.g., `C:\Go` on Windows or `/usr/local/go` on macOS and Linux).

- **GOPATH:** This variable specifies the location of your Go workspace (discussed in the next section). By default, you can set it to a directory like ~/go (or %USERPROFILE%\go on Windows).

To set these variables:

- **Windows:**
  - Right-click on "This PC" and select "Properties."
  - Click on "Advanced system settings."
  - Click on "Environment Variables."
  - Under "System variables," click "New" and add GOROOT and GOPATH.
  - Edit the "Path" variable under "System variables" and add %GOROOT%\bin to the end.
- **macOS and Linux:**
  - Edit your shell profile file (e.g., ~/.bash_profile, ~/.bashrc, or ~/.zshrc).
  - Add the following lines (replace with your actual Go installation path):

    ```
    export GOROOT=/usr/local/go
    export GOPATH=$HOME/go
    export PATH=$PATH:$GOROOT/bin
    ```

  - Save the file and source it (source ~/.bash_profile).

6. Verifying the Installation

Open a new terminal window and type the following command:

```
go version
```

You should see output similar to this:

```
go version go1.20 darwin/amd64
```

This indicates that Go is installed correctly, and you're ready to start coding!

Choosing a Code Editor or IDE

Selecting the right code editor or Integrated Development Environment (IDE) is crucial for a productive and enjoyable Go development experience. Fortunately, there are several excellent options available, each with its own strengths and features. Let's explore some popular choices:

1. Visual Studio Code (VS Code)

- **Free and Open Source:** VS Code is a free, open-source code editor developed by Microsoft. It's lightweight, fast, and highly customizable.
- **Rich Extension Ecosystem:** VS Code boasts a vast library of extensions, including the official Go extension, which provides essential features like code completion, linting, debugging, and code navigation.
- **Cross-Platform:** VS Code is available for Windows, macOS, and Linux, making it a versatile choice for developers.
- **Ideal for Beginners:** VS Code's intuitive interface and extensive documentation make it an excellent choice for beginners who are new to Go development.

2. GoLand

- **Powerful Go IDE:** Developed by JetBrains, GoLand is a full-featured IDE specifically designed for Go development. It offers advanced code analysis, refactoring tools, integrated testing, and debugging capabilities.

- **Intelligent Code Completion:** GoLand's code completion is highly intelligent, suggesting relevant code snippets and automatically importing necessary packages.
- **Ergonomic Design:** GoLand's interface is designed for productivity, with features like code navigation, quick fixes, and project management tools readily available.
- **Suited for Experienced Developers:** GoLand's comprehensive feature set and advanced tools make it an excellent choice for experienced Go developers who demand a powerful IDE.

3. Sublime Text

- **Lightweight and Fast:** Sublime Text is a popular code editor known for its speed and minimalist design. It's highly customizable and extensible through packages.
- **GoSublime Package:** The GoSublime package provides Go-specific features like code completion, linting, and build systems.
- **Good for Minimalists:** Sublime Text is a great option for developers who prefer a lightweight and customizable editor without the overhead of a full-fledged IDE.

Choosing the Right Tool for You

The best code editor or IDE for you depends on your personal preferences, experience level, and the specific requirements of your project. Consider the following factors:

- **Ease of Use:** If you're a beginner, VS Code's intuitive interface and extensive documentation might be a good starting point.
- **Features:** GoLand offers the most comprehensive set of features, making it ideal for complex projects and experienced developers.
- **Performance:** Sublime Text is known for its speed and responsiveness, making it a good choice for those who prioritize performance.
- **Customizability:** Both VS Code and Sublime Text are highly customizable, allowing you to tailor them to your workflow.

Ultimately, the best way to choose is to try out different options and see which one feels most comfortable and productive for you. Regardless of your choice, make sure to install the necessary Go extensions or packages to enhance your development experience.

Understanding the Go Workspace

The Go workspace is a structured directory on your file system that serves as the central hub for your Go development projects. It provides a standardized way to organize your source code, compiled packages, and executable binaries. Understanding the Go workspace is essential for managing Go projects effectively.

Directory Structure

A Go workspace typically has the following three subdirectories:

1. `src` **(Source):** This directory contains your Go source code files. You'll organize your code into packages (each package is a directory containing `.go` files) within this directory. For example, a project named `myproject` would have its source code in the `src/myproject` directory.
2. `pkg` **(Package Objects):** When you build your Go packages, the compiled package objects (`.a` files on most systems) are stored in the `pkg` directory. These package objects can be reused by other Go projects, speeding up compilation times. The `pkg` directory is further organized by operating system and architecture (e.g., `pkg/darwin_amd64`, `pkg/windows_amd64`).
3. `bin` **(Binaries):** This directory is where the executable binaries generated by `go install` are placed. These binaries can be run from your terminal without needing to specify their full path.

The GOPATH Environment Variable

The GOPATH environment variable is crucial for the Go toolchain to function correctly. It points to the root directory of your Go workspace. The Go tools use GOPATH to find your source code, packages, and binaries.

- **Setting GOPATH:** You can set the GOPATH environment variable as described in the previous section on installing Go. By default, you can set it to a directory like ~/go (or %USERPROFILE%\go on Windows).
- **Multiple Workspaces:** You can have multiple Go workspaces by setting GOPATH to a colon-separated list of directories (e.g., GOPATH=/path/to/workspace1:/path/to/workspace2). However, it's generally recommended to have a single workspace for simplicity.

Creating and Managing Go Projects

Let's see how to create and manage Go projects within the workspace:

1. **Creating a Project:**
   - Choose a directory within your src directory to hold your project. Let's call it myproject.
   - Inside the myproject directory, create your Go source code files (e.g., main.go).
2. **Building and Installing:**
   - Open a terminal and navigate to the myproject directory.
   - Run go build to compile your source code. This will create an executable binary in the current directory.
   - Run go install to compile and install your package. This will place the executable binary in the bin directory of your workspace.
3. **Running the Binary:**
   - Since the binary is now in your PATH, you can simply type myproject in the terminal to run it.

Example Project Structure:

```
GOPATH/
├── bin/
│   └── myproject (executable)
├── pkg/
│   └── <os_arch>/
│       └── myproject.a (package object)
└── src/
    └── myproject/
        ├── main.go
        ├── utils.go
        └── ... (other source files)
```

Important Note: In Go 1.11 and later, Go modules have become the preferred way to manage dependencies and build Go projects. Modules offer a more flexible and decentralized approach than the traditional GOPATH workspace. While GOPATH is still supported, it's recommended to learn and adopt Go modules for new projects. However, understanding the GOPATH workspace is still valuable, especially when working with older projects or legacy codebases.

Exploring Go Tools

Go comes bundled with a powerful set of command-line tools that streamline the development, testing, and documentation of your Go projects. These tools are essential for every Go developer and understanding how to use them effectively will significantly enhance your workflow.

go build

The `go build` command is used to compile your Go source code into executable binaries. It takes one or more file names as arguments, which can be either individual .go files or package names.

Example:

```
go build main.go # Compiles main.go and produces an executable named main (or main.exe on Windows)
go build ./mypackage # Compiles the mypackage package
```

Explanation:

- `go build` analyzes your source code, checks for errors, and compiles it into machine code.
- By default, it produces an executable binary with the same name as the package or file you specified.
- You can use the -o flag to specify a different output file name (e.g., `go build -o myapp main.go`).

go run

The `go run` command is a convenient way to compile and run Go programs directly without creating separate executable files. It's particularly useful for quick testing and experimentation.

Example:

```
go run main.go # Compiles and runs main.go
```

Explanation:

- `go run` combines the compilation and execution steps into a single command.
- It's ideal for small scripts or programs that you want to run quickly without generating binaries.

go get

The `go get` command is used to download and install Go packages from remote repositories like GitHub. It automatically fetches the package's source code, resolves its dependencies, and installs it in your Go workspace.

Example:

```
go get github.com/gin-gonic/gin # Downloads and installs the Gin web framework
```

Explanation:

- `go get` downloads the package's source code and places it in the `src` directory of your workspace.
- It also downloads and installs any dependencies that the package requires.
- You can use the -u flag to update an already installed package to its latest version.

go test

The go test command is used to run tests for your Go packages. It automatically discovers test functions (functions that start with Test and take a *testing.T argument) and executes them.

Example:

```
go test ./mypackage # Runs tests for the mypackage package
```

Explanation:

- go test compiles your test code and runs the test functions.
- It reports the results of the tests, including whether they passed or failed.
- You can use the -v flag to get more verbose output, including details about each test case.

go doc

The go doc command provides access to Go's extensive documentation from the command line. You can use it to view documentation for packages, types, functions, and methods.

Example:

```
go doc fmt.Println # Shows documentation for the fmt.Println function
go doc net/http # Shows documentation for the net/http package
```

Explanation:

- go doc fetches the documentation from your local Go installation or from online sources if necessary.
- It presents the documentation in a clear and readable format in your terminal.
- You can use the -all flag to view the complete documentation for a package, including private members.

These Go tools are indispensable for any Go developer. By mastering their usage, you can streamline your workflow, ensure code quality, and leverage Go's rich documentation to write efficient and reliable applications.

Hello, World! Your First Go Program

It's time to write your very first Go program! As is tradition in the programming world, we'll start with the classic "Hello, World!" example. This simple program will introduce you to the basic structure of a Go program and demonstrate how to print output to the console.

Creating the Program

1. **Open Your Code Editor:** Launch your chosen code editor or IDE.
2. **Create a New File:** Create a new file and save it as main.go. The .go extension is the standard for Go source code files.
3. **Write the Code:** Enter the following code into your main.go file:

   ```
   package main

   import "fmt"

   func main() {
       fmt.Println("Hello, World!")
   }
   ```

Understanding the Code

Let's break down this simple program:

- `package main`: This line declares that this file belongs to the `main` package. In Go, every program must start with a `main` package, and the `main` package must contain a `main` function.
- `import "fmt"`: This line imports the `fmt` package, which provides formatting and output functions. We'll use the `Println` function from this package to print our message.
- `func main() { ... }`: This defines the `main` function, which is the entry point of every Go program. The code inside the curly braces `{}` will be executed when the program runs.
- `fmt.Println("Hello, World!")`: This line calls the `Println` function from the `fmt` package. It takes a string argument (`"Hello, World!"`) and prints it to the console, followed by a newline character.

Running the Program

1. **Open Your Terminal:** Open a terminal or command prompt.
2. **Navigate to Your Project:** Use the `cd` command to navigate to the directory where you saved `main.go`.
3. **Run the Program:** Type the following command and press Enter:

```
go run main.go
```

Output:

You should see the following output in your terminal:

Hello, World!

Congratulations! You've just written and run your first Go program. This simple example demonstrates the basic structure of a Go program and how to use the `fmt` package for output. As you progress through this book, you'll build upon this foundation and learn how to create more complex and powerful applications using Go.

Chapter Summary

In this chapter, we've taken the essential steps to set up your Go development environment. You've learned how to install Go on your system, choose a suitable code editor or IDE, understand the Go workspace structure, and familiarize yourself with the essential Go tools. We've also dipped our toes into Go programming by creating and running the classic "Hello, World!" program.

With your development environment in place, you're now equipped to dive deeper into the Go language and explore its vast capabilities. The next chapter will introduce you to the fundamental syntax, data types, and operators that form the building blocks of Go programs. Get ready to embark on an exciting journey into the world of Go programming!

Go Fundamentals: Syntax, Data Types, and Operators

Outline

- Basic Syntax and Structure
- Comments and Documentation
- Data Types
- Variables
- Constants
- Operators
- Chapter Summary

Basic Syntax and Structure

Go's syntax and structure are designed to be clean, simple, and easy to read. Let's delve into the fundamental elements that make up a Go program:

Case Sensitivity

Go, like many programming languages, is case-sensitive. This means that `myVariable` and `myvariable` are treated as two distinct variables. Similarly, function names, keywords, and identifiers are all case-sensitive.

```go
var myVariable = 10
var myvariable = 20 // Different variable

func myFunction() { ... }
func MyFunction() { ... } // Different function
```

Statements

In Go, statements are the individual instructions that make up a program. Each statement typically ends with a semicolon (;). However, Go has an automatic semicolon insertion (ASI) mechanism that often eliminates the need for explicit semicolons.

```go
fmt.Println("Hello, world!") // Semicolon is optional

x := 10; y := 20; // Multiple statements on one line
```

The ASI rules can be a bit complex, so it's generally considered good practice to include semicolons for clarity, especially when writing multiple statements on a single line.

Code Blocks

Code blocks in Go are defined by curly braces (`{}`). They group together multiple statements that should be treated as a single unit. Code blocks are used in various contexts, such as function bodies, conditional statements (`if`, `else`), loops (`for`, `while`), and more.

```go
func main() { // Function body is a code block
    message := "Hello, world!"
    fmt.Println(message)
```

```
}

if x > 0 { // Conditional block
    fmt.Println("x is positive")
} else { // Another conditional block
    fmt.Println("x is not positive")
}
```

The `main` Function and Packages

Every Go program must have a `main` function. This function is the starting point of execution when you run your Go program. It's declared within the `main` package, which is the special package that denotes an executable program.

```
package main // Package declaration

func main() { // Main function
    // Your program's logic goes here
}
```

In Go, code is organized into packages. A package is a collection of related source files that are compiled together. Packages provide a way to modularize code, making it easier to manage and reuse. The `main` package is unique in that it indicates that the code is meant to be compiled into an executable program.

In summary, Go's basic syntax and structure are designed for clarity and simplicity. Case sensitivity, optional semicolons, code blocks, and the `main` function within the `main` package are fundamental concepts that you'll encounter throughout your Go programming journey. Understanding these basics lays the foundation for writing well-organized and readable Go code.

Comments and Documentation

Comments and documentation are essential for making your Go code understandable and maintainable. Comments provide explanations and context within the code itself, while documentation generates external documentation that can be accessed by other developers.

Single-line and Multi-line Comments

Go supports two types of comments:

1. **Single-line Comments:** These comments start with two forward slashes (`//`) and continue until the end of the line. They are typically used for short explanations or notes about specific lines of code.

   ```
   // This is a single-line comment explaining the following line
   x := 10 // Assign 10 to the variable x
   ```

2. **Multi-line Comments:** These comments begin with `/*` and end with `*/`. They can span multiple lines and are often used for longer explanations, documenting functions or sections of code, or temporarily commenting out blocks of code.

   ```
   /*
   This is a multi-line comment
   that can span multiple lines.
   It's often used for detailed explanations.
   */
   func calculateAverage(numbers []float64) float64 {
   ```

```
        // ... (function implementation)
}
```

Godoc

Godoc is a tool that comes with the Go installation. It automatically extracts documentation from your code comments and generates formatted documentation in HTML or plain text format. Godoc comments are special comments that follow a specific format and are used to document packages, types, functions, and methods.

Writing Effective Godoc Comments

To write effective Godoc comments, follow these guidelines:

- **Placement:** Place the Godoc comment immediately above the declaration of the package, type, function, or method it documents.
- **Format:** Start the comment with the name of the item being documented, followed by a period. Then, write a concise summary sentence that describes its purpose. You can include additional paragraphs for more detailed explanations, examples, or notes.
- **Tags:** Use special tags (starting with @) to provide additional information:
    - `@param <name> <description>`: Describes a function parameter.
    - `@return <description>`: Describes the return value of a function.
    - `@example`: Provides an example of how to use the documented item.
    - `@see`: Creates a link to related documentation.

Example:

```
// Package calculator provides basic arithmetic operations.
package calculator

// Add returns the sum of two integers.
func Add(a, b int) int {
    return a + b
}

// Subtract returns the difference of two integers.
//
// Examples:
//
//   Subtract(5, 3) // Returns 2
//   Subtract(10, 7) // Returns 3
func Subtract(a, b int) int {
    return a - b
}
```

In this example, the godoc tool would generate documentation for the `calculator` package, including descriptions for the Add and Subtract functions, along with an example for Subtract.

Generating Documentation

To generate documentation for your project, run the following command in your project's root directory:

```
godoc -http=:6060
```

This will start a local web server that serves your documentation. You can then open a web browser and navigate to `http://localhost:6060` to view the generated documentation.

By following these guidelines for comments and documentation, you can make your Go code more understandable, maintainable, and accessible to other developers.

Data Types

In Go, data types define the kind of values that a variable can hold and the operations that can be performed on those values. Go offers a rich set of built-in data types to represent various types of information, which can be categorized into two main categories: basic types and composite types.

Basic Types

Go's basic types are the fundamental building blocks for representing numbers, text, and logical values. Let's explore each of them:

1. **Numeric Types**
   Go provides several numeric types to accommodate different sizes and types of numbers:
   - **Integers (int, int8, int16, int32, int64):** Used to represent whole numbers (positive, negative, or zero). The size of an integer type determines its range of values. For example, int8 can hold values from -128 to 127, while int64 can hold much larger values.
   - **Unsigned Integers (uint, uint8, uint16, uint32, uint64):** Similar to integers, but they can only hold non-negative values. The range of an unsigned integer is double that of its signed counterpart (e.g., uint8 can hold values from 0 to 255).
   - **Floating-Point Numbers (float32, float64):** Used to represent numbers with fractional parts (e.g., 3.14, -0.5). float32 provides single-precision floating-point numbers, while float64 provides double-precision for greater accuracy.
   - **Complex Numbers (complex64, complex128):** Used to represent numbers with real and imaginary parts (e.g., 3 + 4i). complex64 has float32 components, and complex128 has float64 components.

   Examples:

   ```go
   var age int = 30            // Integer
   var price float64 = 9.99 // Floating-point number
   var isStudent bool = true // Boolean
   ```

2. **String Type (string)**
   Strings in Go are sequences of characters enclosed in double quotes ("). They are used to represent text.

   Example:

   ```go
   var message string = "Hello, Go!"
   ```

3. **Boolean Type (bool)**
   Booleans represent logical values: true or false. They are used for conditional statements and logical operations.

   Example:

   ```go
   var isActive bool = false
   ```

Composite Types

Go also offers composite data types, which are built from basic types or other composite types. We'll cover these in more detail in later chapters:

- **Arrays:** Fixed-size collections of elements of the same type.
- **Slices:** Dynamically-sized sequences of elements of the same type.
- **Maps:** Collections of key-value pairs.
- **Structs:** Custom data types that group together related fields.

Choosing the Right Data Type

Selecting the appropriate data type for a variable is crucial for efficient memory usage and ensuring correct program behavior. Consider the following factors:

- **Type of Data:** Choose a data type that matches the kind of information you need to store (e.g., integer for age, string for names, boolean for flags).
- **Range of Values:** Select a numeric type that can accommodate the range of values you expect (e.g., `int8` for small numbers, `float64` for precise calculations).
- **Memory Usage:** Be mindful of memory usage, especially when dealing with large datasets. Choose data types that balance precision with memory efficiency.

By understanding Go's fundamental data types, you lay the groundwork for working with variables, expressions, and operations in your programs.

Variables

Variables are fundamental building blocks in Go programming, used to store and manipulate data within your programs. They provide a way to label and access information, making your code more flexible and reusable. In this section, you'll learn how to declare, assign values to, and work with variables in Go.

Variable Declaration

In Go, you declare a variable using the `var` keyword, followed by the variable name, its type, and an optional initial value.

Syntax:

```
var variableName dataType = initialValue
```

Examples:

```
var age int = 30           // Integer variable
var name string = "Alice"  // String variable
var pi float64 = 3.14159 // Floating-point variable
var isActive bool = true   // Boolean variable
```

Type Inference (Short Variable Declaration):

Go offers a convenient shorthand for variable declaration using type inference. Instead of explicitly specifying the data type, you can use the `:=` operator. Go will infer the data type based on the initial value assigned to the variable.

Example:

```
age := 30          // Inferred as int
name := "Alice"    // Inferred as string
pi := 3.14159 // Inferred as float64
isActive := true   // Inferred as bool
```

Variable Assignment

Once you've declared a variable, you can assign a value to it using the assignment operator (=).

Example:

```
var message string  // Declare a string variable
message = "Hello, Go!" // Assign a value to the variable
```

You can also declare and assign a value to a variable in a single statement using the := operator:

```
message := "Hello, Go!" // Declare and assign in one step
```

Variable Naming Conventions

Go follows certain conventions for naming variables:

- **CamelCase:** Use camelCase for variable names (e.g., `firstName`, `isValid`).
- **Meaningful Names:** Choose names that clearly reflect the purpose or content of the variable (e.g., age instead of x, `totalPrice` instead of p).
- **Avoid Reserved Keywords:** Don't use Go's reserved keywords (e.g., `if`, `else`, `for`) as variable names.
- **Start with a Letter or Underscore:** Variable names must start with a letter or underscore.
- **Case Matters:** Go is case-sensitive, so `count` and `Count` are different variables.

Scope

The scope of a variable determines where it can be accessed and modified within your code. Go has two main types of variable scope:

1. **Local Scope:** Variables declared within a function or block have local scope. They can only be accessed and modified within that function or block.

    ```
    func calculateArea(length, width int) int {
        area := length * width // Local variable
        return area
    }
    ```

    In this example, the `area` variable is local to the `calculateArea` function and cannot be accessed outside of it.

2. **Global Scope:** Variables declared outside of any function have global scope. They can be accessed and modified from anywhere within the package.

    ```
    var message string = "Hello, Go!" // Global variable

    func main() {
        fmt.Println(message) // Accessing the global variable
    }

    func anotherFunction() {
        message = "Goodbye, Go!" // Modifying the global variable
    }
    ```

    In this example, the `message` variable is global and can be accessed and modified from both the `main` function and the `anotherFunction` function.

Understanding variable scope is crucial for writing well-structured and organized code. It helps prevent unintended modifications of variables and makes your code easier to reason about.

By mastering variable declaration, assignment, naming conventions, and scope, you'll be well-equipped to manage data effectively in your Go programs.

Constants

Constants, like variables, are used to store values in Go. However, unlike variables, the value of a constant cannot be changed once it has been assigned. This makes constants ideal for representing fixed values that shouldn't be altered during the execution of your program.

Constant Declaration

To declare a constant in Go, you use the `const` keyword, followed by the constant name, its type, and the value it should hold.

Syntax:

```
const constantName dataType = value
```

Examples:

```
const pi float64 = 3.14159 // Mathematical constant
const daysInWeek int = 7      // Number of days in a week
const message string = "Hello, Go!" // A string constant
```

Similar to variable declarations, you can omit the data type if the compiler can infer it from the value. This is called a short constant declaration:

```
const pi = 3.14159    // Inferred as float64
const daysInWeek = 7 // Inferred as int
```

Typed and Untyped Constants

Go has two types of constants: typed and untyped.

1. **Typed Constants:** Typed constants have a specific data type associated with them. This means that the compiler enforces type safety, preventing you from assigning a value of a different type to the constant.

    ```
    const pi float64 = 3.14159 // Typed constant (float64)
    ```

2. **Untyped Constants:** Untyped constants, on the other hand, do not have a fixed data type. The compiler can automatically determine their type based on the context in which they are used. This flexibility allows you to use untyped constants in various situations without explicitly casting them.

    ```
    const a = 42 // Untyped integer constant
    const b = 3.14 // Untyped floating-point constant
    ```

Enumerated Constants

Go provides a convenient way to create a set of related constants called enumerated constants. You can use the `iota` identifier to automatically assign incrementing integer values to these constants.

Example:

```
const (
```

```
    Sunday    = iota // 0
    Monday           // 1
    Tuesday          // 2
    Wednesday        // 3
    Thursday         // 4
    Friday           // 5
    Saturday         // 6
)
```

In this example, Sunday is assigned the value 0, Monday is assigned 1, Tuesday is assigned 2, and so on. The `iota` identifier starts at 0 and increments by 1 for each subsequent constant in the `const` group.

By understanding the different types of constants and how to use them effectively, you can make your Go code more readable, maintainable, and less error-prone. Constants provide a way to represent fixed values that should not change, ensuring consistency and clarity throughout your program.

Operators

Operators are symbols or keywords that perform specific operations on values (operands) within your Go code. They are essential for manipulating data and controlling the flow of your programs. Let's explore the various types of operators available in Go:

Arithmetic Operators

Arithmetic operators perform mathematical operations on numeric values.

Operator	Description	Example
+	Addition	`result := 5 + 3`
-	Subtraction	`result := 10 - 4`
*	Multiplication	`result := 6 * 7`
/	Division	`result := 15 / 5`
%	Modulus (remainder)	`result := 13 % 3`

Comparison Operators

Comparison operators compare two values and return a boolean result (`true` or `false`).

Operator	Description	Example
==	Equal to	`isEqual := 5 == 5`
!=	Not equal to	`isNotEqual := 10 != 8`
>	Greater than	`isGreater := 7 > 3`
<	Less than	`isLess := 2 < 6`
>=	Greater than or equal to	`isGreaterOrEqual := 8 >= 8`

<=	Less than or equal to	`isLessOrEqual := 4 <= 4`

Logical Operators

Logical operators combine boolean expressions and return a boolean result.

Operator	Description	Example
&&	Logical AND	`isValid := (x > 0) && (y < 10)`
||	Logical OR	`isEligible := (age >= 18) || (hasLicense == true)`
!	Logical NOT	`isNotValid := !isValid`

Bitwise Operators

Bitwise operators perform operations on the individual bits of integer values.

Operator	Description	Example
&	Bitwise AND	`result := 5 & 3`
|	Bitwise OR	`result := 7 | 2`
^	Bitwise XOR	`result := 6 ^ 4`
<<	Left shift	`result := 3 << 2`
>>	Right shift	`result := 8 >> 1`

Assignment Operators

Assignment operators assign values to variables.

Operator	Description	Example	Equivalent to
=	Simple assignment	x = 5	x = 5
+=	Add and assign	x += 3	x = x + 3
-=	Subtract and assign	y -= 2	y = y - 2
*=	Multiply and assign	z *= 4	z = z * 4
/=	Divide and assign	a /= 2	a = a / 2
%=	Modulus and assign	b %= 5	b = b % 5
&=	Bitwise AND and assign	c &= 1	c = c & 1
|=	Bitwise OR and assign	d |= 8	d = d | 8

^=	Bitwise XOR and assign	e ^= 15	e = e ^ 15
<<=	Left shift and assign	f <<= 1	f = f << 1
>>=	Right shift and assign	g >>= 2	g = g >> 2

Other Operators

Go also has other operators, such as the address operator (&) and the dereference operator (*), which are used to work with pointers. We will cover these operators in detail in the chapter on pointers and memory management.

Understanding how operators work is essential for building expressions and performing calculations in your Go programs. As you progress through this book, you'll encounter these operators frequently and learn how to use them to manipulate data effectively.

Chapter Summary

In this chapter, we've laid the groundwork for your Go programming journey by exploring the language's fundamental syntax, data types, and operators. We've covered:

- **Basic Syntax and Structure:** You learned about case sensitivity, statements, code blocks, and the importance of the `main` function and package.
- **Comments and Documentation:** You discovered how to write comments to explain your code and use the `godoc` tool to generate documentation.
- **Data Types:** You were introduced to Go's basic and composite data types, understanding their purpose and how to use them to represent different kinds of information.
- **Variables:** You learned how to declare, assign values to, and work with variables, including concepts like type inference and scope.
- **Constants:** You explored constants, understanding the difference between typed and untyped constants and how to create enumerated constants.
- **Operators:** You got acquainted with the various operators available in Go, including arithmetic, comparison, logical, bitwise, and assignment operators.

With these fundamental concepts under your belt, you're well-prepared to start writing your own Go programs. In the upcoming chapters, we'll delve deeper into Go's control flow statements, functions, data structures, and more advanced topics, enabling you to build sophisticated and efficient applications. Get ready to unlock the full potential of Go programming!

Section II:
Building Blocks of Go Programs

Working with Variables, Constants, and Control Flow

Outline

- Declaring and Using Variables
- Constants: Fixed Values
- Control Flow: Directing Program Execution
- Conditional Statements: Making Decisions
- Loops: Repeating Actions
- Switch Statements: Multi-way Branching
- Breaking and Continuing: Controlling Loops
- Chapter Summary

Declaring and Using Variables

In the realm of programming, variables act as containers that hold data. They allow you to store information, manipulate it, and reference it later in your code. Think of variables as labeled boxes where you can store different types of items, like numbers, text, or true/false values.

Declaring Variables

In Go, you declare a variable using the `var` keyword, followed by the variable name, its data type, and an optional initial value.

- **Syntax**

```
var variableName dataType = initialValue // With initialization
var variableName dataType                // Without initialization
```

- **Examples:**

```
var age int = 30        // Declare an integer variable named 'age' and initialize it with the value 30.
var name string         // Declare a string variable named 'name' without an initial value.
var pi float64 = 3.14159 // Declare a floating-point variable named 'pi' and initialize it.
var isActive bool       // Declare a boolean variable named 'isActive' without an initial value.
```

Shorthand Declaration (:=)

Go also provides a shorthand way to declare and initialize variables using the `:=` operator. This approach is often preferred for its conciseness.

- **Example:**

  ```
  count := 10        // Declare and initialize an integer variable named 'count'
                     with the value 10.
  greeting := "Hello, Go!" // Declare and initialize a string variable named
  'greeting'.
  ```

Type Inference

When you use the shorthand declaration (:=), Go's compiler employs *type inference*. This means it automatically determines the data type of the variable based on the value you assign to it.

- **Example:**

  ```
  radius := 5.0 // The compiler infers that 'radius' is of type `float64`.
  ```

Assigning Values

You can assign a value to a variable using the assignment operator (=).

- **Example:**

  ```
  var message string
  message = "Welcome to Go Programming!"
  ```

- **Updating Values:**

  You can also update the value of an existing variable using the assignment operator.

  - **Example**

    ```
    count := 10
    count = 25        // Update the value of 'count' to 25.
    ```

By skillfully utilizing variables, you can effectively store, manage, and manipulate data within your Go programs, making your code more dynamic and adaptable.

Constants: Fixed Values

In the dynamic world of programming, where variables can change their values throughout the execution of a program, constants provide a sense of stability and predictability. In Go, constants represent immutable values that, once assigned, remain unchanged throughout the lifetime of your program. This characteristic makes constants ideal for representing fixed values, configuration settings, mathematical constants, or any other data that should not be altered during runtime.

Declaring Constants

You declare a constant in Go using the `const` keyword, followed by the constant's name, its data type (optional), and the value it should hold.

- **Syntax**

  ```
  const constantName dataType = value    // With explicit type declaration
  const constantName = value             // With inferred type
  ```

- **Examples:**

```
const pi float64 = 3.14159      // Declare a typed constant named 'pi' with a value of
3.14159 and type float64.
const daysInWeek = 7            // Declare an untyped constant named 'daysInWeek' with a
value of 7. The type will be inferred.
const gravity = 9.8             // Declare an untyped constant named 'gravity' with a
value of 9.8.
const message = "Hello, Go!"    // Declare an untyped constant named 'message' with a
value of "Hello, Go!".
```

Benefits of Using Constants

- **Readability:** Constants make your code more self-documenting. By using descriptive names for constants, you convey the meaning and purpose of the values they represent, enhancing code readability.
- **Prevent Accidental Modifications:** Constants act as safeguards against unintentional changes to critical values. Once a constant is defined, its value cannot be altered, preventing errors that might occur if a variable were accidentally modified.
- **Maintainability:** When you need to update a value that's used in multiple places throughout your code, changing a single constant is much easier and less error-prone than searching for and modifying every instance of a variable.

Typed vs Untyped Constants

Go distinguishes between two types of constants:

- **Typed constants** have an explicitly declared data type, ensuring type safety. This means that the compiler will prevent you from assigning a value of a different type to the constant.

```
const speedLimit int = 65
speedLimit = 65.5  // This will result in a compilation error as you're trying
to assign a float64 value to an int constant.
```

- **Untyped constants** do not have a fixed data type. Go's compiler intelligently determines their type based on the context in which they are used. This flexibility allows you to use untyped constants in various expressions without the need for explicit type conversions.

```
const two = 2
var x int = two * 5      // 'two' is treated as an int
var y float64 = two * 3.14  // 'two' is treated as a float64
```

In essence, constants provide a way to define fixed values that contribute to the clarity, safety, and maintainability of your Go programs. By using constants judiciously, you can enhance the structure and robustness of your code.

Control Flow: Directing Program Execution

In the realm of programming, control flow is the conductor that orchestrates the execution of your code. It determines the order in which statements are executed, allowing you to create programs that respond to different conditions, make decisions, and repeat actions. Without control flow, your programs would be linear and inflexible, unable to adapt to varying inputs or user interactions.

The Importance of Control Flow

- **Decision Making:** Control flow constructs enable your programs to make decisions based on specific conditions. For instance, you can use an `if` statement to execute a certain block of code only if a particular condition is met.

- **Repetition:** Loops allow you to repeat a set of instructions multiple times, automating tasks and processing data efficiently. This eliminates the need to write the same code repeatedly.
- **Dynamic Behavior:** Control flow enables you to create dynamic and responsive programs that react to user input, environmental changes, or other events. This makes your programs more interactive and adaptable.
- **Code Organization:** By using control flow constructs, you can structure your code in a logical and organized manner, making it easier to understand, debug, and maintain.

Control Flow Constructs in Go

Go provides a variety of control flow constructs to manage the execution of your programs:

- **Conditional Statements:** These statements, such as `if`, `else if`, and `else`, allow you to execute different code blocks based on specific conditions.
- **Loops:** Go offers the `for` loop for repeating actions a certain number of times or until a condition is met. It also provides the `for-range` loop for iterating over elements in collections like arrays, slices, and maps.
- **Switch Statements:** The `switch` statement provides a concise way to handle multiple conditions and their corresponding actions.
- **Breaking and Continuing:** The `break` and `continue` statements allow you to control the flow within loops, enabling you to exit a loop prematurely or skip the remaining iterations of the current loop cycle.

Creating Dynamic Programs

By combining these control flow constructs, you can create Go programs that exhibit dynamic behavior. For example, you can:

- **Validate User Input:** Use conditional statements to check if user input is valid before processing it, ensuring that your program handles unexpected inputs gracefully.
- **Process Data:** Use loops to iterate over data structures, performing calculations, filtering information, or transforming data according to specific criteria.
- **Implement Game Logic:** Use control flow to create interactive game experiences, responding to user actions and updating the game state accordingly.
- **Build Responsive Web Applications:** Use control flow in your web server logic to handle different HTTP requests, generate dynamic content, and interact with databases.

Conclusion

Control flow is the backbone of any Go program. It gives you the power to direct the execution of your code, making decisions, repeating actions, and responding to various conditions. By mastering control flow constructs, you can create dynamic, responsive, and well-structured Go programs that solve real-world problems and provide engaging user experiences. In the following sections, we will explore each control flow construct in detail, providing you with the knowledge and skills to harness the full potential of control flow in your Go programming endeavors.

Conditional Statements: Making Decisions

The `if` Statement

In the dynamic world of programming, decisions are paramount. The `if` statement in Go empowers you to make these decisions by executing specific code blocks conditionally based on the truth or falsehood of a boolean expression.

Syntax

The basic syntax of an `if` statement is as follows:

```
if condition {
    // Code to execute if the condition is true
}
```

- **condition:** This is a boolean expression that evaluates to either `true` or `false`.
- **Code block:** The code within the curly braces `{}` will only be executed if the `condition` evaluates to `true`.

Examples

- **Simple Condition**

    ```
    age := 25

    if age >= 18 {
        fmt.Println("You are an adult.")
    }
    ```

    In this example, the code within the `if` block will only be executed if the age variable is greater than or equal to 18.

- **Comparison Operators**

    You can use comparison operators (==, !=, >, <, >=, <=) to create conditions.

    ```
    score := 85

    if score >= 90 {
        fmt.Println("Excellent!")
    } else if score >= 80 {
        fmt.Println("Good!")
    } else {
        fmt.Println("Needs improvement.")
    }
    ```

- **Logical Operators**

    Combine multiple conditions using logical operators (&& for AND, || for OR, ! for NOT).

    ```
    isSunny := true
    isWarm := false

    if isSunny && isWarm {
        fmt.Println("Perfect weather for a picnic!")
    } else if isSunny || isWarm {
        fmt.Println("It's either sunny or warm.")
    } else {
        fmt.Println("Not the best weather.")
    }
    ```

Key Points

- The `condition` in an `if` statement must be a boolean expression.

- The code block associated with the `if` statement is executed only if the condition is `true`.
- You can use comparison and logical operators to create complex conditions.
- The `else if` and `else` clauses provide alternative code paths for when the initial condition is `false`.

The `if` statement is a cornerstone of decision-making in Go programs. By mastering its usage and combining it with comparison and logical operators, you can create programs that respond intelligently to different situations and user inputs.

The `else` Clause

The `else` clause complements the `if` statement by providing an alternative code path to execute when the condition in the `if` statement evaluates to `false`. It acts as a safety net, ensuring that your program has a course of action even when the initial condition isn't met.

Syntax

The syntax for using the `else` clause with an `if` statement is:

```go
if condition {
    // Code to execute if the condition is true
} else {
    // Code to execute if the condition is false
}
```

Examples

- **Basic if-else**

    ```go
    number := 7

    if number%2 == 0 {
        fmt.Println("The number is even.")
    } else {
        fmt.Println("The number is odd.")
    }
    ```

    In this example, if the `number` is even (divisible by 2), the first code block is executed. Otherwise, the `else` block is executed.

- **Handling User Input**

    ```go
    reader := bufio.NewReader(os.Stdin)
    fmt.Print("Enter your age: ")
    input, _ := reader.ReadString('\n')
    age, _ := strconv.Atoi(strings.TrimSpace(input))

    if age >= 18 {
        fmt.Println("You are eligible to vote.")
    } else {
        fmt.Println("You are not yet eligible to vote.")
    }
    ```

    This code snippet takes user input for their age and checks if they are eligible to vote. If the age is 18 or greater, the first message is printed; otherwise, the second message is displayed.

- **File Operations**

```go
file, err := os.Open("data.txt")
if err != nil {
    fmt.Println("Error opening file:", err)
} else {
    defer file.Close()
    // ... (Read or write to the file)
}
```

In this scenario, we attempt to open a file. If an error occurs (indicated by `err` not being `nil`), we print an error message. Otherwise, we proceed to work with the file and ensure it's closed using `defer` when the function exits.

Key Points

- The `else` clause is optional but provides a fallback action when the `if` condition is not met.
- You can only have one `else` clause associated with an `if` statement.
- The `else` clause immediately follows the `if` block, and its code block is executed if the `if` condition is `false`.

The `else` clause enhances the decision-making capabilities of your Go programs. It allows you to handle alternative scenarios gracefully, ensuring that your code has a well-defined behavior even when the initial condition isn't satisfied.

The `else if` Statement

When you need to evaluate multiple conditions in a sequence and execute different code blocks based on which condition is true, the `else if` statement comes to the rescue. It allows you to create a chain of conditional checks, providing a more structured and organized way to handle complex decision-making logic in your Go programs.

Syntax

The syntax for using the `else if` statement is:

```
if condition1 {
    // Code to execute if condition1 is true
} else if condition2 {
    // Code to execute if condition1 is false and condition2 is true
} else if condition3 {
    // Code to execute if condition1 and condition2 are false and condition3 is true
} else {
    // Code to execute if all previous conditions are false
}
```

- **Multiple Conditions:** You can have as many `else if` clauses as needed to handle different scenarios.
- **Evaluation Order:** The conditions are evaluated sequentially from top to bottom. The first condition that evaluates to `true` will have its corresponding code block executed, and the remaining `else if` and `else` clauses will be skipped.
- **The `else` Clause:** The `else` clause is optional but provides a fallback action if none of the previous conditions are met.

Examples

- **Grading System**

    ```
    score := 85

    if score >= 90 {
        fmt.Println("Grade: A")
    } else if score >= 80 {
        fmt.Println("Grade: B")
    } else if score >= 70 {
        fmt.Println("Grade: C")
    } else if score >= 60 {
        fmt.Println("Grade: D")
    } else {
        fmt.Println("Grade: F")
    }
    ```

    This example demonstrates how to use `else if` to assign letter grades based on a student's score.

- **Handling User Input**

    ```
    reader := bufio.NewReader(os.Stdin)
    fmt.Print("Enter a command: ")
    command, _ := reader.ReadString('\n')
    command = strings.TrimSpace(command)

    if command == "start" {
        fmt.Println("Starting the process...")
    } else if command == "stop" {
        fmt.Println("Stopping the process...")
    } else if command == "restart" {
        fmt.Println("Restarting the process...")
    } else {
        fmt.Println("Invalid command.")
    }
    ```

    In this example, `else if` helps handle different user commands, providing appropriate responses based on the input.

- **Complex Conditions**

    You can combine comparison and logical operators to create more intricate conditions within your `else if` statements.

    ```
    age := 30
    hasLicense := true

    if age >= 18 && hasLicense {
        fmt.Println("You can drive.")
    } else if age >= 16 && hasLicense {
        fmt.Println("You can drive with supervision.")
    } else {
        fmt.Println("You cannot drive.")
    }
    ```

Key Points

- `else if` statements allow you to check multiple conditions sequentially.

- The first `true` condition triggers the execution of its associated code block, and the rest are skipped.
- The `else` clause provides a fallback action if none of the `else if` conditions are met.
- You can create complex decision-making logic by combining multiple `else if` statements and using logical operators.

The `else if` statement enhances the flexibility and expressiveness of your Go programs by allowing you to handle a variety of scenarios in a structured and organized way. By mastering its usage, you can create code that makes informed decisions and responds intelligently to different inputs or conditions.

Loops: Repeating Actions

The `for` Loop

Loops are the workhorses of programming, allowing you to automate repetitive tasks and process collections of data efficiently. In Go, the `for` loop is a versatile tool for iterating over code blocks multiple times. It gives you precise control over the repetition process, making it suitable for a wide range of scenarios.

Structure of a `for` Loop

A typical `for` loop in Go consists of three components:

1. **Initialization:** This statement is executed once at the beginning of the loop. It's often used to declare and initialize a counter variable that controls the loop's iterations.
2. **Condition:** This boolean expression is checked before each iteration. If it evaluates to `true`, the loop body is executed. If it's `false`, the loop terminates.
3. **Post Statement:** This statement is executed at the end of each iteration. It's commonly used to update the counter variable.

Syntax

```
for initialization; condition; post statement {
    // Code to be repeated (loop body)
}
```

Types of `for` Loops

Go's `for` loop is flexible enough to be used in various ways, resembling different loop constructs found in other programming languages. Let's explore some common patterns:

1. **Traditional `for` Loop**

    This is the most familiar form of a `for` loop, using a counter variable to control the number of iterations.

    ```
    for i := 0; i < 5; i++ {
        fmt.Println("Iteration:", i)
    }
    ```

    This loop will print "Iteration: 0" through "Iteration: 4".

2. **`for` Loop as a `while` Loop**

You can omit the initialization and post statement to create a loop that behaves like a `while` loop. The loop continues as long as the condition remains `true`.

```
count := 0
for count < 10 {
    fmt.Println("Count:", count)
    count++
}
```

3. **Infinite `for` Loop**

You can create an infinite loop by omitting all three components of the `for` loop. This loop will run indefinitely until you explicitly break out of it using the `break` statement.

```
for {
    // ... (some code)
    if someCondition {
        break // Exit the loop
    }
}
```

4. **`for-range` Loop**

The `for-range` loop is a specialized loop for iterating over elements in arrays, slices, maps, and strings. It provides a convenient way to access each element and its index (or key-value pair in the case of maps).

```
numbers := []int{1, 2, 3, 4, 5}
for index, value := range numbers {
    fmt.Println("Index:", index, "Value:", value)
}
```

Key Points

- The `for` loop is a versatile construct for repeating code blocks.
- It consists of three components: initialization, condition, and post statement.
- Go's `for` loop can mimic the behavior of `while` loops and infinite loops.
- The `for-range` loop simplifies iteration over collections.

The `for` loop is a fundamental tool for controlling the flow of your Go programs. By understanding its different forms and how to use them effectively, you can create efficient and dynamic programs that handle repetitive tasks and process data with ease.

Switch Statements: Multi-way Branching

When you're faced with the need to make decisions based on multiple possible values or types, the `switch` statement in Go provides an elegant and concise solution. It acts as a multi-way branch, allowing you to evaluate an expression and execute different code blocks based on its value. The `switch` statement can enhance the readability and maintainability of your code, especially when dealing with numerous conditions.

Syntax

The basic syntax of a `switch` statement is as follows:

```
switch expression {
case value1:
    // Code to execute if expression matches value1
case value2:
    // Code to execute if expression matches value2
// ... (more cases)
default:
    // Code to execute if expression doesn't match any of the cases
}
```

- **expression**: This is the value that you want to compare against the cases. It can be of any comparable type (e.g., `int`, `string`, `bool`).
- **case value1, case value2, etc.**: These are the possible values that the `expression` might match.
- **default**: This is an optional case that is executed if none of the other cases match.

How Cases are Evaluated

The `switch` statement evaluates the `expression` and compares it to the values in each `case`. If a match is found, the code block associated with that `case` is executed. If no match is found, the `default` case (if present) is executed.

The `fallthrough` Keyword

By default, after a matching case's code block is executed, the `switch` statement terminates. However, you can use the `fallthrough` keyword at the end of a case to allow execution to continue to the next case, even if it doesn't match the expression.

Examples

- **Handling Days of the Week**

    ```
    day := "Wednesday"

    switch day {
    case "Monday":
        fmt.Println("It's the start of the workweek.")
    case "Friday":
        fmt.Println("It's almost the weekend!")
    case "Saturday", "Sunday":
        fmt.Println("It's the weekend!")
    default:
        fmt.Println("It's a weekday.")
    }
    ```

    In this example, the `switch` statement checks the value of day and prints an appropriate message based on the day of the week. Notice how multiple cases (`"Saturday"` and `"Sunday"`) can be combined on a single line.

- **Type Switch**

    You can also use a `switch` statement to check the type of a variable using a type switch.

    ```
    var data interface{} = 3.14
    ```

```
switch v := data.(type) {
case int:
    fmt.Println("data is an integer:", v)
case float64:
    fmt.Println("data is a float64:", v)
case string:
    fmt.Println("data is a string:", v)
default:
    fmt.Println("data is of another type")
}
```

This example demonstrates how to use a type switch to determine the type of the `data` variable and perform different actions based on its type.

Key Points

- The `switch` statement provides a concise way to handle multiple conditions.
- Cases are evaluated sequentially until a match is found.
- The `default` case is optional and handles scenarios where no other case matches.
- The `fallthrough` keyword allows execution to continue to the next case.
- You can use `switch` statements to handle different values or types.

The `switch` statement is a valuable tool for creating clean and organized code when dealing with multiple conditions. It can improve code readability and make your programs more maintainable by consolidating decision-making logic into a single construct. By understanding how to use `switch` statements effectively, you can write more efficient and expressive Go code.

Breaking and Continuing: Controlling Loops

The break Statement

In the dynamic world of programming, there are times when you need to interrupt the normal flow of a loop and exit it prematurely. The `break` statement in Go serves this purpose, allowing you to terminate a loop before its natural conclusion based on specific conditions or events.

How the break Statement Works

- **Immediate Termination:** When the `break` statement is encountered within a loop, the loop is immediately terminated, and the program execution continues with the first statement after the loop.
- **Nested Loops:** In the case of nested loops, the `break` statement only terminates the innermost loop in which it is placed. The outer loops continue their execution.

Using break in for Loops

```
for i := 0; i < 10; i++ {
    if i == 5 {
        break // Exit the loop when i reaches 5
    }
    fmt.Println(i)
}
```

In this example, the loop will iterate from 0 to 4, and when i becomes 5, the `break` statement will terminate the loop. The output will be:

```
0
1
2
3
4
```

Using break in switch Statements

```
switch day {
case "Monday":
    fmt.Println("Start of the workweek")
case "Friday":
    fmt.Println("Almost weekend!")
    break // Exit the switch after handling Friday
case "Saturday", "Sunday":
    fmt.Println("Weekend!")
default:
    fmt.Println("Weekday")
}
```

In this switch statement, if the day is "Friday", the corresponding message will be printed, and then the break statement will prevent the execution from falling through to the next case ("Saturday" or "Sunday").

Key Points:

- The break statement provides a way to exit a loop prematurely based on a condition.
- It can be used within for loops, switch statements, and even within nested loops.
- In nested loops, break only terminates the innermost loop.

The break statement offers you greater control over the flow of your loops, allowing you to handle scenarios where you need to exit a loop early based on specific conditions. This flexibility is crucial for creating responsive and efficient programs that can adapt to various situations. Next, we will explore the continue statement, which provides another way to control loop iterations.

The continue Statement

While the break statement allows you to exit a loop entirely, the continue statement provides a way to skip the remaining code within the current iteration of a loop and move on to the next iteration. This can be useful when you want to bypass certain actions based on specific conditions while still keeping the loop running.

How the continue Statement Works

- **Skip to Next Iteration:** When the continue statement is encountered within a loop, the remaining code within the loop body for the current iteration is skipped. The loop then proceeds to the next iteration, evaluating the loop's condition and continuing if it's still true.
- **Nested Loops:** Similar to break, in nested loops, continue only affects the innermost loop in which it's placed.

Using continue in for Loops

```
for i := 0; i < 10; i++ {
    if i%2 == 0 { // Check if 'i' is even
        continue // Skip even numbers
    }
```

```
    fmt.Println(i)
}
```

In this example, the loop iterates from 0 to 9. If `i` is even, the `continue` statement is executed, skipping the `fmt.Println(i)` statement and moving on to the next iteration. The output will be:

1
3
5
7
9

Key Points

- The `continue` statement is used to skip the remaining code within the current loop iteration and proceed to the next iteration.
- It's helpful when you want to bypass certain actions based on specific conditions.
- It can be used within `for` loops and nested loops.
- In nested loops, `continue` only affects the innermost loop.

The `continue` statement, in conjunction with the `break` statement, provides fine-grained control over the execution flow within your loops. By using these statements strategically, you can create more efficient and adaptable programs that handle various scenarios and data manipulations with ease.

Chapter Summary

In this chapter, we've explored the fundamental building blocks that empower you to control the flow and manipulate data within your Go programs. You've learned how to:

- **Declare and Use Variables:** You can now create variables to store different types of data, assign values to them, and update their values as needed. You also understand the concept of variable scope and how it affects accessibility within your code.
- **Define Constants:** You've learned how to declare constants to represent fixed values that remain unchanged throughout your program's execution. You now understand the distinction between typed and untyped constants and the benefits they offer in terms of code readability and maintainability.
- **Control Program Flow:** You've mastered the art of directing the execution of your code using control flow constructs like conditional statements (`if`, `else if`, `else`) and loops (`for`, `for-range`).
- **Make Decisions:** You can now use conditional statements to execute specific code blocks based on the truth or falsehood of conditions, enabling your programs to make intelligent decisions.
- **Repeat Actions:** You've explored the power of loops to automate repetitive tasks and process collections of data efficiently. You've learned how to use different types of `for` loops, including traditional `for` loops, while-like loops, infinite loops, and `for-range` loops.
- **Handle Multiple Conditions:** You've learned how to use `switch` statements to handle multiple conditions and their corresponding actions concisely.
- **Control Loop Iterations:** You've gained the ability to control the flow within loops using the `break` and `continue` statements, allowing you to exit loops prematurely or skip specific iterations based on conditions.

These fundamental concepts form the foundation of Go programming. By mastering variables, constants, and control flow, you've equipped yourself with the essential tools to create dynamic, responsive, and well-structured Go programs.

Functions: The Backbone of Go Code

Outline

- Understanding Functions
- Defining and Calling Functions
- Function Parameters and Arguments
- Return Values
- Multiple Return Values
- Named Return Values
- Variadic Functions
- Anonymous Functions and Closures
- Recursion
- Defer Statements
- Function Types and First-Class Functions
- Chapter Summary

Understanding Functions

Functions are the building blocks of well-structured and maintainable Go programs. At their core, functions are self-contained blocks of code designed to perform specific tasks. They encapsulate a set of instructions that can be executed repeatedly throughout your code, promoting reusability and modularity.

Think of functions as miniature programs within your larger program. Each function has a name, a set of inputs (parameters), and a defined output (return value). When you call a function, you provide it with the necessary inputs, and it performs its designated task, optionally returning a result.

Benefits of Using Functions

1. **Code Modularity:** Functions allow you to break down complex tasks into smaller, more manageable units. This modular approach makes your code easier to understand, debug, and modify.
2. **Reusability:** Once you define a function, you can call it multiple times from different parts of your program, avoiding code duplication and promoting efficiency.
3. **Readability:** Functions make your code more readable by encapsulating specific tasks within well-defined boundaries. This improves the overall structure and clarity of your code.
4. **Code Organization:** Functions help organize your code into logical sections, making it easier to navigate and understand the flow of your program.
5. **Maintainability:** When you need to update a specific functionality, you can modify the corresponding function without affecting the rest of your code. This makes your codebase easier to maintain and evolve over time.
6. **Testing:** Functions are inherently testable. You can write unit tests for individual functions to ensure their correctness and identify potential bugs early in the development process.

Analogy

Imagine you're building a house. Instead of constructing every element from scratch every time you need it (e.g., building a door, a window, or a wall), you can create reusable components (functions) that you can assemble to construct different parts of the house. This modular approach simplifies the building process, makes it easier to modify or replace components, and allows you to focus on the overall design and structure of the house.

In the context of Go

Go embraces functions as a core principle of its design. The language encourages you to write modular code by breaking down tasks into functions. This philosophy aligns with the broader software engineering principle of "separation of concerns," where different parts of your code are responsible for distinct tasks, leading to cleaner, more maintainable, and easier-to-test codebases.

In the following sections, we'll delve deeper into the mechanics of defining and using functions in Go. You'll learn how to create functions, pass arguments, return values, and leverage advanced features like multiple return values, named return values, variadic functions, anonymous functions, closures, and more. By mastering these concepts, you'll be well-equipped to harness the power of functions and build well-structured, reusable, and efficient Go programs.

Defining and Calling Functions

Functions in Go are defined using the `func` keyword, followed by the function name, a list of parameters (if any) enclosed in parentheses, an optional return type, and the function body enclosed in curly braces {}. Let's break down the syntax and explore how to define and call functions in Go.

Syntax for Defining Functions

```
func functionName(parameter1 dataType1, parameter2 dataType2, ...) returnType {
    // Function body (code to be executed)
    // ...
    return returnValue // Optional return statement
}
```

- **func:** The keyword that indicates you're defining a function.
- **functionName:** The name you choose for your function. It should be descriptive and follow Go's naming conventions (camelCase).
- **parameter1 dataType1, parameter2 dataType2, ...:** A comma-separated list of parameters, each with its name and data type. Parameters act as placeholders for values that will be passed to the function when it's called.
- **returnType:** The data type of the value that the function will return. If the function doesn't return a value, you can omit this part or use the keyword `void`.
- **{ and }:** Curly braces enclose the function body, which contains the code that will be executed when the function is called.
- **return returnValue:** An optional statement that specifies the value to be returned by the function.

Examples of Defining Simple Functions

1. **Function without Parameters or Return Value**

```
func greet() {
    fmt.Println("Hello, Go!")
}
```

2. **Function with Parameters**

```
func add(x int, y int) int {
    sum := x + y
    return sum
}
```

3. Function with Multiple Return Values

```
func divide(x, y float64) (float64, error) {
    if y == 0 {
        return 0, errors.New("division by zero")
    }
    return x / y, nil
}
```

Calling Functions

To execute the code within a function, you need to *call* it. You do this by using the function's name followed by parentheses, passing any required arguments within the parentheses.

Examples of Calling Functions

```
greet() // Calling the greet function

result := add(5, 3) // Calling the add function and storing the returned value in 'result'

quotient, err := divide(10, 2) // Calling the divide function and handling multiple return values
if err != nil {
    fmt.Println("Error:", err)
} else {
    fmt.Println("Quotient:", quotient)
}
```

In these examples, we're calling the functions we defined earlier, providing the necessary arguments, and, in the case of add and `divide`, capturing the returned values.

Key Points

- Functions encapsulate reusable blocks of code.
- The `func` keyword is used to define functions.
- Functions can have parameters, return values, or both.
- Go supports multiple return values.
- You call a function by using its name followed by parentheses and passing any required arguments.

By mastering the art of defining and calling functions, you'll be able to create modular, reusable, and well-organized Go programs.

Function Parameters and Arguments

In the realm of Go functions, parameters and arguments play a crucial role in enabling communication and data exchange between different parts of your program. Understanding the distinction between these two concepts and how they work together is essential for writing flexible and reusable functions.

Parameters: Placeholders for Values

- Think of function parameters as placeholders or variables that are defined within a function's signature. They act as temporary containers for values that will be passed to the function when it's called.
- When defining a function, you specify its parameters along with their data types.
- **Syntax:**

```
func functionName(parameter1 dataType1, parameter2 dataType2, ...) returnType
{
    // ... function body
}
```

- **Example:**

```
func greet(name string) {
    fmt.Println("Hello,", name, "!")
}
```

In this example, name is a parameter of type string. It acts as a placeholder for the actual name that will be provided when the function is called.

Arguments: Actual Values

- Arguments are the concrete values that you supply to a function when you call it. They fill in the placeholders defined by the function's parameters.
- When calling a function, you provide arguments within parentheses, matching the order and types of the parameters.
- **Example:**

```
greet("Alice")
```

In this call to the greet function, "Alice" is the argument that corresponds to the name parameter.

Passing Different Types of Arguments

Go allows you to pass various types of arguments to functions, including:

- **Basic Types:** You can pass basic data types like int, float64, string, and bool as arguments.

```
func calculateArea(length, width int) int {
    return length * width
}

area := calculateArea(5, 3)
```

- **Composite Types:** You can pass composite data types like arrays, slices, maps, and structs as arguments.

```
func printPerson(person struct{ name string; age int }) {
    fmt.Println("Name:", person.name, "Age:", person.age)
}

p := struct{ name string; age int }{name: "Bob", age: 25}
printPerson(p)
```

Key Points

- Parameters are placeholders defined in the function signature.
- Arguments are the actual values passed to the function when it's called.
- Go supports passing various data types as arguments, including basic and composite types.
- The number and types of arguments must match the function's parameters.

By understanding the relationship between function parameters and arguments, you can create flexible and reusable functions that can operate on different inputs. This modular approach promotes code organization, maintainability, and testability, leading to more robust and efficient Go programs.

Return Values

Functions in Go can produce output or results by returning values. The `return` statement is used to specify the value that a function sends back to the caller. This allows you to capture and utilize the results of a function's computations or actions elsewhere in your program.

Specifying Return Types

When defining a function, you can declare its return type after the parameter list. The return type indicates the kind of value the function will produce.

- **Syntax:**

```go
func functionName(parameters...) returnType {
    // ... function body
    return returnValue
}
```

- **Examples:**

```go
func square(x int) int { // Returns an integer
    return x * x
}

func isEven(num int) bool { // Returns a boolean
    return num%2 == 0
}

func greet(name string) string { // Returns a string
    return "Hello, " + name + "!"
}
```

Returning Values

The `return` statement within the function body specifies the value to be returned. The returned value must match the declared return type of the function.

- **Example:**

```go
func calculateAverage(numbers []float64) float64 {
    var sum float64
    for _, num := range numbers {
        sum += num
    }
    average := sum / float64(len(numbers))
    return average
}
```

In this example, the `calculateAverage` function calculates the average of a slice of `float64` numbers and returns the result as a `float64`.

Returning Different Data Types

Go functions can return values of various data types, including:

- **Basic Types:** You can return basic data types like `int`, `float64`, `string`, and `bool`.
- **Composite Types:** You can also return composite data types like arrays, slices, maps, and structs.

```go
func createPerson(name string, age int) struct {
    Name string
    Age  int
} {
    return struct {
        Name string
        Age  int
    }{name, age}
}
```

In this example the function `createPerson` returns a struct containing the Name and Age of a person.

Key Points:

- The `return` statement is used to specify the value a function sends back to the caller.
- The return type is declared after the parameter list in the function signature.
- The returned value must match the declared return type.
- Functions can return various data types, including basic and composite types.

By understanding how to define return types and use the `return` statement, you can create functions that produce meaningful outputs, enabling you to build more complex and sophisticated Go programs. In the next section, we'll explore Go's unique ability to return multiple values from a single function.

Multiple Return Values

One of Go's distinctive features is its ability to return multiple values from a function. This capability adds flexibility and expressiveness to your code, allowing you to convey more information from a function in a clear and concise manner.

Defining Functions with Multiple Return Values

To define a function that returns multiple values, you specify the return types within parentheses after the parameter list.

Syntax:

```go
func functionName(parameters...) (returnType1, returnType2, ...) {
    // ... function body
    return value1, value2, ...
}
```

Example:

```go
func divide(x, y float64) (float64, error) {
    if y == 0 {
        return 0, errors.New("division by zero")
    }
    return x / y, nil
}
```

In this example, the `divide` function returns both the quotient of the division and an `error` value. If the divisor (y) is zero, it returns an error indicating division by zero. Otherwise, it returns the calculated quotient and a `nil` error, signifying successful execution.

Assigning Multiple Return Values

When calling a function that returns multiple values, you can assign the returned values to multiple variables using a comma-separated list on the left side of the assignment operator (=).

Example:

```
quotient, err := divide(10, 2)
if err != nil {
    fmt.Println("Error:", err)
} else {
    fmt.Println("Quotient:", quotient)
}
```

In this example, the `quotient` and `err` variables receive the two values returned by the `divide` function. The code then checks if an error occurred and handles it accordingly.

Common Use Case: Returning Result and Error

A prevalent use case for multiple return values is to return both a result and an error status. This pattern is idiomatic in Go and promotes explicit error handling.

- **Successful Execution:** When a function executes successfully, it returns the desired result along with a `nil` error value.
- **Error Condition:** If an error occurs during the function's execution, it returns a zero value for the result and a non-`nil` error value that describes the error.

Key Points:

- Go functions can return multiple values.
- You specify the return types within parentheses in the function signature.
- Use a comma-separated list of variables to assign multiple return values.
- Returning a result and an error status is a common pattern in Go.

By leveraging Go's ability to return multiple values, you can write more expressive and informative functions. This feature enhances code clarity, promotes explicit error handling, and contributes to the overall robustness of your Go programs.

Named Return Values

Go offers a unique feature called named return values, which allows you to assign names to the values that a function returns. This seemingly subtle enhancement can significantly improve the readability and clarity of your code, especially when dealing with functions that return multiple values.

Defining Functions with Named Return Values

When defining a function with named return values, you include the names of the return values along with their types in the function signature.

Syntax

```
func functionName(parameters...) (result1 returnType1, result2 returnType2, ...) {
```

```
    // ... function body
    return // You can omit the values after 'return'
}
```

How Named Return Values Work

- **Implicit Declaration:** Named return values are implicitly declared as variables within the function's scope. You can use them directly within the function body, just like any other local variable.
- **"Naked" Return:** When using named return values, you can use a "naked" `return` statement (without specifying any values) at the end of the function. This will automatically return the current values of the named return variables.

Improved Readability

Named return values enhance code readability in several ways:

- **Self-Documenting Code:** The names of the return values act as documentation, conveying their purpose and meaning directly in the function signature. This makes it easier to understand what the function returns without having to delve into its implementation.
- **Clearer Assignments:** When calling a function with named return values, you can directly see which variable is assigned to which returned value, improving code clarity.
- **Reduced Errors:** By explicitly naming the return values, you reduce the risk of accidentally assigning them to the wrong variables or using them incorrectly.

Examples

```
func calculateStats(numbers []int) (min, max, avg int) {
    // ... (calculate min, max, and avg)
    return // Return the calculated values
}

func main() {
    numbers := []int{5, 2, 9, 1, 7}
    min, max, avg := calculateStats(numbers)
    fmt.Println("Min:", min, "Max:", max, "Avg:", avg)
}
```

In this example, the `calculateStats` function uses named return values (`min`, `max`, `avg`) to clearly indicate what it returns. When calling the function, the returned values are directly assigned to variables with the same names, making the code more readable and self-explanatory.

Key Points

- Named return values improve code readability and clarity.
- They are implicitly declared as variables within the function.
- You can use a "naked" `return` statement to return the current values of the named return variables.
- Named return values are particularly useful for functions that return multiple values.

By leveraging named return values, you can write Go functions that are not only functional but also elegant and easy to understand. This feature encourages self-documenting code, reduces errors, and contributes to the overall maintainability of your Go projects.

Variadic Functions

Variadic functions in Go offer a powerful way to handle scenarios where you need a function to accept a variable number of arguments. This flexibility is particularly useful when you don't know in advance how many arguments will be passed to the function.

Defining Variadic Functions

You define a variadic function by using the ellipsis (...) operator before the type of the final parameter in the function's signature. This indicates that the function can accept zero or more arguments of that specific type.

Syntax:

```go
func functionName(params ...dataType) returnType {
    // ... function body
}
```

How Variadic Functions Work

- **Slice of Arguments:** Inside the function, the variadic parameter is treated as a slice of the specified data type. This slice contains all the arguments passed to the function for that parameter.
- **Accessing Arguments:** You can access the individual arguments within the slice using indexing or iteration, just like you would with any other slice.
- **Zero or More Arguments:** Variadic functions can be called with zero, one, or multiple arguments of the specified type.

Examples

- **Calculating the Sum of Numbers**

    ```go
    func sum(numbers ...int) int {
        total := 0
        for _, num := range numbers {
            total += num
        }
        return total
    }

    func main() {
        result := sum(1, 2, 3, 4, 5)
        fmt.Println("Sum:", result) // Output: Sum: 15
    }
    ```

    In this example, the sum function accepts a variadic parameter numbers of type int. It calculates the sum of all the numbers passed as arguments and returns the total.

- **Formatting Strings**

    ```go
    func formatMessage(format string, values ...interface{}) string {
        return fmt.Sprintf(format, values...)
    }

    func main() {
        message := formatMessage("Hello, %s! You are %d years old.", "Alice", 30)
        fmt.Println(message) // Output: Hello, Alice! You are 30 years old.
    }
    ```

    The formatMessage function uses a variadic parameter values of type interface{} to accept any number of values to be formatted into the provided string using fmt.Sprintf.

Key Points

- Variadic functions can accept a variable number of arguments.
- The ellipsis (...) operator is used to define a variadic parameter.
- Inside the function, the variadic parameter is treated as a slice.
- Variadic functions can be called with zero or more arguments.

Variadic functions provide a powerful mechanism for handling scenarios where the number of arguments is not predetermined. They enhance the flexibility and adaptability of your Go code, enabling you to create functions that can operate on a varying number of inputs.

Anonymous Functions and Closures

Go empowers you to define functions without explicitly assigning them names. These functions, known as *anonymous functions*, can be declared and used directly within your code, providing a concise way to express functionality in specific contexts.

Defining Anonymous Functions

Anonymous functions are defined using the `func` keyword, followed by the parameter list, return type (if any), and the function body enclosed in curly braces {}.

Syntax:

```
func(parameters...) returnType {
    // ... function body
}
```

Closures: Capturing Variables

One of the powerful features of anonymous functions in Go is their ability to form *closures*. A closure is a combination of an anonymous function and its surrounding environment (the variables within its enclosing scope). This means that an anonymous function can access and modify variables from the scope in which it's defined, even after that scope has exited.

Use Cases

Anonymous functions and closures are particularly useful in several scenarios:

1. **Event Handlers and Callbacks:**

    ```
    button.OnClick(func() {
        fmt.Println("Button clicked!")
    })
    ```

    In this example, an anonymous function is passed as an argument to the `OnClick` method of a button. This function will be executed when the button is clicked, and it can access variables from the surrounding scope (e.g., variables related to the button or the application's state).

2. **Goroutines:**

    ```
    go func(message string) {
        fmt.Println(message)
    }("Hello from a goroutine!")
    ```

Here, an anonymous function is used to create a goroutine that prints a message. The closure allows the goroutine to access the message variable even though it's defined outside the goroutine's scope.

3. **Higher-Order Functions:**

```
func applyOperation(numbers []int, operation func(int) int) []int {
    result := make([]int, len(numbers))
    for i, num := range numbers {
        result[i] = operation(num)
    }
    return result
}

func main() {
    numbers := []int{1, 2, 3, 4, 5}
    doubled := applyOperation(numbers, func(x int) int { return x * 2 })
    fmt.Println(doubled) // Output: [2 4 6 8 10]
}
```

In this scenario, the applyOperation function takes a slice of integers and an anonymous function (operation) as arguments. The anonymous function performs a specific operation on each element of the slice, demonstrating the use of closures in higher-order functions.

Key Points

- Anonymous functions are functions without names defined inline within your code.
- Closures allow anonymous functions to access and modify variables from their surrounding scope.
- Anonymous functions and closures are useful for event handlers, callbacks, goroutines, and higher-order functions.

Anonymous functions and closures offer a powerful way to express functionality directly where it's needed, enhancing code conciseness and flexibility. By mastering these concepts, you can write more expressive and adaptable Go programs that leverage the benefits of closures and functional programming patterns.

Recursion

Recursion is a powerful programming technique where a function calls itself to solve a problem by breaking it down into smaller, similar subproblems. This approach can lead to elegant and concise solutions for problems that exhibit a recursive structure.

The Essence of Recursion

- **Self-Reference:** A recursive function contains a call to itself within its body.
- **Base Case:** Every recursive function must have a base case, which is a condition that stops the recursion. Without a base case, the function would call itself infinitely, leading to a stack overflow.
- **Recursive Case:** The recursive case defines how the problem is broken down into smaller subproblems and how the function calls itself to solve those subproblems.

Example: Calculating Factorials

The factorial of a non-negative integer n (denoted by n!) is the product of all positive integers less than or equal to n.

- **Mathematical Definition:**

0! = 1
n! = n * (n-1)! (for n > 0)

- **Recursive Implementation in Go:**

```
func factorial(n int) int {
    if n == 0 {
        return 1 // Base case: 0! = 1
    } else {
        return n * factorial(n-1) // Recursive case: n! = n * (n-1)!
    }
}
```

In this example:

- The base case is when n is 0, and the function returns 1.
- The recursive case calculates the factorial of n by multiplying n with the factorial of n-1.

Example: Traversing a Tree

Consider a binary tree data structure where each node has a value and references to its left and right children. Recursion is often used to traverse such tree-like structures.

```
type Node struct {
    Value int
    Left  *Node
    Right *Node
}

func inOrderTraversal(node *Node) {
    if node == nil {
        return // Base case: empty tree or reached a leaf node
    }
    inOrderTraversal(node.Left)  // Traverse the left subtree
    fmt.Println(node.Value)      // Visit the current node
    inOrderTraversal(node.Right) // Traverse the right subtree
}
```

In this example:

- The base case is when the node is nil (empty tree or reached a leaf node).
- The recursive case traverses the left subtree, visits the current node, and then traverses the right subtree.

Key Points

- Recursion is a technique where a function calls itself.
- Every recursive function must have a base case to stop the recursion.
- The recursive case defines how the problem is broken down and how the function calls itself to solve subproblems.
- Recursion is often used for problems with a recursive structure, such as calculating factorials, traversing trees, or solving mathematical puzzles.

Recursion can lead to elegant and efficient solutions for certain types of problems. However, it's important to use recursion carefully, as excessive or improper recursion can lead to stack overflow errors. In general, prefer iterative solutions when they are straightforward and efficient. But when a problem naturally lends itself to a recursive approach, recursion can be a powerful tool in your Go programming toolkit.

Defer Statements

The `defer` statement in Go is a powerful tool that allows you to schedule a function call to be executed at the end of the current function's execution, regardless of how the function exits. This delayed execution provides a convenient way to handle resource cleanup, ensure that certain actions are always performed, and improve the clarity and maintainability of your code.

How `defer` Works

- **Delayed Execution:** When you use the `defer` keyword before a function call, that function call is not executed immediately. Instead, it is added to a stack of deferred calls associated with the current function.
- **LIFO Order:** The deferred calls are executed in Last-In-First-Out (LIFO) order at the end of the function's execution. This means that the last function call that was deferred will be the first one to be executed.
- **Panic Handling:** Even if the function panics (encounters a runtime error), the deferred calls will still be executed before the panic propagates further up the call stack. This ensures that crucial cleanup actions are always performed.

Use Cases for `defer`

1. **Resource Cleanup:**

   `defer` is commonly used to ensure that resources like files, network connections, or database handles are properly closed, even if an error occurs or the function panics.

   ```go
   func processFile(filename string) error {
       file, err := os.Open(filename)
       if err != nil {
           return err
       }
       defer file.Close() // Close the file when the function exits

       // ... (read or write to the file)
   }
   ```

2. **Locking and Unlocking:**

   In concurrent programs, `defer` can be used to ensure that locks are released after they are acquired, preventing deadlocks.

   ```go
   func updateData(mutex *sync.Mutex, data []int) {
       mutex.Lock()
       defer mutex.Unlock() // Unlock the mutex when the function exits

       // ... (update the data)
   }
   ```

3. **Error Handling:**

`defer` can be used in conjunction with error handling to ensure that error messages or logs are always recorded before a function returns, even if an error occurs within nested function calls.

```
func performOperation() error {
    defer func() {
        if err := recover(); err != nil {
            log.Println("Error:", err)
        }
    }()

    // ... (code that might panic)
}
```

Key Points

- The `defer` statement schedules a function call to be executed at the end of the current function.
- Deferred calls are executed in LIFO order.
- `defer` is useful for resource cleanup, locking/unlocking, and error handling.
- Even if a function panics, the deferred calls will still be executed.

The `defer` statement provides a powerful mechanism for managing resources, ensuring cleanup actions, and improving the overall structure and robustness of your Go code. By using `defer` strategically, you can write cleaner, safer, and more maintainable programs.

Function Types and First-Class Functions

In Go, functions are not just blocks of executable code; they are also *first-class values*. This means that functions can be treated like any other data type in Go. You can assign them to variables, pass them as arguments to other functions, and even return them from functions. This powerful feature unlocks a world of possibilities for creating flexible and expressive code.

Defining Function Types

To work with functions as values, you need to define *function types*. A function type specifies the signature of a function, including its parameters and return types.

Syntax:

```
type functionTypeName func(parameterTypes...) returnTypes
```

Creating Variables that Hold Functions

Once you've defined a function type, you can create variables of that type to store functions.

Example:

```
type operation func(int, int) int

func add(x, y int) int {
    return x + y
}

func multiply(x, y int) int {
    return x * y
}
```

```
func main() {
    var op operation // Declare a variable of type 'operation'
    op = add         // Assign the 'add' function to 'op'
    result := op(5, 3)
    fmt.Println(result) // Output: 8

    op = multiply    // Assign the 'multiply' function to 'op'
    result = op(5, 3)
    fmt.Println(result) // Output: 15
}
```

In this example, we define a function type `operation` that represents functions that take two integers and return an integer. We then create a variable op of type `operation` and assign different functions (add and `multiply`) to it, demonstrating how functions can be treated as values.

Use Cases

1. **Callbacks:** Function types are commonly used to implement callbacks, where you pass a function as an argument to another function to be executed at a later time or under specific conditions.
2. **Higher-Order Functions:** Higher-order functions are functions that take other functions as arguments or return functions as results. Function types enable you to create such higher-order functions in Go.
3. **Functional Programming Patterns:** Go's support for function types allows you to implement various functional programming patterns, such as map, filter, and reduce, which can lead to more concise and expressive code.

Key Points

- Functions in Go are first-class values.
- You can define function types to represent function signatures.
- Variables of function types can hold functions.
- Function types enable callbacks, higher-order functions, and functional programming patterns.

By treating functions as first-class values and using function types, you can write more flexible and adaptable Go code. This feature promotes code reusability, modularity, and the application of functional programming principles, leading to more elegant and maintainable solutions.

Chapter Summary

In this chapter, you have embarked on a journey to understand the power and versatility of functions in Go. We have covered:

- The concept of functions as reusable blocks of code that promote modularity, reusability, and readability.
- Defining and calling functions, including specifying parameters, return types, and the function body.
- The distinction between function parameters (placeholders) and arguments (actual values passed to the function).
- Go's ability to return multiple values from a function, enhancing code expressiveness.
- The concept of named return values, which improve code readability and clarity.
- Variadic functions, which allow you to handle a variable number of arguments.
- Anonymous functions and closures, providing concise and flexible ways to define and use functions inline.
- Recursion as a technique for solving problems by breaking them down into smaller, similar subproblems.

- The `defer` statement, enabling you to schedule function calls to be executed at the end of a function, even in the presence of panics.
- Function types and first-class functions, showcasing Go's ability to treat functions as values, leading to callbacks, higher-order functions, and functional programming patterns.

By mastering these concepts, you've gained a solid understanding of how functions work in Go and how to leverage their power to create well-structured, reusable, and efficient code. In the next chapter, we'll dive into the world of Go data structures, exploring arrays, slices, and maps, which are essential tools for organizing and manipulating collections of data in your programs.

Mastering Go Data Structures: Arrays, Slices, and Maps

Outline

- Understanding Data Structures
- Arrays: Fixed-Size Collections
- Slices: Dynamic Arrays
- Maps: Key-Value Stores
- Chapter Summary

Understanding Data Structures

In the world of programming, data structures act as the organizational backbone for handling and managing information. They provide systematic ways to arrange, store, and retrieve data efficiently. Without data structures, your programs would be limited to working with individual pieces of data, making it difficult to manage large datasets or perform complex operations.

The Role of Data Structures

- **Organization:** Data structures bring order to chaos by arranging data in a predictable and accessible manner. This organization allows for efficient storage and retrieval, enabling you to quickly locate specific pieces of information.
- **Efficiency:** Data structures are designed to optimize various operations on data, such as insertion, deletion, search, and sorting. By choosing the appropriate data structure, you can significantly improve the performance of your algorithms and programs.
- **Abstraction:** Data structures provide a layer of abstraction, allowing you to work with data at a higher level without worrying about the low-level details of memory management. This simplifies development and makes your code more readable and maintainable.

Essential Data Structures in Go

Go provides several built-in data structures that serve as the foundation for managing data in your programs. In this chapter, we'll focus on three core data structures:

1. **Arrays:** Arrays are fixed-size collections of elements of the same type. They offer a straightforward way to store and access data sequentially using indices.
2. **Slices:** Slices are dynamic, flexible views into underlying arrays. They provide a more convenient and efficient way to work with collections of data, as they can grow or shrink as needed.
3. **Maps:** Maps are unordered collections of key-value pairs. They allow you to store and retrieve values based on unique keys, providing efficient lookup and retrieval capabilities.

These three data structures, along with other composite types like structs, empower you to handle a wide range of data management tasks in your Go programs. By understanding their strengths, limitations, and appropriate use cases, you can make informed decisions about how to organize and manipulate data effectively, leading to more performant and maintainable code.

In the following sections, we'll dive deeper into each of these data structures, exploring their syntax, operations, and internal workings. Get ready to master the art of data organization and manipulation in Go!

Arrays: Fixed-Size Collections

Introduction to Arrays

Arrays in Go serve as the foundation for storing and organizing collections of elements. They are characterized by two key attributes:

1. **Homogeneous:** All elements within an array must be of the same data type. This ensures type safety and allows for efficient memory allocation and access.
2. **Fixed Size:** Once an array is declared, its size cannot be changed. This means you need to know the number of elements you'll need to store in advance.

Declaring and Initializing Arrays

You declare an array in Go using the following syntax:

```
var arrayName [size]dataType
```

- `arrayName`: The name you choose for your array.
- `size`: The number of elements the array will hold. This must be a constant or a literal value known at compile time.
- `dataType`: The data type of the elements within the array.

Examples:

```go
var numbers [5]int        // An array of 5 integers
var names [3]string       // An array of 3 strings
var isLoggedIn [10]bool   // An array of 10 booleans
```

You can also initialize an array with values during declaration:

```go
var numbers = [5]int{10, 20, 30, 40, 50}
var fruits = [3]string{"apple", "banana", "orange"}
```

Accessing Elements

You can access individual elements within an array using their index, which starts at 0 for the first element.

```go
fmt.Println(numbers[0])   // Output: 10
fmt.Println(fruits[2])    // Output: orange
```

Key Points

- Arrays store collections of elements of the same type.
- Arrays have a fixed size determined at compile time.
- You can declare and initialize arrays using the `var` keyword and square brackets `[ ]`.
- Access elements within an array using their index (starting at 0).

Arrays provide a simple and efficient way to store and access data sequentially. However, their fixed size can be a limitation in scenarios where you need to add or remove elements dynamically.

Working with Arrays

Once you've created an array, you'll often need to access and manipulate its elements. Go provides several ways to work with arrays, making it easy to iterate over their contents, modify individual elements, and perform other operations.

Iterating over Arrays

You can iterate over the elements of an array using a traditional `for` loop:

```
numbers := [5]int{10, 20, 30, 40, 50}

for i := 0; i < len(numbers); i++ {
    fmt.Println(numbers[i])
}
```

In this example, we use the `len` function to get the length of the `numbers` array and iterate over its elements using the index `i`.

Alternatively, you can use the `range` keyword to iterate over the array more concisely:

```
for index, value := range numbers {
    fmt.Println("Index:", index, "Value:", value)
}
```

The `range` keyword provides both the index and the value of each element in the array, making it a convenient way to access both pieces of information during iteration.

Modifying Elements

You can modify elements within an array by assigning new values to them using their index.

```
numbers[2] = 99 // Change the third element to 99
```

Limitations of Arrays

While arrays are useful for storing collections of data, they have some limitations:

1. **Fixed Size:** The size of an array is fixed at the time of declaration and cannot be changed later. This can be inconvenient if you need to add or remove elements dynamically.
2. **Index Out-of-Bounds Errors:** If you try to access an element at an index that is outside the bounds of the array (less than 0 or greater than or equal to the array's length), your program will panic with an "index out of range" error.
3. **Pass-by-Value:** When you pass an array to a function, a copy of the entire array is made. This can be inefficient for large arrays, as it consumes more memory and can impact performance.

Key Points

- You can iterate over arrays using `for` loops or the `range` keyword.
- Modify elements within an array using their index.
- Arrays have a fixed size and can lead to index out-of-bounds errors.
- Arrays are passed by value to functions.

While arrays provide a basic way to store collections of data, their limitations can make them less suitable for certain scenarios.

Multidimensional Arrays

While single-dimensional arrays store elements in a linear sequence, multidimensional arrays allow you to organize data in a grid-like or tabular structure. In essence, a multidimensional array is an array of arrays, where each element of the outer array is itself an array.

Declaring and Initializing Multidimensional Arrays

The syntax for declaring a multidimensional array in Go is as follows:

```
var arrayName [rows][columns]dataType
```

- `arrayName`: The name of the multidimensional array
- `rows`: The number of rows in the array (outer array's size)
- `columns`: The number of columns in each row (inner arrays' size)
- `dataType`: The type of elements stored in the array

Examples

```
var matrix [3][3]int // A 3x3 matrix of integers
var board [8][8]string // A chessboard represented as an 8x8 array of strings
```

You can also initialize a multidimensional array during declaration:

```
var matrix = [2][3]int{
    {1, 2, 3},
    {4, 5, 6},
}
```

Accessing and Modifying Elements

You access and modify elements in a multidimensional array using multiple indices, one for each dimension.

```
fmt.Println(matrix[0][1]) // Output: 2 (first row, second column)
matrix[1][2] = 99         // Change the element in the second row, third column to 99
```

Key Points:

- Multidimensional arrays are arrays of arrays, providing a way to store data in a grid-like structure
- Declare multidimensional arrays using multiple sets of square brackets [ ][ ]
- Access and modify elements using multiple indices, one for each dimension

Multidimensional arrays are valuable when you need to represent data that has a natural row-and-column structure, such as matrices, game boards, or spreadsheets. However, like single-dimensional arrays, they have a fixed size, which can be a limitation. In the next section, we will explore slices, which offer a more dynamic and flexible approach to working with collections of data in Go.

Slices: Dynamic Arrays

Introduction to Slices

While arrays offer a basic way to store collections of data in Go, their fixed size can be limiting in scenarios where you need to add or remove elements dynamically. Slices come to the rescue by providing a more flexible and convenient approach to working with collections of data. In essence, slices are dynamic, resizable views into underlying arrays.

The Relationship Between Slices and Arrays

- **Built on Arrays:** At their core, slices are built upon arrays. They provide a way to reference a contiguous portion of an underlying array.
- **Dynamic Size:** Unlike arrays, slices don't have a fixed size. They can grow or shrink as you add or remove elements.
- **Flexibility:** Slices offer greater flexibility than arrays, allowing you to work with collections of data that might change in size during program execution.

- **Efficiency:** Slices provide efficient memory usage by sharing the underlying array's memory. When you create a slice from an array, the slice doesn't copy the entire array; it simply references a portion of it.

Advantages of Slices over Arrays

- **Dynamic Resizing:** Slices can grow or shrink as needed, eliminating the need to know the exact number of elements in advance.
- **Pass-by-Reference:** When you pass a slice to a function, you're essentially passing a reference to the underlying array. This means that modifications made to the slice within the function will affect the original slice, enabling efficient data sharing.
- **Built-in Functions:** Go provides a rich set of built-in functions for working with slices, making it easy to perform common operations like appending elements, slicing, and finding elements.

Illustrative Analogy

Think of an array as a fixed-size bookshelf, where each slot can hold a single book. A slice, on the other hand, is like a window into that bookshelf. You can adjust the size of the window to view different sections of the bookshelf, and you can even add more shelves to the bookshelf if needed, allowing the window to expand.

Key Points:

- Slices are dynamic, resizable views into underlying arrays.
- They offer greater flexibility and efficiency than arrays.
- Slices can grow or shrink as needed.
- They are passed by reference, enabling efficient data sharing.
- Go provides built-in functions for working with slices.

Let's delve deeper into the mechanics of creating, manipulating, and understanding the internals of slices. By mastering these concepts, you'll be equipped to handle collections of data effectively and efficiently in your Go programs.

Creating and Manipulating Slices

Slices in Go offer versatile ways to create and manage collections of data dynamically. You can create slices from array literals, use the make function, or extract portions of existing arrays or slices through slicing operations.

1. Creating Slices from Array Literals

You can directly create a slice from an array literal using square brackets [ ] without specifying a size.

```
numbers := []int{1, 2, 3, 4, 5}
fruits := []string{"apple", "banana", "orange"}
```

2. Creating Slices using the make Function

The make function allows you to create a slice with an initial length and an optional capacity.

```
data := make([]int, 5)       // Creates a slice with length 5 and capacity 5
moreData := make([]int, 3, 10) // Creates a slice with length 3 and capacity 10
```

- **Length:** The initial number of elements in the slice.
- **Capacity:** The number of elements the underlying array can hold before needing to be resized.

3. Creating Slices using Slicing Operations

You can extract a portion of an existing array or slice to create a new slice using slicing syntax.

```
original := []int{10, 20, 30, 40, 50}
subSlice := original[1:4] // Creates a slice containing elements from index 1 to 3 (exclusive)
```

Adding Elements: The append Function

The append function is used to add elements to the end of a slice. If the slice's capacity is insufficient, a new underlying array with a larger capacity is allocated, and the elements are copied over.

```
numbers := []int{1, 2, 3}
numbers = append(numbers, 4, 5)
fmt.Println(numbers) // Output: [1 2 3 4 5]
```

Removing Elements: Slicing

You can effectively remove elements from a slice by creating a new slice that excludes the unwanted elements.

```
numbers := []int{1, 2, 3, 4, 5}
newNumbers := append(numbers[:2], numbers[3:]...) // Removes the element at index 2
fmt.Println(newNumbers) // Output: [1 2 4 5]
```

Common Slice Operations

- **Iteration:** You can iterate over slices using `for` loops or the `range` keyword, similar to arrays.

    ```
    for i, value := range numbers {
        fmt.Println("Index:", i, "Value:", value)
    }
    ```

- **Accessing Elements:** Access elements using their index, just like arrays.

    ```
    firstElement := numbers[0]
    ```

- **Modifying Elements:** Modify elements using their index.

    ```
    numbers[1] = 99
    ```

Key Points

- Create slices using array literals, the `make` function, or slicing operations.
- Add elements to a slice using the append function.
- Remove elements using slicing techniques.
- Iterate over, access, and modify slice elements similar to arrays

Slices are a cornerstone of Go programming, offering a dynamic and efficient way to manage collections of data. By understanding how to create, manipulate, and work with slices, you'll be well-equipped to handle a wide range of data-related tasks in your Go programs.

Slice Internals

Understanding the internal representation of slices is crucial for grasping their behavior and optimizing their performance in your Go programs. While slices provide a convenient and flexible abstraction for working with collections of data, they are built upon underlying arrays and have specific internal mechanics that influence how they operate.

Internal Representation

A slice in Go is represented by a data structure that consists of three components:

1. **Pointer:** A pointer to the underlying array that stores the actual elements of the slice. This pointer indicates the starting memory address of the slice's data within the array.
2. **Length:** The number of elements currently present in the slice. This represents the accessible portion of the underlying array that the slice "views."
3. **Capacity:** The total number of elements that the underlying array can hold. This determines how much the slice can grow before a new underlying array needs to be allocated.

Influence on Behavior and Performance

- **Dynamic Resizing:** When you append elements to a slice, its length increases. If the length exceeds the capacity, the Go runtime automatically allocates a new underlying array with a larger capacity, copies the existing elements, and updates the slice's pointer to point to the new array. This dynamic resizing allows slices to grow as needed, but it can incur some performance overhead when reallocation occurs.
- **Pass-by-Reference:** Slices are passed by value, but the value itself is a descriptor containing a pointer to the underlying array. This means that when you pass a slice to a function, any modifications made to the slice's elements within the function will affect the original slice, as they both refer to the same underlying array.
- **Memory Efficiency:** Slices are memory-efficient because they share the underlying array's memory. When you create a slice from an array or another slice, no new memory is allocated for the elements; the slice simply references a portion of the existing array.

Slice Capacity and Appending Efficiency

The capacity of a slice plays a significant role in the efficiency of appending elements.

- **Sufficient Capacity:** If the slice has enough capacity to accommodate new elements, appending is a fast operation. The new elements are simply added to the end of the slice, and the length is incremented.
- **Insufficient Capacity:** If the slice's capacity is reached, appending triggers a reallocation. A new underlying array with a larger capacity is created, the existing elements are copied, the new elements are appended, and the slice's pointer is updated. This reallocation can be computationally expensive, especially for large slices.

Key Points

- A slice is represented internally by a pointer, length, and capacity.
- The pointer points to the underlying array that stores the slice's data.
- The length indicates the number of accessible elements in the slice.
- The capacity determines how much the slice can grow before reallocation.
- Slice capacity influences the efficiency of appending elements.
- Understanding slice internals helps you write more performant code and avoid potential pitfalls.

By understanding the internal workings of slices, you can make informed decisions about their usage and optimize their performance in your Go programs. Consider the potential for reallocation when appending elements and use the make function with appropriate capacity hints to minimize reallocation overhead in performance-critical scenarios.

Slice Gotchas

While slices offer flexibility and convenience, they also come with certain nuances that can trip up even experienced Go developers. Understanding these potential pitfalls is crucial for writing correct and efficient code. Let's explore some common slice gotchas:

1. **Pass-by-Value (but with a Twist)**
   - **Misconception:** Slices are often described as being passed by reference, leading to the assumption that modifications to a slice within a function create a copy and don't affect the original slice.
   - **Reality:** Slices are technically passed by value, but the value itself is a descriptor containing a pointer to the underlying array. This means that when you pass a slice to a function, any modifications made to the slice's elements within the function will indeed affect the original slice, as they both share the same underlying array.
   - **Example:**

   ```go
   func modifySlice(s []int) {
       s[0] = 99 // Modifies the first element of the slice
       s = append(s, 100) // This creates a new underlying array and doesn't affect the original slice
   }

   func main() {
       numbers := []int{1, 2, 3}
       modifySlice(numbers)
       fmt.Println(numbers) // Output: [99 2 3] (first element modified)
   }
   ```

   In this example, modifying an element within the slice affects the original slice, but appending to the slice within the function creates a new underlying array, leaving the original slice unchanged.

2. **Capacity vs. Length**
   - **Confusion:** It's easy to confuse the capacity and length of a slice.
   - **Clarification:**
     - **Length:** The number of elements currently present and accessible in the slice.
     - **Capacity:** The total number of elements the underlying array can hold before needing to be resized.
   - **Example:**

   ```go
   s := make([]int, 3, 5) // Length: 3, Capacity: 5
   fmt.Println(len(s), cap(s)) // Output: 3 5
   ```

   Understanding the distinction is crucial for performance optimization. Appending elements to a slice is efficient as long as the capacity allows it. However, when the length reaches the capacity, appending triggers a reallocation, which can be costly.

3. **Nil Slices**
   - **Misunderstanding:** A nil slice (`nil`) is not the same as an empty slice (`[]T{}`).
   - **Explanation:**
     - **Nil Slice:** A nil slice has no underlying array and a length and capacity of 0.
     - **Empty Slice:** An empty slice has an underlying array (albeit empty) and a length of 0 but a non-zero capacity.
   - **Checking for Nil or Empty:**

   ```go
   if s == nil {
       fmt.Println("Slice is nil")
   } else if len(s) == 0 {
       fmt.Println("Slice is empty")
   }
   ```

Key Takeaways

- Be mindful of how slice modifications within functions affect the original slice due to the pass-by-value nature with underlying array sharing.
- Understand the difference between slice capacity and length, especially when appending elements for performance considerations.
- Distinguish between nil slices and empty slices and use appropriate checks to handle them correctly.

By being aware of these slice gotchas and understanding the underlying mechanics, you can avoid common pitfalls and write more robust and efficient Go code that leverages the power and flexibility of slices.

Maps: Key-Value Stores

Introduction to Maps

In the world of data structures, maps, also known as dictionaries or associative arrays, provide a powerful way to store and retrieve data based on unique keys. In Go, maps are unordered collections of key-value pairs, where each key is associated with a corresponding value.

Key Characteristics of Maps:

- **Key-Value Pairs:** Maps store data in the form of key-value pairs. Each key acts as a unique identifier for its associated value.
- **Unordered:** Maps do not maintain any specific order for the key-value pairs they store. The order in which elements are iterated over a map is not guaranteed to be consistent.
- **Efficient Lookup:** Maps are designed for efficient lookup and retrieval of values based on their keys. They use hash tables internally to achieve fast access times.
- **Dynamic Size:** Maps can grow or shrink dynamically as you add or remove key-value pairs.

Declaring and Initializing Maps

You declare a map in Go using the following syntax:

```
var mapName map[keyType]valueType
```

- **mapName:** The name you choose for your map
- **keyType:** The data type of the keys in the map
- **valueType:** The data type of the values associated with the keys

Examples:

```
var studentGrades map[string]int     // A map to store student names (keys) and their grades (values)
var wordCounts map[string]int        // A map to store words (keys) and their frequencies (values)
var isLoggedIn map[int]bool          // A map to store user IDs (keys) and their login status (values)
```

To initialize a map, you need to use the make function:

```
studentGrades := make(map[string]int)
wordCounts := make(map[string]int)
isLoggedIn := make(map[int]bool)
```

You can also initialize a map with some initial key-value pairs using a map literal:

```
studentGrades := map[string]int{
```

```
    "Alice": 95,
    "Bob": 88,
    "Charlie": 72,
}
```

Key Points

- Maps store key-value pairs, where keys are unique identifiers for their associated values
- Maps are unordered collections
- Maps provide efficient lookup of values based on keys
- Maps can grow or shrink dynamically
- Declare maps using the map keyword and initialize them using the `make` function or a map literal

Maps offer a powerful way to organize and access data based on keys. They are particularly useful when you need to store and retrieve information associated with specific identifiers, such as user profiles, product catalogs, or configuration settings.

Working with Maps

Once you've created a map, you'll need to interact with its key-value pairs. Go provides straightforward ways to add, retrieve, modify, and delete entries within a map, allowing you to manage and manipulate your data effectively.

1. Adding Key-Value Pairs

You can add a new key-value pair to a map using the following syntax:

```
mapName[key] = value
```

Example:

```
studentGrades := make(map[string]int)
studentGrades["Alice"] = 95
studentGrades["Bob"] = 88
```

2. Retrieving Values

You can retrieve the value associated with a key using the following syntax:

```
value := mapName[key]
```

Example:

```
aliceGrade := studentGrades["Alice"]
fmt.Println(aliceGrade) // Output: 95
```

3. Modifying Values

You can modify the value associated with an existing key by simply assigning a new value to it.

Example:

```
studentGrades["Bob"] = 92 // Update Bob's grade
```

4. Deleting Key-Value Pairs

You can delete a key-value pair from a map using the `delete` function.

```
delete(mapName, key)
```

Example:

```
delete(studentGrades, "Charlie") // Remove Charlie's entry from the map
```

5. Checking if a Key Exists: The Comma-ok Idiom

Go provides a convenient way to check if a key exists in a map using the "comma-ok idiom."

```
value, ok := mapName[key]
if ok {
    // Key exists, and 'value' contains the associated value
} else {
    // Key doesn't exist
}
```

Example:

```
grade, exists := studentGrades["David"]
if exists {
    fmt.Println("David's grade:", grade)
} else {
    fmt.Println("David is not in the map")
}
```

6. Iterating over Maps

You can iterate over the key-value pairs in a map using a `for-range` loop.

```
for key, value := range studentGrades {
    fmt.Println("Student:", key, "Grade:", value)
}
```

Key Points

- Add key-value pairs using `mapName[key] = value`.
- Retrieve values using `value := mapName[key]`.
- Modify values by assigning new values to existing keys.
- Delete key-value pairs using the `delete` function.
- Check if a key exists using the comma-ok idiom (`value, ok := mapName[key]`).
- Iterate over maps using `for-range` loops.

By mastering these operations, you can effectively manage and manipulate data stored in maps, enabling you to build dynamic and data-driven Go programs. Remember that maps are unordered, so the order of iteration might not be consistent.

Map Internals

Under the hood, Go implements maps using hash tables. A hash table is a data structure that allows for efficient storage and retrieval of key-value pairs. It achieves this by using a hash function to compute an index (or hash code) for each key, which determines where the corresponding value is stored in an underlying array.

Key Components of a Hash Table:

- **Hash Function:** A hash function takes a key as input and produces a hash code as output. A good hash function distributes keys evenly across the hash table, minimizing collisions (situations where multiple keys map to the same index).

- **Array (Buckets):** The underlying array in a hash table is divided into buckets. Each bucket can hold multiple key-value pairs.
- **Collision Resolution:** When a collision occurs (two or more keys hash to the same index), the hash table needs a mechanism to handle it. Go uses a combination of chaining (storing colliding keys in a linked list within the bucket) and open addressing (finding an alternative empty bucket) to resolve collisions.

How Hash Tables Contribute to Efficiency:

- **Fast Key Lookup:** When you want to retrieve a value from a map, Go calculates the hash code for the key and uses it to directly access the corresponding bucket in the underlying array. This allows for near-constant-time lookup, even for large maps.
- **Efficient Insertion:** When you add a new key-value pair to a map, Go calculates the hash code for the key and inserts the pair into the appropriate bucket. If a collision occurs, the collision resolution mechanism ensures that the new pair is stored correctly.
- **Dynamic Resizing:** Go's map implementation automatically resizes the underlying array (and potentially the hash function) as the number of key-value pairs grows. This ensures that the map remains efficient even as it expands.

Key Points:

- Go implements maps using hash tables.
- Hash tables use hash functions to compute indices for keys, enabling fast lookup and insertion.
- Collision resolution mechanisms handle situations where multiple keys hash to the same index.
- Go's map implementation automatically resizes the hash table as needed, ensuring efficiency even for large maps.

While you don't need to understand the intricate details of hash table implementation to use maps effectively in Go, having a basic grasp of their internal workings can help you appreciate their efficiency and make informed decisions about their usage in your programs.

Map Gotchas

While maps are incredibly useful for storing and retrieving data based on keys, there are some important considerations and potential pitfalls to be aware of when working with them in Go. Understanding these nuances will help you avoid common errors and write more robust code.

1. **Unordered Nature**
    - **Key Point:** Maps in Go do not guarantee any specific order of key-value pairs. The order in which elements are iterated over a map can change between runs or even during the same run.
    - **Implication:** If you need to maintain a specific order for your data, you'll need to use a different data structure, such as a slice, or implement your own sorting mechanism.
    - **Example:**

```go
myMap := map[string]int{
    "apple":  1,
    "banana": 2,
    "orange": 3,
}

for key, value := range myMap {
    fmt.Println(key, value)
}

// Output might be in any order, e.g.:
// banana 2
```

```
// orange 3
// apple 1
```

2. **Nil Maps**
   - **Key Point:** A nil map (`nil`) is a map that has not been initialized using the `make` function. Attempting to access or modify a nil map will result in a runtime panic.
   - **Checking for Nil Maps:** Always check if a map is nil before working with it.

```
var myMap map[string]int // nil map

if myMap == nil {
    fmt.Println("Map is nil")
}

myMap = make(map[string]int) // Initialize the map
```

   - **Empty Maps:** An empty map is a map that has been initialized but contains no key-value pairs. You can check if a map is empty by comparing its length to 0 using the `len` function.

```
if len(myMap) == 0 {
    fmt.Println("Map is empty")
}
```

3. **Concurrent Access**
   - **Key Point:** Maps in Go are not inherently safe for concurrent access. If multiple goroutines try to read from and write to the same map simultaneously, it can lead to data races and unpredictable behavior.
   - **Synchronization:** To ensure safe concurrent access to maps, you need to use synchronization mechanisms like mutexes or channels.

```
var mutex sync.Mutex
myMap := make(map[string]int)

// Read from the map
mutex.Lock()
value := myMap["key"]
mutex.Unlock()

// Write to the map
mutex.Lock()
myMap["newKey"] = newValue
mutex.Unlock()
```

In this example, a `sync.Mutex` is used to protect the map from concurrent access. The `Lock` method is called before accessing the map, and the `Unlock` method is called afterward to release the lock.

Additional Considerations

- **Key Types:** Not all data types can be used as keys in a map. Keys must be comparable, meaning you can use the `==` and `!=` operators to compare them. Common key types include basic types like `int`, `string`, and `bool`, as well as some composite types like structs with comparable fields.
- **Iterating over Large Maps:** Iterating over large maps can be computationally expensive. If you need to perform frequent iterations over a large map, consider alternative data structures or optimization techniques.

By understanding these map gotchas and taking necessary precautions, you can leverage the power of maps effectively in your Go programs. Remember to handle nil maps gracefully, be mindful of their unordered nature, and synchronize access in concurrent scenarios to ensure data integrity and avoid unexpected behavior.

Chapter Summary

In this chapter, you have embarked on a journey to understand the essential data structures that underpin data organization and manipulation in Go. We have covered:

- **The concept of data structures** as ways to arrange and store data efficiently, facilitating access, modification, and manipulation.
- **Arrays:** You learned about arrays as fixed-size collections of elements of the same type, their declaration, initialization, accessing elements using indices, and their limitations.
- **Multidimensional Arrays:** You were introduced to multidimensional arrays (arrays of arrays) for representing data in a grid-like or tabular structure. You learned how to declare, initialize, and access elements in multidimensional arrays.
- **Slices:** You explored slices as dynamic views into underlying arrays, offering flexibility and efficiency in managing collections of data. You learned how to create slices from arrays, literals, and the make function. You also explored various slice operations, including appending, slicing, and iterating.
- **Slice Internals:** You delved into the internal representation of slices, understanding their components (pointer, length, and capacity) and how they influence slice behavior and performance.
- **Slice Gotchas:** You learned about common pitfalls and misconceptions related to slices, such as pass-by-value semantics, the difference between capacity and length, and nil slices.
- **Maps:** You discovered maps as unordered collections of key-value pairs, offering efficient lookup and retrieval based on keys. You learned how to declare, initialize, add, retrieve, modify, and delete key-value pairs in maps.
- **Map Internals:** You were briefly introduced to the internal implementation of maps using hash tables, highlighting how they contribute to efficient key lookup and insertion.
- **Map Gotchas:** You became aware of common considerations when working with maps, such as their unordered nature, nil maps, and the need for synchronization in concurrent access scenarios.

By mastering these essential data structures, you have acquired valuable tools for organizing, managing, and manipulating data in your Go programs. Arrays provide a simple way to store fixed-size collections, while slices offer dynamic resizing and efficient memory usage. Maps enable you to associate values with unique keys, providing fast lookup and retrieval capabilities. Understanding the strengths and limitations of each data structure allows you to choose the most appropriate one for your specific needs, leading to more efficient, readable, and maintainable Go code.

In the next chapter, we will explore structs, which allow you to create custom data types that group together related fields. This will further expand your ability to model and represent complex data in your Go programs.

Understanding Structs and Custom Types in Go

Outline

- Introduction to Structs
- Defining Structs
- Creating and Initializing Structs
- Accessing and Modifying Struct Fields
- Nested Structs
- Anonymous Structs
- Methods: Adding Behavior to Structs
- Custom Types: Type Aliases and New Types
- Chapter Summary

Introduction to Structs

In the world of Go programming, structs serve as the architects of organized and meaningful data representation. They allow you to group together related data fields into a single, cohesive unit known as a *composite type*. Think of structs as blueprints for creating custom data structures that mirror the entities and concepts you encounter in the real world.

The Power of Structs

- **Data Encapsulation:** Structs encapsulate multiple pieces of information that belong together logically. For instance, a Person struct might include fields for name, age, and address.
- **Modeling Real-World Entities:** Structs provide a natural way to represent real-world objects and concepts within your code. You can create structs to model things like Book, Car, Employee, or any other entity with multiple attributes.
- **Code Organization:** By grouping related data into structs, you promote better code organization and clarity. Instead of having scattered variables, you have a single struct that represents a complete entity.
- **Readability:** Structs make your code more readable and self-documenting. The struct's name and its field names convey the meaning and purpose of the data, making your code easier to understand.
- **Flexibility:** Structs can be nested, meaning they can contain other structs as fields. This allows you to model complex relationships and hierarchies within your data.
- **Methods:** Structs can have methods associated with them, allowing you to define behavior and operations that are specific to the struct's data.

Illustrative Analogy

Consider a car. It has various attributes like its make, model, year, color, and number of doors. Instead of representing each attribute as a separate variable, you can create a Car struct that encapsulates all these related pieces of information:

```go
type Car struct {
    Make   string
    Model  string
    Year   int
    Color  string
    Doors  int
}
```

Now, you can create instances of the Car struct to represent different cars, each with its own set of attributes:

```
myCar := Car{Make: "Toyota", Model: "Camry", Year: 2022, Color: "Silver", Doors: 4}
```

Key Points

- Structs are composite data types that group related fields together.
- They enable you to model real-world entities and create more organized code.
- Structs enhance code readability and maintainability.
- They can be nested to represent complex relationships.
- Methods can be associated with structs to define their behavior.

In the following sections, we'll delve deeper into the mechanics of defining, creating, and working with structs in Go. You'll learn how to access and modify struct fields, nest structs, define methods, and leverage custom types to create even more powerful and expressive data representations.

Defining Structs

Structs in Go are blueprints for creating custom data types that encapsulate related fields. You define a struct using the `type` and `struct` keywords, followed by the struct's name and a list of its fields enclosed in curly braces `{}`. Each field within a struct has a name and a data type, representing a specific attribute of the entity the struct models.

Syntax

```
type structName struct {
    fieldName1 dataType1
    fieldName2 dataType2
    // ... more fields
}
```

- **type**: The keyword used to introduce a new type definition.
- **structName**: The name you choose for your struct. It should be descriptive and follow Go's naming conventions (CamelCase).
- **struct**: The keyword that indicates you're defining a struct type.
- **fieldName1 dataType1, fieldName2 dataType2, etc.**: A list of fields within the struct, each with its name and data type.
- **{ and }**: Curly braces enclose the list of fields.

Examples

1. **Person Struct**

    ```
    type Person struct {
        Name  string
        Age   int
        Email string
    }
    ```

2. **Book Struct**

    ```
    type Book struct {
        Title  string
        Author string
        ISBN   string
    ```

```
        Pages    int
}
```

3. **Product Struct**

```
type Product struct {
    ID          int
    Name        string
    Price       float64
    Description string
    InStock     bool
}
```

Key Points

- Use the `type` and `struct` keywords to define a struct.
- Each field within a struct has a name and a data type.
- Field names should be descriptive and follow Go's naming conventions.
- You can define structs to represent various entities, objects, or concepts in your program.

By defining structs, you create custom data types that encapsulate related information, making your code more organized, readable, and maintainable.

Creating and Initializing Structs

Once you've defined a struct, you can create instances (variables) of that struct to represent specific entities or objects. Go provides several ways to create and initialize struct instances, offering flexibility and convenience.

1. Struct Literals

The most common way to create a struct instance is using a struct literal. A struct literal uses curly braces `{}` to enclose a comma-separated list of field-value pairs.

- **Syntax**

```
variableName := structName{field1: value1, field2: value2, ...}
```

- **Example:**

```
type Person struct {
    Name string
    Age  int
}

p1 := Person{Name: "Alice", Age: 30}
```

This creates a `Person` struct instance named p1 with Name set to "Alice" and Age set to 30.

2. The new Keyword

You can also create a struct instance using the new keyword. This allocates memory for the struct and returns a pointer to it. The fields of the struct are initialized to their zero values (e.g., 0 for numeric types, "" for strings, `false` for booleans).

- **Syntax**

```
variableName := new(structName)
```

- **Example:**

```
p2 := new(Person)
p2.Name = "Bob"
p2.Age = 25
```

This creates a `Person` struct instance named p2 with all fields initially set to their zero values. You then assign values to the Name and Age fields using the dot notation.

3. Initializing with Positional Values

You can initialize struct fields using positional values, where the values are provided in the same order as the fields are declared in the struct definition.

- **Example:**

```
p3 := Person{"Charlie", 35}
```

This creates a `Person` struct instance named p3 with Name set to "Charlie" and Age set to 35. Note that this approach requires you to provide values for all fields in the struct, and the order of the values must match the order of the fields.

Key Points:

- Create struct instances using struct literals or the new keyword
- Initialize struct fields using field-value pairs, positional values, or the new function
- Struct literals are the most common and convenient way to create and initialize structs
- The new keyword allocates memory for the struct and returns a pointer to it
- Positional values can be used for initialization but require providing values for all fields in the correct order

By understanding these different ways to create and initialize structs, you have the flexibility to choose the most appropriate approach based on your specific needs and coding style. Remember that proper initialization is crucial for ensuring that your struct instances contain valid and meaningful data.

Accessing and Modifying Struct Fields

Once you've created a struct instance, you'll often need to access and manipulate its individual fields. Go provides a straightforward way to do this using the dot notation (`.`). The dot notation allows you to reference a specific field within a struct by combining the struct instance's name, a dot, and the field's name.

Accessing Struct Fields

To access the value of a struct field, use the following syntax:

```
structInstance.fieldName
```

Example

```
type Person struct {
    Name string
    Age  int
}
```

```go
p := Person{Name: "Alice", Age: 30}

fmt.Println(p.Name) // Output: Alice
fmt.Println(p.Age)  // Output: 30
```

In this example, we access the Name and Age fields of the p struct instance using the dot notation.

Modifying Struct Fields

You can modify the value of a struct field by assigning a new value to it using the dot notation and the assignment operator (=).

Example:

```go
p.Age = 31 // Update Alice's age to 31
```

Key Points

- Use the dot notation (.) to access and modify struct fields
- Combine the struct instance's name, a dot, and the field's name to reference a specific field
- Assign new values to fields using the assignment operator (=)

By mastering the dot notation, you gain the ability to interact with the individual components of your struct instances, enabling you to read their values, update them as needed, and perform various operations on the encapsulated data. This flexibility empowers you to build dynamic and data-driven Go programs that model real-world entities and processes effectively.

Nested Structs

In the real world, objects and entities often have complex relationships and hierarchical structures. Go's support for nested structs allows you to mirror these complexities within your code, providing a way to model intricate data representations and express relationships between different entities.

The Essence of Nested Structs

- A nested struct is simply a struct that contains one or more fields that are themselves structs.
- This nesting enables you to create hierarchical structures and represent relationships between different entities.

Modeling Complex Relationships

Nested structs are particularly useful when you need to model data that has multiple levels of organization or relationships between different components.

- **Example: Representing an Address**

```go
type Address struct {
    Street     string
    City       string
    State      string
    PostalCode string
}

type Person struct {
    Name    string
    Age     int
    Address Address
```

}

In this example, the `Person` struct has a field named `Address`, which is itself a struct representing a person's address. This nesting allows you to encapsulate the address information within the `Person` struct, creating a more organized and meaningful representation of a person's data.

Working with Nested Structs

You can access and modify fields within nested structs using multiple levels of dot notation.

```go
func main() {
    p := Person{
        Name: "Alice",
        Age:  30,
        Address: Address{
            Street:     "123 Main St",
            City:       "Anytown",
            State:      "CA",
            PostalCode: "12345",
        },
    }

    fmt.Println(p.Name)              // Output: Alice
    fmt.Println(p.Address.City)      // Output: Anytown
    p.Address.PostalCode = "54321"   // Modify the postal code
}
```

Key Points

- Nested structs allow you to represent complex relationships and hierarchies within your data.
- You can access and modify fields within nested structs using multiple levels of dot notation.
- Nested structs can be used to model a wide range of real-world scenarios, such as customer profiles with billing and shipping addresses, employee records with department information, or product catalogs with nested categories.

By leveraging the power of nested structs, you can create Go programs that accurately reflect the complexities of the real world, leading to more intuitive, organized, and maintainable code.

Anonymous Structs

In Go, you have the flexibility to define structs without assigning them explicit names. These nameless structures are aptly called *anonymous structs*. They provide a concise way to create temporary or lightweight data structures directly within your code, without the need to define a separate named struct type.

Defining Anonymous Structs

You define an anonymous struct using the `struct` keyword, followed by a list of fields enclosed in curly braces `{}`. Since there's no name associated with the struct, you typically create an instance of it directly during declaration.

Syntax

```go
variableName := struct {
    fieldName1 dataType1
    fieldName2 dataType2
    // ... more fields
```

```
}{field1: value1, field2: value2, ...}
```

Use Cases

Anonymous structs are handy in situations where:

- **Temporary Structures:** You need a quick and lightweight way to group related data together for a specific purpose, without the overhead of defining a named struct.
- **One-off Data Representations:** You're working with data that doesn't warrant a full-fledged named struct, perhaps for a single function or a specific code block.
- **Function Return Values:** You want to return multiple values from a function in a structured way, without creating a separate named struct.

Example

```
func getCoordinates() struct {
    X int
    Y int
} {
    // ... (calculate coordinates)
    return struct {
        X int
        Y int
    }{10, 20}
}

func main() {
    coords := getCoordinates()
    fmt.Println("Coordinates:", coords.X, coords.Y)
}
```

In this example, the `getCoordinates` function returns an anonymous struct containing the X and Y coordinates. The `main` function receives this struct and accesses its fields using the dot notation.

Key Points

- Anonymous structs are structs without explicitly defined names
- They are useful for creating temporary or lightweight data structures
- You define and create an instance of an anonymous struct in a single statement
- Anonymous structs can be used to return multiple values from a function in a structured manner

Anonymous structs offer a convenient way to create ad-hoc data structures directly within your code. They enhance code conciseness and flexibility, especially when dealing with temporary or one-off data representations. However, for more complex or reusable data structures, it's generally recommended to define named structs to improve code readability and maintainability.

Methods: Adding Behavior to Structs

While structs are excellent for encapsulating data, they become even more powerful when you associate functions with them. In Go, these associated functions are called *methods*. Methods allow you to define behavior and operations that are specific to the struct's data, making your code more organized, readable, and object-oriented.

Defining Methods

You define a method in Go by associating a function with a specific struct type. This association is established through a special parameter called the *receiver* in the function's signature. The receiver specifies the type of struct the method operates on.

Syntax

```
func (receiver structType) methodName(parameters...) returnType {
    // ... method body
}
```

- `receiver`: This is a variable that represents an instance of the struct the method is associated with. You can choose any name for the receiver, but it's common to use a shortened version of the struct name (e.g., p for `Person`, c for `Circle`).
- `structType`: The type of struct the method is associated with.
- `methodName`: The name of the method. It should be descriptive and follow Go's naming conventions (CamelCase).
- `parameters...`: A comma-separated list of parameters (if any) that the method accepts.
- `returnType`: The data type of the value that the method returns (if any).

Calling Methods

You call a method on a struct instance using the dot notation (`.`), similar to accessing struct fields.

Syntax

```
structInstance.methodName(arguments...)
```

Examples

```
type Circle struct {
    Radius float64
}

// Method to calculate the area of a circle
func (c Circle) area() float64 {
    return math.Pi * c.Radius * c.Radius
}

func main() {
    myCircle := Circle{Radius: 5}
    area := myCircle.area()
    fmt.Println("Area:", area)
}
```

In this example, we define a `Circle` struct with a `Radius` field. We then associate a method named `area` with the `Circle` struct. The `area` method calculates and returns the area of the circle based on its radius. In the `main` function, we create a `Circle` instance and call its `area` method to get the calculated area.

Key Points

- Methods associate functions with specific struct types.
- The receiver parameter in a method's signature specifies the struct type the method operates on.
- Methods can access and modify the fields of the struct instance they are called on.

- Methods provide a way to add behavior and operations to structs, making your code more object-oriented and organized.

By mastering the concept of methods, you can create Go programs that are not only data-centric but also behavior-driven. Methods allow you to encapsulate logic and operations within your structs, leading to more modular, reusable, and expressive code.

Custom Types: Type Aliases and New Types

Type Aliases

In the realm of Go programming, where clarity and expressiveness are paramount, type aliases emerge as a valuable tool for enhancing code readability and tailoring your code to specific domains or contexts. A type alias, as the name suggests, provides an alternative name for an existing type, allowing you to create more meaningful and self-documenting code.

Creating Type Aliases

You create a type alias in Go using the `type` keyword, followed by the new alias name, the = operator, and the existing type you want to alias.

Syntax

```
type aliasName existingType
```

Example:

```
type ID int64 // Create a new type 'ID' that is an alias for int64
type Name string // Create a new type 'Name' that is an alias for string

func main() {
    var userID ID = 12345
    var userName Name = "Alice"

    fmt.Println(userID, userName)
}
```

In this example, we define two type aliases: ID for `int64` and Name for `string`. We then use these aliases to declare variables `userID` and `userName`, making the code more readable and self-explanatory.

Benefits of Type Aliases

- **Readability:** Type aliases can make your code more readable by providing meaningful names for types that might otherwise be represented by less descriptive built-in types.
- **Domain-Specific Language:** Type aliases can help you create a domain-specific language within your Go code, making it easier to understand and reason about the concepts and entities relevant to your application's domain.
- **Code Refactoring:** If you need to change the underlying type of a variable in the future, you can simply modify the type alias definition, and all occurrences of the alias will automatically reflect the change.
- **Documentation:** Type aliases can serve as a form of documentation, indicating the intended use or meaning of a variable based on its type.

Key Points

- Type aliases provide alternative names for existing types.

- They enhance code readability, expressiveness, and maintainability.
- Type aliases can be used to create domain-specific languages and facilitate code refactoring.

By leveraging type aliases, you can tailor your Go code to specific domains, improve its readability, and make it more self-documenting. Now, let's explore how to create entirely new types in Go, which offer even more flexibility and control over your data representations.

New Types

While type aliases provide alternative names for existing types, Go also allows you to create entirely new types using the `type` keyword. These new types, distinct from their underlying types, offer a powerful way to encapsulate data and behavior, enhancing code organization, type safety, and expressiveness.

Creating New Types

You create a new type in Go using the `type` keyword, followed by the new type's name, and the underlying type it's based on.

Syntax

```
type newTypeName underlyingType
```

Example:

```
type Temperature float64  // New type 'Temperature' based on float64
type Length int           // New type 'Length' based on int
```

Inheritance and Methods

New types inherit the underlying type's behavior, meaning you can perform the same operations on them as you would on the underlying type. However, the crucial distinction is that you can define methods specifically for these new types, adding custom behavior and functionality.

Example:

```
type Celsius Temperature

// Method to convert Celsius to Fahrenheit
func (c Celsius) ToFahrenheit() Fahrenheit {
    return Fahrenheit((c * 9 / 5) + 32)
}

type Fahrenheit Temperature

// Method to convert Fahrenheit to Celsius
func (f Fahrenheit) ToCelsius() Celsius {
    return Celsius((f - 32) * 5 / 9)
}
```

In this example, we create two new types, `Celsius` and `Fahrenheit`, both based on the underlying type `Temperature` (which is itself an alias for `float64`). We then define methods `ToFahrenheit` on `Celsius` and `ToCelsius` on `Fahrenheit` to provide conversion functionality specific to each temperature scale.

Benefits of New Types

- **Type Safety:** New types create distinct types in Go, even if they share the same underlying type. This enforces type safety, preventing you from accidentally mixing values of different new types, even if their underlying representations are compatible.

- **Encapsulation:** New types allow you to encapsulate data and behavior together. By defining methods on new types, you can create self-contained units that manage their own data and operations.
- **Code Organization:** New types promote better code organization by providing meaningful names for specific data representations and their associated operations.
- **Expressiveness:** New types enable you to create a more expressive and domain-specific language within your Go code, making it easier to understand and reason about the concepts and entities relevant to your application.

Key Points

- Use the `type` keyword to create new types based on existing types.
- New types inherit the behavior of their underlying types.
- You can define methods specifically for new types, adding custom behavior.
- New types enforce type safety and promote encapsulation, code organization, and expressiveness.

By mastering the creation and use of new types, you can elevate your Go programming skills and build more robust, maintainable, and expressive code. New types provide a powerful way to model real-world concepts, encapsulate data and behavior, and create a domain-specific language within your Go programs.

Chapter Summary

In this chapter, you've explored the powerful concepts of structs and custom types in Go, which enable you to model real-world entities, encapsulate data and behavior, and create more organized and expressive code.

Here are the key takeaways:

- **Structs:** You learned how to define structs using the `type` and `struct` keywords, grouping related data fields into a single composite type. You also saw how to create struct instances using struct literals or the new keyword, and how to access and modify struct fields using the dot notation.
- **Nested Structs:** You explored how nested structs allow you to represent complex relationships and hierarchies within your data, providing a more natural and intuitive way to model real-world entities.
- **Anonymous Structs:** You were introduced to anonymous structs as a concise way to create temporary or lightweight data structures directly within your code.
- **Methods:** You learned how to define methods on structs, associating functions with specific struct types to add behavior and operations related to the struct's data.
- **Custom Types:** You discovered how to create type aliases using the `type` keyword to provide alternative names for existing types, enhancing code readability and expressiveness. You also learned how to create entirely new types, which inherit the underlying type's behavior but can have their own methods defined on them, promoting type safety and encapsulation.

By mastering these concepts, you've added valuable tools to your Go programming arsenal. Structs and custom types enable you to model data more effectively, organize your code, and create a more domain-specific and expressive language within your programs. In the next chapter, we'll dive into the world of pointers and memory management in Go, exploring how to work with memory directly and optimize your code for performance and efficiency.

Section III:
Intermediate Go Concepts

Pointers and Memory Management in Go

Outline

- Understanding Memory and Pointers
- Declaring and Using Pointers
- The new Function and Heap Allocation
- Pointer Arithmetic
- Pointers and Functions
- Pointers and Structs
- Common Pointer Use Cases
- Pointers and Safety
- When to Use Pointers
- Chapter Summary

Understanding Memory and Pointers

In the heart of every Go program lies its memory, the dynamic storage space where data resides during execution. Variables, data structures, and even the program's instructions themselves all find their temporary abode within this memory landscape. Understanding how Go manages memory is key to writing efficient and performant code. At the core of memory management in Go are **pointers**, special variables that act as signposts, guiding you to the exact locations where your data is stored.

Memory: The Data Warehouse

Think of your computer's memory as a vast warehouse filled with countless storage units. Each unit has a unique address, and your program's data is stored within these units during execution. Variables, which you've already encountered, serve as labels for these storage units, allowing you to conveniently access and manipulate the data they contain.

Pointers: The Memory Navigators

- **Memory Addresses:** Every piece of data stored in memory has a unique address, much like a street address identifies a specific house.
- **Pointers as Variables:** Pointers are special variables that store these memory addresses. Instead of holding the actual data, they hold the location where the data resides.
- **Indirect Access:** By using a pointer, you can indirectly access and manipulate the data stored at the memory address it points to.
- **References:** You can think of pointers as references or aliases to variables. They provide an alternative way to access the same underlying data.

The Relationship Between Pointers and Variables

- **Variables and Memory:** When you declare a variable in Go, the compiler allocates a suitable storage unit in memory to hold its value. The variable's name then becomes associated with that memory location.
- **Creating Pointers:** You can create a pointer to a variable using the address-of operator (&). This operator returns the memory address of the variable.
- **Dereferencing Pointers:** To access the value stored at the memory address held by a pointer, you use the dereference operator (*). This operator "follows" the pointer to its target location and retrieves the data stored there.

Benefits of Pointers

- **Efficient Data Sharing:** Pointers enable you to share large data structures between different parts of your program without making expensive copies.
- **Modifying Data in Functions:** By passing pointers to functions, you allow those functions to modify the original values of variables, rather than just working with copies.
- **Dynamic Data Structures:** Pointers are essential for building dynamic data structures like linked lists and trees, where each node contains pointers to other nodes, creating a flexible and interconnected network of data.

Key Takeaways

- Memory is the storage space where data is stored during program execution.
- Pointers are variables that store memory addresses.
- Pointers provide indirect access to data stored in memory.
- Pointers and variables are closely related, with pointers referencing the memory locations of variables.

By understanding the relationship between memory, variables, and pointers, you gain a deeper insight into how Go manages data and how pointers can be leveraged to optimize your code, enable data sharing, and build dynamic data structures.

Declaring and Using Pointers

Pointers in Go are like special keys that unlock the ability to directly manipulate data stored in memory. By understanding how to declare, assign, and dereference pointers, you gain precise control over your data and can build efficient and flexible programs.

Declaring Pointer Variables

To declare a pointer variable in Go, you use the asterisk (*) operator followed by the data type that the pointer will point to.

- **Syntax:**

```
var pointerName *dataType
```

- **Example:**

```
var numPtr *int        // Pointer to an integer
var strPtr *string     // Pointer to a string
var personPtr *Person  // Pointer to a Person struct
```

Getting the Memory Address: The & Operator

The address-of operator (&) is used to obtain the memory address of a variable. This address can then be assigned to a pointer variable.

- **Example:**

    ```
    var num int = 10
    numPtr := &num // Assign the address of 'num' to 'numPtr'
    ```

Accessing the Value: The * Operator (Dereferencing)

The dereference operator (*) is used to access the value stored at the memory address pointed to by a pointer.

- **Example:**

    ```
    value := *numPtr // Access the value stored at the address pointed to by 'numPtr'
    fmt.Println(value) // Output: 10
    ```

Examples of Declaring, Assigning, and Dereferencing Pointers

```
var x int = 42
var xPtr *int = &x    // Declare and assign a pointer to 'x'

fmt.Println(xPtr)   // Output: 0xc0000140a0 (memory address)
fmt.Println(*xPtr) // Output: 42 (value at the memory address)

*xPtr = 99 // Modify the value at the memory address
fmt.Println(x)   // Output: 99 (the original variable 'x' is also modified)

var name string = "Alice"
var namePtr *string = &name

fmt.Println(*namePtr) // Output: Alice
```

Key Points

- Declare pointer variables using the * operator followed by the data type.
- Get the memory address of a variable using the & operator.
- Access the value stored at a memory address using the * operator (dereferencing).
- Modifying the value through a pointer also modifies the original variable.

Pointers provide a powerful way to indirectly access and manipulate data stored in memory. By understanding how to declare, assign, and dereference pointers, you gain finer control over your data and can implement more efficient and flexible algorithms in Go. In the next section, we'll explore how to allocate memory on the heap using the new function and how pointers are essential for working with heap-allocated data.

The new Function and Heap Allocation

In Go, the new function serves as a bridge between your code and the dynamic memory allocation capabilities of the operating system. It allows you to request a block of memory from the heap, a region of memory used for storing data whose lifetime is not tied to a specific function's execution.

How new Works

1. **Memory Allocation:** When you call the new function with a data type as its argument, it requests a block of memory from the heap large enough to hold a value of that type.

2. **Zero Initialization:** The allocated memory is initialized to the zero value for the specified data type (e.g., 0 for numeric types, `false` for booleans, " " for strings).
3. **Pointer Return:** The new function returns a pointer to the newly allocated memory. This pointer allows you to access and manipulate the data stored on the heap.

Syntax:

```
pointer := new(dataType)
```

Example:

```
func main() {
    intPtr := new(int)          // Allocate memory for an integer on the heap
    *intPtr = 42                // Assign a value to the allocated memory
    fmt.Println(*intPtr)        // Output: 42

    strPtr := new(string)       // Allocate memory for a string on the heap
    *strPtr = "Hello, heap!"    // Assign a value to the allocated memory
    fmt.Println(*strPtr)        // Output: Hello, heap!
}
```

Stack vs. Heap

- **Stack:** The stack is a region of memory used for storing local variables and function call information. It's managed automatically by the Go runtime, and memory allocated on the stack is automatically freed when a function returns.
- **Heap:** The heap is a larger, more flexible region of memory used for storing data whose lifetime is not directly tied to a function's execution. Memory allocated on the heap must be explicitly freed (in languages like C) or managed by a garbage collector (as in Go) to avoid memory leaks.

Importance of Pointers for Heap Allocation

- **Accessing Heap Data:** Since memory allocated on the heap doesn't have a directly associated variable name, you need pointers to access and manipulate that data.
- **Dynamic Data Structures:** Pointers are crucial for building dynamic data structures like linked lists and trees, where nodes are typically allocated on the heap and linked together using pointers.
- **Sharing Data:** Pointers enable you to share data between different parts of your program without making copies, improving efficiency, especially for large data structures.

Key Points

- The new function allocates memory on the heap and returns a pointer to it.
- Pointers are essential for accessing and managing data stored on the heap.
- Use the new function to create variables on the heap and access them using pointers.
- Heap allocation provides flexibility for storing data whose lifetime is not tied to a function's execution.

By understanding heap allocation and the role of pointers, you gain the ability to create and manage dynamic data structures, share data efficiently, and optimize memory usage in your Go programs.

Pointer Arithmetic

Pointer arithmetic in Go empowers you to perform basic arithmetic operations on pointers, enabling you to navigate through memory and access data directly. While this capability provides low-level control and can lead to performance optimizations, it also requires careful handling to avoid potential pitfalls.

Understanding Pointer Arithmetic

- **Memory Addresses and Offsets:** When you perform arithmetic operations on a pointer, you're essentially adjusting the memory address it holds by a certain offset. The offset is calculated based on the size of the data type the pointer points to.
- **Arrays and Slices:** Pointer arithmetic is particularly useful when working with arrays and slices, as they are represented in memory as contiguous blocks of elements. By incrementing or decrementing a pointer, you can move it to point to different elements within the array or slice.

Syntax

- **Incrementing a Pointer:** `pointer++` (moves the pointer to the next element)
- **Decrementing a Pointer:** `pointer--` (moves the pointer to the previous element)
- **Adding an Offset:** `pointer + offset` (moves the pointer forward by `offset` elements)
- **Subtracting an Offset:** `pointer - offset` (moves the pointer backward by `offset` elements)

Examples

- **Iterating over an Array**

```go
numbers := [5]int{10, 20, 30, 40, 50}
var ptr *int = &numbers[0] // Pointer to the first element

for i := 0; i < len(numbers); i++ {
    fmt.Println(*ptr) // Access the value at the current pointer location
    ptr++             // Move the pointer to the next element
}
```

- **Modifying Slice Elements**

```go
data := []int{1, 2, 3, 4, 5}
ptr := &data[0] // Pointer to the first element

for i := 0; i < len(data); i++ {
    *ptr *= 2 // Double the value at the current pointer location
    ptr++
}

fmt.Println(data) // Output: [2 4 6 8 10]
```

Key Points

- Pointer arithmetic allows you to navigate through memory by adjusting the memory address held by a pointer
- It is particularly useful when working with arrays and slices
- Use pointer arithmetic carefully to avoid accessing memory outside the bounds of your data structures, which can lead to undefined behavior and crashes

Pointer arithmetic provides a low-level mechanism for interacting with data in memory. While it can lead to performance optimizations in certain scenarios, it's essential to use it with caution and ensure that you stay within the valid bounds of your data structures.

Pointers and Functions

In Go, when you pass arguments to a function, they are typically passed by value. This means that the function receives a copy of the argument's value, and any modifications made to that copy within the function do not affect the original variable. However, by using pointers as function parameters, you can enable functions to directly modify the values of the original variables, providing a powerful mechanism for data manipulation and efficient data passing.

Pass by Value vs. Pass by Pointer

- **Pass by Value:** When you pass a variable by value to a function, a copy of the variable's value is created and passed to the function. Any changes made to this copy within the function do not affect the original variable.
- **Pass by Pointer:** When you pass a pointer to a function, you're essentially passing the memory address of the variable. The function receives a reference to the original variable, allowing it to directly access and modify its value.

Modifying Variables Using Pointers

```go
func double(x *int) {
    *x *= 2 // Modify the value at the memory address pointed to by 'x'
}

func main() {
    num := 5
    double(&num) // Pass the address of 'num'
    fmt.Println(num) // Output: 10 (the original 'num' is modified)
}
```

In this example, the `double` function takes a pointer to an integer as its parameter. Inside the function, it dereferences the pointer using the `*` operator and multiplies the value at that memory address by 2. This modification affects the original `num` variable in the `main` function.

Efficient Data Passing

Passing pointers can be particularly beneficial when dealing with large data structures like structs or arrays. Instead of creating a copy of the entire structure, which can be memory-intensive, you pass a pointer, allowing the function to access and modify the original data directly.

```go
type Person struct {
    Name string
    Age  int
}

func updateAge(p *Person, newAge int) {
    p.Age = newAge
}

func main() {
    person := Person{Name: "Alice", Age: 30}
    updateAge(&person, 35)
    fmt.Println(person.Age) // Output: 35
}
```

In this example, the `updateAge` function takes a pointer to a `Person` struct and updates its `Age` field. This modification directly affects the original `person` struct in the `main` function.

Key Points

- Pointers as function parameters enable functions to modify the original values of variables.
- Pass by value creates a copy of the argument, while pass by pointer passes a reference.

- Use pointers for efficient data passing of large data structures and when you need functions to modify variables.

By understanding how pointers interact with functions, you can write more flexible and efficient Go code. You can now choose between pass by value and pass by pointer based on your specific needs, allowing you to control whether functions modify the original data or work with copies.

Pointers and Structs

Pointers and structs form a powerful combination in Go, enabling you to create references to struct instances and manipulate their fields directly in memory. This capability offers several advantages, particularly when dealing with large structs or when you need to modify the original struct instance within a function.

Creating Pointers to Structs

You can create a pointer to a struct instance using the address-of operator (&) and assign it to a pointer variable of the corresponding struct type.

```go
type Person struct {
    Name string
    Age  int
}

func main() {
    person := Person{Name: "Alice", Age: 30}
    personPtr := &person // Create a pointer to the 'person' struct
}
```

Accessing and Modifying Struct Fields Using Pointers

To access or modify the fields of a struct through a pointer, you use the dereference operator (*) followed by the dot notation (.).

```go
fmt.Println((*personPtr).Name)  // Output: Alice
(*personPtr).Age = 31           // Modify the Age field
fmt.Println(person.Age)         // Output: 31 (the original struct is modified)
```

Go provides a shorthand syntax for accessing and modifying struct fields through pointers:

```go
fmt.Println(personPtr.Name) // Output: Alice
personPtr.Age = 31          // Modify the Age field
```

Benefits of Using Pointers with Structs

1. **Avoiding Copying:** When you pass a large struct to a function by value, a copy of the entire struct is created, which can be memory-intensive and impact performance. By passing a pointer to the struct instead, you avoid copying the entire struct, improving efficiency.
2. **Modifying the Original Struct:** When a function receives a pointer to a struct, it can directly modify the fields of the original struct instance, eliminating the need to return the modified struct from the function.
3. **Representing Optional Values:** Pointers can be used to represent optional struct values. A `nil` pointer indicates the absence of a struct instance.

Key Points

- Use the address-of operator (&) to create pointers to struct instances.
- Access and modify struct fields through pointers using the dereference operator (*) and dot notation (.).
- Go provides a shorthand syntax for accessing and modifying struct fields through pointers.
- Pointers with structs can improve performance by avoiding copying large structs and enable direct modification of the original struct instance.

By understanding how to use pointers with structs, you gain more control over your data and can write more efficient and flexible Go code. Pointers enable you to share large structs without incurring the overhead of copying, and they allow you to modify the original struct instance directly within functions, leading to cleaner and more expressive code.

Common Pointer Use Cases

Pointers play a vital role in various programming scenarios, offering flexibility, efficiency, and the ability to manipulate data directly in memory. Let's delve into some common use cases where pointers shine in Go:

1. Dynamic Data Structures

- **Linked Lists and Trees:** Pointers are the backbone of dynamic data structures like linked lists and trees. Each node in these structures contains pointers to other nodes, creating a chain or a hierarchical network of interconnected elements. This dynamic linking allows for efficient insertion, deletion, and traversal of elements, as you can simply modify pointers to rearrange the structure without moving large chunks of data.
- **Example (Linked List):**

```go
type Node struct {
    Value int
    Next  *Node
}

func main() {
    head := &Node{Value: 1, Next: nil}
    head.Next = &Node{Value: 2, Next: nil}
    // ... add more nodes
}
```

In this example, each `Node` contains a `Next` pointer that points to the next node in the list, forming a chain of interconnected nodes.

2. Sharing Data

- **Avoiding Copies:** When dealing with large data structures, passing them by value to functions can be inefficient, as it creates a copy of the entire structure. Pointers offer a solution by allowing you to pass a reference to the data, enabling multiple parts of your program to access and modify the same underlying data without the overhead of copying.
- **Example:**

```go
type BigData struct {
    // ... large number of fields
}

func processData(data *BigData) {
    // ... modify data directly
}
```

```go
func main() {
    bigData := BigData{/* ... initialize fields */}
    processData(&bigData) // Pass a pointer to avoid copying
}
```

3. Function Parameters

- **Modifying Arguments:** As discussed earlier, pointers as function parameters allow functions to modify the original values of variables passed to them. This is useful when you want a function to produce side effects or update the state of objects.
- **Example:**

```go
func swap(x, y *int) {
    temp := *x
    *x = *y
    *y = temp
}
```

The swap function takes pointers to two integers and swaps their values by directly modifying the data at the memory addresses pointed to by the pointers.

4. System Calls and C Interoperability

- **Low-Level Interactions:** When interacting with low-level system calls or C libraries, you might need to use pointers to pass memory addresses or interface with C data structures that rely on pointers.
- **Example (hypothetical):**

```go
// C function signature: void processData(int* data, int size);
func ProcessData(data []int) {
    C.processData(&data[0], C.int(len(data))) // Pass a pointer to the first element of the slice and its length
}
```

Choosing When to Use Pointers

While pointers offer flexibility and efficiency, it's important to use them judiciously. Consider using pointers when:

- You need to modify the original value of a variable within a function.
- You're working with large data structures and want to avoid copying them.
- You're building dynamic data structures like linked lists or trees.
- You need to interact with low-level system calls or C libraries.

Remember that pointers introduce the potential for null pointer dereferences and other memory-related errors. Use them carefully and with proper error handling to ensure the safety and correctness of your Go programs.

Pointers and Safety

While pointers are a powerful tool in Go, they also come with potential risks and challenges that, if not handled carefully, can lead to runtime errors, crashes, and memory leaks. Understanding these potential pitfalls is crucial for writing safe and reliable Go code.

1. Null Pointers

- **Concept:** A null pointer is a pointer that does not point to any valid memory location. In Go, null pointers are represented by the value `nil`.
- **Risk:** Attempting to dereference a null pointer (access the value it points to) will result in a runtime panic, causing your program to crash.
- **Prevention:** Always check if a pointer is `nil` before dereferencing it.

```
func processValue(ptr *int) {
    if ptr != nil {
        fmt.Println(*ptr)
    } else {
        fmt.Println("Pointer is nil")
    }
}
```

2. Dangling Pointers

- **Concept:** A dangling pointer is a pointer that points to memory that has been freed or deallocated. This can happen if you free memory while a pointer still references it, or if you have multiple pointers to the same memory location and one of them is used to free the memory.
- **Risk:** Accessing or modifying data through a dangling pointer can lead to unpredictable behavior, data corruption, or crashes.
- **Prevention:** Be cautious when freeing memory or reassigning pointers. Ensure that no other pointers are still referencing the freed memory.

3. Memory Leaks

- **Concept:** A memory leak occurs when memory allocated on the heap is no longer in use by the program but is not properly freed or garbage collected. This can lead to gradual accumulation of unused memory, eventually causing your program to run out of memory and crash.
- **In C:** In languages like C, where manual memory management is required, memory leaks are a common issue if you forget to call the `free` function to deallocate memory after you're done using it.
- **In Go:** Go's garbage collector helps prevent memory leaks by automatically reclaiming memory that is no longer reachable by the program. However, subtle memory leaks can still occur if you inadvertently create circular references or keep references to objects that are no longer needed.

Key Points

- Null pointers can lead to runtime panics if dereferenced.
- Dangling pointers can cause unpredictable behavior and crashes.
- Memory leaks can occur if memory allocated on the heap is not properly freed or garbage collected.
- Be cautious when working with pointers, especially when freeing memory or reassigning pointers.
- Go's garbage collector helps prevent memory leaks, but you still need to be mindful of potential circular references or unnecessary object retention.

While pointers offer power and flexibility, they also demand careful handling to ensure the safety and stability of your Go programs. By understanding the potential risks and taking preventive measures, you can leverage the benefits of pointers while minimizing the chances of encountering these pitfalls.

When to Use Pointers

Pointers, with their ability to directly manipulate memory and provide references to data, are a powerful tool in the Go programmer's toolkit. However, like any powerful tool, they should be wielded with care and understanding. Let's explore some scenarios where pointers are particularly useful in Go, along with considerations for their safe and effective use.

1. Modifying Data within Functions

- **Scenario:** You need a function to modify the original value of a variable passed to it, not just a copy.
- **Why Pointers:** Pointers allow you to pass the memory address of a variable to a function, enabling the function to directly access and modify the value at that address.
- **Example:**

```
func increment(x *int) {
    *x++
}
```

2. Large Data Structures

- **Scenario:** You're working with large data structures like structs or arrays, and passing them by value would lead to significant memory overhead due to copying.
- **Why Pointers:** By passing a pointer to the data structure, you avoid copying the entire structure, improving performance, especially for large datasets.
- **Example:**

```
type Image struct {
    // ... (potentially large data)
}

func processImage(img *Image) {
    // ... modify the image directly
}
```

3. Dynamic Data Structures

- **Scenario:** You're building dynamic data structures like linked lists, trees, or graphs, where elements need to be linked together using references.
- **Why Pointers:** Pointers are essential for creating the links between nodes in dynamic data structures, enabling you to build flexible and adaptable structures that can grow and shrink as needed.

4. Optional Values

- **Scenario:** You need to represent a value that might be present or absent (optional).
- **Why Pointers:** A pointer can be `nil` to indicate the absence of a value, providing a clear and concise way to represent optional data.

```
type Person struct {
    Name    string
    Address *Address // Optional address
}
```

Caution and Best Practices

While pointers offer numerous benefits, it's crucial to use them judiciously and with caution.

- **Avoid Unnecessary Complexity:** If you don't need to modify a variable within a function or if the data structure is small, passing by value is often simpler and less error-prone.
- **Handle Null Pointers:** Always check if a pointer is `nil` before dereferencing it to prevent runtime panics.

- **Mind Memory Management:** Be mindful of memory allocation and deallocation, especially when working with pointers to heap-allocated data. Ensure that you don't create memory leaks or dangling pointers.

Key Takeaways

- Pointers are powerful but should be used judiciously.
- Consider using pointers when modifying data within functions, working with large data structures, building dynamic data structures, or representing optional values.
- Always handle null pointers carefully and be mindful of memory management to avoid errors and ensure the safety of your Go programs.

By understanding when and how to use pointers effectively, you can leverage their capabilities to write efficient, flexible, and well-structured Go code while minimizing the risks associated with their use.

Chapter Summary

In this chapter, we delved into the world of pointers and memory management in Go, exploring how pointers provide a way to directly access and manipulate data stored in memory.

We covered the following key concepts:

- **Memory and Pointers:** We discussed the concept of memory as the storage space for data during program execution and introduced pointers as variables that store memory addresses.
- **Declaring and Using Pointers:** We learned how to declare pointer variables using the * operator, obtain memory addresses using the & operator, and access values using the * operator (dereferencing).
- **The new Function and Heap Allocation:** We explained how the new function allocates memory on the heap and returns a pointer to the allocated memory. We also discussed the distinction between stack and heap allocation.
- **Pointer Arithmetic:** We introduced the concept of pointer arithmetic, allowing you to navigate through memory by performing arithmetic operations on pointers.
- **Pointers and Functions:** We explored how pointers can be used as function parameters to enable functions to modify the original values of variables. We also discussed the difference between pass by value and pass by pointer.
- **Pointers and Structs:** We demonstrated how pointers can be used with structs to create references to struct instances and access and modify their fields directly.
- **Common Pointer Use Cases:** We discussed common scenarios where pointers are used, including dynamic data structures, sharing data, function parameters, and system calls.
- **Pointers and Safety:** We addressed the potential risks and challenges associated with pointers, such as null pointers, dangling pointers, and memory leaks.
- **When to Use Pointers:** We provided guidance on when to use pointers, considering factors like modifying data, working with large data structures, building dynamic data structures, and representing optional values.

By understanding pointers and memory management in Go, you've gained a deeper understanding of how Go programs interact with memory. You can now leverage pointers to write more efficient, flexible, and powerful code. However, remember to use pointers judiciously and with caution to avoid potential pitfalls and ensure the safety and correctness of your programs.

In the next chapter, we will explore error handling in Go, learning how to gracefully handle errors that might occur during program execution and create robust and reliable applications.

Error Handling: Gracefully Handling Errors in Go

Outline

- The Importance of Error Handling
- Go's Approach to Error Handling
- The `error` Interface
- Functions Returning Errors
- Handling Errors with `if err != nil`
- Error Wrapping
- Custom Error Types
- Panics and `recover`
- Best Practices for Error Handling
- Chapter Summary

The Importance of Error Handling

In the intricate world of software development, where even the most meticulously crafted programs can encounter unexpected situations, error handling emerges as a guardian of robustness and reliability. Without proper error handling, your applications become fragile, prone to crashes, data corruption, and security vulnerabilities.

The Perils of Unhandled Errors

Imagine a scenario where your program attempts to read data from a file, but the file is missing or inaccessible. Without error handling, this situation could trigger a runtime panic, abruptly halting your program's execution and leaving the user with a frustrating crash. Similarly, a network request might fail due to connectivity issues, or a database operation might encounter an unexpected constraint violation. In the absence of error handling, these situations could lead to data inconsistencies, security breaches, or even system-wide failures.

The Role of Anticipation and Graceful Handling

Effective error handling involves not just reacting to errors when they occur but also *anticipating* potential failure points and designing your code to handle them gracefully. By proactively considering what could go wrong and implementing appropriate error handling mechanisms, you can:

- **Prevent Crashes:** When an error occurs, your program can catch it, log it, and potentially recover from it, rather than crashing and disrupting the user's experience.
- **Protect Data Integrity:** By handling errors related to data input, validation, or storage, you can ensure that your data remains consistent and accurate, preventing corruption or loss.
- **Enhance Security:** Proper error handling helps mitigate security risks by preventing attackers from exploiting vulnerabilities that arise from unhandled exceptions or unexpected input.
- **Improve User Experience:** When errors occur, providing clear and informative error messages helps users understand the problem and take corrective action, instead of being left confused and frustrated.
- **Facilitate Debugging and Maintenance:** Well-structured error handling makes it easier to identify and diagnose issues, streamlining the debugging and maintenance process.

Error Handling as a Core Principle

Error handling should not be an afterthought but rather an integral part of your software development process. By embedding error handling mechanisms throughout your code, you create resilient applications that can gracefully handle unexpected situations, ensuring a seamless user experience and safeguarding the integrity and security of your data.

In the following sections, we'll explore Go's unique approach to error handling, which emphasizes explicitness, readability, and fine-grained control. You'll learn how to use the error interface, handle errors returned from functions, wrap errors for additional context, create custom error types, and manage panics using recover. By mastering these techniques, you'll be well-equipped to build robust and reliable Go programs that can withstand the challenges of the real world.

Go's Approach to Error Handling

Go takes a distinctive and pragmatic approach to error handling that sets it apart from many other programming languages. It embraces an explicit and idiomatic style where errors are treated as values, not exceptions. This means that functions that can potentially encounter errors explicitly return an error value, along with their regular results.

Explicit Error Handling

In contrast to languages like Java or Python, where exceptions are thrown and caught using try-catch blocks, Go's error handling is woven into the fabric of the language itself. Functions that might encounter errors typically return an error value as their last return value. The caller is then responsible for checking this error value and taking appropriate action.

Benefits of Go's Approach

1. **Explicitness:** Go's error handling is explicit and transparent. Errors are not hidden or thrown; they are explicitly returned and handled, making the potential for errors and their handling more visible in the code.
2. **Readability:** Error handling code is seamlessly integrated into the normal flow of the program, eliminating the need for separate try-catch blocks. This results in code that is easier to read, understand, and reason about.
3. **Control:** Go's approach gives developers fine-grained control over how errors are handled at each level of the call stack. You can decide whether to handle an error immediately, propagate it up the call stack, or take specific corrective actions.
4. **Simplicity:** Go's error handling mechanism is relatively simple and straightforward, requiring less boilerplate code compared to exception handling in some languages.
5. **Testability:** Explicit error handling makes it easier to write unit tests that cover various error scenarios, ensuring the robustness of your code.

Contrast with Exception Handling

- **Exceptions:** In exception-based languages, errors are represented as exceptions, which are thrown when an error occurs. The program's control flow is interrupted, and the exception is propagated up the call stack until it's caught by a try-catch block.
- **Go's Approach:** In Go, errors are values returned from functions. The caller explicitly checks for errors and decides how to handle them. This approach avoids the potential complexities and hidden control flow associated with exception handling.

Example:

```
func divide(x, y float64) (float64, error) {
```

```go
    if y == 0 {
        return 0, errors.New("division by zero")
    }
    return x / y, nil
}

func main() {
    result, err := divide(10, 0)
    if err != nil {
        fmt.Println("Error:", err)
    } else {
        fmt.Println("Result:", result)
    }
}
```

In this example, the `divide` function explicitly returns an `error` value along with the result. The `main` function checks for the error and handles it appropriately.

Go's explicit error handling promotes clear and maintainable code by making error handling an integral part of the program's logic. While it might require a slight shift in thinking compared to exception-based languages, its benefits in terms of readability, control, and testability make it a powerful and effective approach to error management in Go.

The `error` Interface

At the heart of Go's error-handling mechanism lies the `error` interface. This simple yet powerful interface acts as the cornerstone for representing and handling errors throughout your Go programs. It provides a standardized way to encapsulate error information and communicate it between different parts of your code.

The `error` Interface Definition

The `error` interface is defined in the standard library as follows:

```go
type error interface {
    Error() string
}
```

This interface has a single method, `Error()`, which returns a string representation of the error. Any type that implements this method can be used as an error value in Go.

Built-in Error Types

Go's standard library provides several built-in types that implement the `error` interface, representing common error scenarios:

- **`io.EOF`:** This error indicates that an end-of-file condition has been reached while reading data.
- **`os.PathError`:** This error represents an error related to file paths, such as a file not being found or a permission issue.
- **`errors.New("...")`:** The `errors.New` function creates a new error with a custom error message.

Custom Error Types

You can also define your own custom error types by creating types that implement the Error() method. This allows you to provide more specific error information and tailor your error handling to your application's needs.

```go
type ValidationError struct {
    Field string
    Message string
}

func (e *ValidationError) Error() string {
    return fmt.Sprintf("Validation error in field '%s': %s", e.Field, e.Message)
}
```

In this example, we define a custom error type ValidationError that includes the field name and a descriptive error message.

Key Points

- The error interface is the core of Go's error handling.
- Any type that implements the Error() method can be used as an error value.
- Go provides built-in error types for common scenarios.
- You can create custom error types for more specific error handling.

The error interface provides a flexible and extensible mechanism for representing and handling errors in Go. By understanding how to work with the error interface and leverage built-in or custom error types, you can write code that gracefully handles errors, providing informative feedback to users and ensuring the robustness of your applications.

Functions Returning Errors

In Go, it's a common and idiomatic practice for functions that can potentially encounter errors to return an error value as their last return value. This convention provides a clear and explicit way for functions to signal errors to the caller, allowing the caller to check for and handle those errors appropriately.

The Error Return Convention

- **Last Return Value:** Functions that might encounter errors typically have a signature where the last return value is of type error.
- **Successful Execution:** If the function executes successfully without encountering any errors, it returns a nil error value along with its regular results.
- **Error Condition:** If an error occurs during the function's execution, it returns a non-nil error value that describes the error, along with zero values for any other return types.

Signaling Errors to the Caller

By returning an error value, a function can signal to the caller that something went wrong during its execution. The caller can then check the error value and take appropriate action, such as:

- **Logging the error:** Record the error message for debugging or analysis purposes.
- **Returning the error:** Propagate the error up the call stack to a higher-level function that can handle it.
- **Taking corrective action:** Attempt to recover from the error or provide alternative functionality.
- **Informing the user:** Display an error message to the user, explaining the problem and suggesting possible solutions.

Examples of Functions Returning Errors

1. **File Operations:**

```go
func readFile(filename string) ([]byte, error) {
    data, err := os.ReadFile(filename)
    if err != nil {
        return nil, err // Return nil data and the error
    }
    return data, nil
}
```

The `readFile` function attempts to read the contents of a file. If an error occurs (e.g., the file doesn't exist), it returns `nil` for the data and the corresponding error.

2. **Network Requests:**

```go
func fetchURL(url string) ([]byte, error) {
    resp, err := http.Get(url)
    if err != nil {
        return nil, err
    }
    defer resp.Body.Close()

    data, err := io.ReadAll(resp.Body)
    if err != nil {
        return nil, err
    }
    return data, nil
}
```

The `fetchURL` function makes an HTTP GET request to a URL. If the request fails or there's an error reading the response body, it returns `nil` for the data and the error.

3. **Database Interactions:**

```go
func getUser(db *sql.DB, userID int) (*User, error) {
    // ... (query the database to retrieve the user)
    if err != nil {
        return nil, err
    }
    return user, nil
}
```

The `getUser` function queries a database to retrieve a user record. If the query fails, it returns `nil` for the user and the error.

Key Points

- Functions that can encounter errors often return an `error` value as their last return value.
- A `nil` error value indicates successful execution.
- A non-`nil` error value signals an error condition.
- Callers should check for errors and handle them appropriately.

By adhering to this convention, Go promotes explicit error handling, making your code more robust and reliable. In the next section, we'll explore how to handle errors using the common `if err != nil` pattern and discuss techniques for providing more informative error messages.

Handling Errors with `if err != nil`

In Go, the most common and idiomatic way to check for errors returned from functions is to use the `if err != nil` construct. This simple yet effective pattern allows you to explicitly handle errors and take appropriate actions based on their presence.

The `if err != nil` Pattern

When a function returns an `error` value, you typically assign it to a variable named `err`. You then use an `if` statement to check if `err` is not `nil`. If it's not `nil`, it means an error occurred, and you can handle it within the `if` block.

```
result, err := someFunction()
if err != nil {
    // Handle the error
} else {
    // Use the result (no error occurred)
}
```

Accessing the Error Message

The `error` interface has a single method, `Error()`, which returns a string representation of the error. You can use this method to access the error message and provide more informative feedback to the user or log it for debugging purposes.

```
if err != nil {
    fmt.Println("An error occurred:", err.Error())
}
```

Handling Errors Appropriately

The specific way you handle an error depends on the context and the nature of the error. Here are some common approaches:

1. **Logging the Error:**

   ```
   if err != nil {
       log.Println("Error:", err) // Log the error for later analysis
   }
   ```

2. **Returning the Error:**

   ```
   func myFunction() error {
       // ... (some code)
       if err != nil {
           return err // Propagate the error up the call stack
       }
       // ...
       return nil // No error occurred
   }
   ```

3. **Taking Corrective Action:**

   ```
   if err != nil {
       // Retry the operation
       // Use an alternative approach
   ```

```
        // Prompt the user for input
        // ...
    }
```

Example

```
data, err := readFile("myfile.txt")
if err != nil {
    fmt.Println("Error reading file:", err.Error())
    // Potentially retry reading the file or provide an alternative action
} else {
    // Process the data read from the file
}
```

Key Points

- Use the `if err != nil` pattern to check for errors returned from functions
- Access the error message using the `Error()` method
- Handle errors appropriately based on the context, such as logging, returning, or taking corrective action

By consistently applying this pattern and handling errors thoughtfully, you can create Go programs that are robust, reliable, and provide a smooth user experience even in the face of unexpected situations. In the next section, we'll explore how to add more context and information to error messages using error wrapping.

Error Wrapping

While Go's explicit error handling mechanism is valuable, sometimes the error messages returned by functions might lack sufficient context to pinpoint the exact location or cause of the error, especially in larger codebases or complex call stacks. Error wrapping comes to the rescue by allowing you to add additional information or context to an existing error, creating more informative and helpful error messages.

The `fmt.Errorf` Function

The `fmt.Errorf` function is a key tool for error wrapping in Go. It allows you to create a new error that incorporates the original error message along with additional context.

Syntax:

```
newError := fmt.Errorf("context: %w", originalError)
```

- **context:** A string that provides additional information about the error, such as the location in your code where the error occurred or the specific operation that failed.
- **%w:** A special format verb that tells `fmt.Errorf` to wrap the `originalError`.
- **originalError:** The original error value that you want to wrap.

Benefits of Error Wrapping

- **Contextual Information:** Error wrapping adds valuable context to error messages, making it easier to understand where and why an error occurred.
- **Preserving the Original Error:** The original error is preserved within the wrapped error, allowing you to access its underlying cause and potentially take specific actions based on the original error type.

- **Improved Debugging:** More informative error messages can significantly speed up the debugging process by providing clues about the root cause of the problem.

Example

```
func openAndReadFile(filename string) ([]byte, error) {
    file, err := os.Open(filename)
    if err != nil {
        return nil, fmt.Errorf("failed to open file %s: %w", filename, err)
    }
    defer file.Close()

    data, err := io.ReadAll(file)
    if err != nil {
        return nil, fmt.Errorf("failed to read file %s: %w", filename, err)
    }
    return data, nil
}
```

In this example, the openAndReadFile function wraps any errors encountered during file opening or reading with additional context, including the filename and the original error message. This creates more informative error messages that help pinpoint the source of the problem.

Key Points:

- Error wrapping adds context and additional information to existing errors
- Use the fmt.Errorf function with the %w verb to wrap errors
- Wrapped errors provide more informative error messages, aiding in debugging and troubleshooting

By incorporating error wrapping into your Go code, you can significantly enhance the clarity and usefulness of your error messages. This practice leads to more maintainable code and a smoother debugging experience, ultimately contributing to the robustness and reliability of your applications.

Custom Error Types

While Go's built-in error types and error wrapping provide a solid foundation for error handling, there are situations where you might want to create your own custom error types. Custom error types allow you to represent specific error scenarios in a more structured and informative way, enhancing the clarity and maintainability of your code.

Defining Custom Error Types

To create a custom error type, you define a new type that implements the error interface. This typically involves creating a struct that includes fields to store relevant error information and implementing the Error() method to provide a string representation of the error.

Example:

```
type ValidationError struct {
    Field   string
    Message string
}

func (e *ValidationError) Error() string {
    return fmt.Sprintf("Validation error in field '%s': %s", e.Field, e.Message)
}
```

In this example, we define a custom error type `ValidationError` that includes fields for the `Field` that caused the error and a descriptive `Message`. The `Error()` method formats these fields into a clear error message.

Benefits of Custom Error Types

1. **Specific Error Information:** Custom error types allow you to include more specific and relevant information about the error, beyond just a generic message. This can be useful for providing detailed feedback to users or for logging purposes.
2. **Type-Based Error Handling:** By defining distinct error types for different error scenarios, you can use type assertions or type switches to handle errors in a more targeted and precise way.

   ```go
   _, err := someFunction()
   if err != nil {
       switch err.(type) {
       case *ValidationError:
           // Handle validation errors
       case *DatabaseError:
           // Handle database errors
       default:
           // Handle other unexpected errors
       }
   }
   ```

3. **Code Organization:** Custom error types promote better code organization by encapsulating error-related information and behavior within dedicated types. This makes your code more modular and easier to maintain.

Using Custom Error Types

You can use custom error types just like built-in error types. Functions that can encounter specific error scenarios can return instances of your custom error types, and callers can use type assertions or type switches to handle those errors appropriately.

```go
func validateAge(age int) error {
    if age < 0 {
        return &ValidationError{Field: "Age", Message: "Age cannot be negative"}
    }
    // ... other validation checks
    return nil
}
```

In this example, the `validateAge` function returns a `ValidationError` if the age is invalid. The caller can then check for this specific error type and handle it accordingly.

Key Points

- Custom error types provide a way to represent specific error scenarios with more detailed information
- They enable type-based error handling using type assertions or type switches
- Define custom error types by creating structs that implement the `error` interface
- Use custom error types to enhance code clarity, organization, and maintainability

By leveraging custom error types, you can create more informative error messages, implement targeted error handling, and improve the overall structure of your Go code. This leads to more robust and user-friendly applications that can gracefully handle a variety of error conditions.

Panics and `recover`

In Go, a **panic** is a runtime error that abruptly terminates the normal flow of your program. It signals an exceptional condition that the program cannot handle gracefully, such as a division by zero, an index out-of-bounds error, or an explicit call to the `panic` function. When a panic occurs, the current goroutine (the lightweight thread executing the code) unwinds its call stack, executing any deferred functions along the way. If the panic is not recovered, the program ultimately crashes.

Causes of Panics

- **Runtime Errors:** Go's runtime can trigger panics in response to various error conditions, such as:
  - **Division by Zero:** Attempting to divide a number by zero.
  - **Index Out of Range:** Accessing an array or slice element at an invalid index.
  - **Nil Pointer Dereference:** Trying to access the value pointed to by a `nil` pointer.
  - **Type Assertion Failure:** Failing to convert an interface value to a specific type using a type assertion.
- **Explicit `panic` Calls:** You can also explicitly trigger a panic using the `panic` function. This is sometimes useful for signaling fatal errors or unrecoverable conditions within your code.

Recovering from Panics with `recover`

While panics can be disruptive, Go provides a mechanism to regain control of a panicking goroutine and handle the error gracefully using the `recover` function.

- **`recover` Function:** The `recover` function can only be called within a deferred function. It captures the value passed to the `panic` function and stops the unwinding of the call stack.
- **`defer` and `recover`:** The typical pattern for recovering from panics involves using a `defer` statement to schedule a function call that attempts to `recover` from a potential panic.

Example

```go
func main() {
    defer func() {
        if r := recover(); r != nil {
            fmt.Println("Recovered from panic:", r)
        }
    }()

    // ... (code that might panic)
    panic("Something went wrong!")
}
```

In this example, the deferred anonymous function attempts to recover from a panic. If a panic occurs, the `recover` function captures the panic value ("Something went wrong!") and prints a recovery message. The program continues to execute after the recovery.

Key Points

- Panics are runtime errors that abruptly terminate a goroutine's execution
- They can be triggered by runtime errors or explicit `panic` calls
- The `recover` function, used within a deferred function, can capture a panic and stop the unwinding of the call stack

- `defer`, `panic`, and `recover` can be used together to handle panics gracefully and prevent program crashes

Panics and `recover` provide a way to handle exceptional situations and prevent your Go programs from crashing. While it's generally recommended to use error handling for expected errors, panics and `recover` can be helpful for dealing with truly exceptional conditions and providing a last line of defense against program failures.

Best Practices for Error Handling

Effective error handling is crucial for building robust and reliable Go programs. By adhering to best practices and adopting a consistent approach, you can ensure that your code gracefully handles unexpected situations, provides informative feedback, and prevents catastrophic failures.

1. Handle Errors Promptly

- **Check Immediately:** Always check for errors immediately after calling functions that might return them. Don't postpone error handling or assume that everything will always work as expected.
- **Avoid Nested `if err != nil`:** While it's tempting to nest multiple `if err != nil` checks, this can lead to deeply nested code and hinder readability. Consider using early returns or helper functions to simplify error handling logic.

2. Provide Context with Error Wrapping

- **Add Context:** Use error wrapping with `fmt.Errorf` to add contextual information to error messages. Include details about the location in your code where the error occurred, the specific operation that failed, or any relevant data that might help in diagnosing the problem.
- **Preserve Original Error:** When wrapping errors, use the %w verb to include the original error, allowing you to access its underlying cause and potentially take specific actions based on the original error type.

3. Use Custom Error Types

- **Specific Errors:** Define custom error types for specific error scenarios within your application. This allows you to provide more targeted error information and enable type-based error handling using type assertions or type switches.
- **Clarity and Maintainability:** Custom error types improve code organization and make your error handling logic more explicit and self-documenting.

4. Handle Panics Gracefully

- **`defer` and `recover`:** Use `defer` and `recover` to handle panics gracefully, preventing them from crashing your entire program. Recover from panics within critical sections of your code and log or report the error before allowing the program to continue or exit gracefully.
- **Avoid Panics for Expected Errors:** Reserve panics for truly exceptional and unrecoverable situations. For expected errors, use regular error handling mechanisms with the `error` interface.

5. Document Error Handling

- **Clear Documentation:** Document the potential errors that a function might return, along with their possible causes and suggested handling approaches. This helps other developers understand how to use your code correctly and handle errors effectively.
- **Godoc Comments:** Use Godoc comments to document the errors returned by your functions, including their types and meanings.

The Importance of Consistent Error Handling

Consistent and thoughtful error handling is a hallmark of well-written and reliable Go programs. By adhering to these best practices and making error handling an integral part of your development process, you can:

- **Prevent Crashes:** Gracefully handle errors to avoid program crashes and ensure a smooth user experience.
- **Protect Data Integrity:** Safeguard your data from corruption or loss by handling errors related to data input, validation, and storage.
- **Enhance Security:** Mitigate security risks by preventing attackers from exploiting vulnerabilities arising from unhandled errors.
- **Improve Maintainability:** Well-structured error handling makes your code easier to understand, debug, and modify, contributing to long-term maintainability.

Remember, error handling is not just about fixing problems; it's about building resilient and user-friendly applications that can gracefully handle the unexpected and provide a positive experience even when things go wrong.

Chapter Summary

In this chapter, we explored the critical aspect of error handling in Go, learning how to build robust and reliable programs that can gracefully respond to unexpected situations.

Key takeaways from this chapter include:

- The significance of error handling in preventing crashes, data corruption, and security vulnerabilities.
- Go's explicit and idiomatic approach to error handling, where errors are represented as values returned from functions.
- The `error` interface as the core of error representation in Go.
- The convention of functions returning an `error` value as their last return value to signal errors to the caller.
- The common pattern of checking for errors using the `if err != nil` construct.
- The technique of error wrapping to add context and additional information to error messages using `fmt.Errorf`.
- The creation of custom error types for specific error scenarios, enabling more targeted error handling.
- The concept of panics as runtime errors and how to recover from them using `defer` and `recover`.
- Best practices for error handling in Go, including handling errors promptly, providing context, using custom error types, handling panics gracefully, and documenting error handling.

By incorporating these error-handling techniques into your Go code, you can create more resilient, maintainable, and user-friendly applications. Remember that effective error handling is not just about fixing problems; it's about anticipating potential issues and designing your code to respond gracefully, ensuring a smooth and reliable experience for your users.

In the next chapter, we will explore packages in Go, learning how to organize and reuse code effectively, leading to more modular and scalable projects.

Packages: Organizing and Reusing Go Code

Outline

- The Importance of Code Organization
- Understanding Packages
- Creating and Using Packages
- Importing Packages
- Exported vs. Unexported Identifiers
- The main Package and Executable Programs
- Organizing Code with Packages
- Standard Library Packages
- Third-Party Packages
- Best Practices for Package Design
- Chapter Summary

The Importance of Code Organization

In the realm of software development, especially when dealing with large and complex Go projects, code organization emerges as a linchpin for success. The ability to structure your code in a logical and coherent manner is not merely a matter of aesthetics; it's a crucial factor that directly impacts the readability, maintainability, and collaborative potential of your projects.

Navigating the Code Labyrinth

Imagine a sprawling metropolis without organized streets and addresses. Finding your way around would be a daunting task, riddled with confusion and inefficiency. Similarly, a large Go codebase without proper organization can quickly become a labyrinthine maze, making it challenging to locate specific functions, understand relationships between different components, and make modifications without introducing unintended side effects.

The Virtues of Well-Organized Code

- **Readability:** Organized code is like a well-written story, with clear chapters, sections, and paragraphs that guide the reader through the narrative. By structuring your code into logical units and using descriptive names, you make it easier for yourself and others to understand the purpose and functionality of each part.
- **Maintainability:** As your project evolves and requirements change, well-organized code simplifies the process of making updates and modifications. You can pinpoint the specific areas that need to be changed without wading through a tangled mess of interconnected code.
- **Collaboration:** When multiple developers work on the same project, code organization becomes even more crucial. A clear and consistent structure facilitates collaboration by enabling developers to understand each other's work, avoid conflicts, and contribute to the codebase effectively.
- **Reusability:** By organizing code into reusable modules, you can avoid duplication and streamline development. Well-defined packages and functions can be easily shared and incorporated into different parts of your project or even across multiple projects.
- **Testability:** Organized code is more conducive to testing. By isolating specific functionalities within packages and functions, you can write targeted unit tests that verify the correctness of each component independently.

Packages: The Cornerstone of Organization

In Go, packages serve as the primary mechanism for achieving code organization. They provide a way to group related code into self-contained units, creating namespaces for identifiers and preventing naming conflicts. By strategically organizing your code into packages, you can create a modular and scalable architecture that facilitates collaboration, reusability, and maintainability.

Key Points:

- Code organization is vital for managing large and complex Go projects.
- Well-organized code improves readability, maintainability, collaboration, reusability, and testability.
- Packages provide a fundamental mechanism for organizing code in Go.

In the following sections, we'll explore the concept of packages in more detail. You'll learn how to create and use packages, understand import paths and aliases, and discover best practices for designing well-structured and maintainable packages. By mastering the art of package organization, you'll be well-equipped to build Go projects that are not only functional but also elegant, scalable, and easy to work with.

Understanding Packages

In Go, packages act as the primary organizational units for structuring and managing code. They provide a way to group together related code, creating self-contained modules that promote modularity, reusability, and maintainability. Think of packages as containers or compartments that hold specific pieces of your Go code, much like folders organize files on your computer.

Namespaces and Naming Conflicts

One of the core benefits of packages is that they create namespaces for the identifiers (variables, functions, types) defined within them. This means that an identifier within one package won't clash with an identifier with the same name in another package.

- **Example:**
  You might have a math package that defines a function named add, and a geometry package that also defines a function named add. Thanks to packages, these two add functions can coexist without conflict, as they belong to different namespaces: math.add and geometry.add.

Packages and Directories

In Go, there's a direct correspondence between packages and directories. Each package is represented by a directory within your Go workspace's src directory. The name of the directory becomes the name of the package.

- **Example:**
  If you have a package named myutils, you would create a directory named myutils within your src directory. Inside this directory, you would place the Go source files that belong to the myutils package.

Key Points

- Packages are containers for organizing related Go code.
- They create namespaces for identifiers, preventing naming conflicts.
- Each package corresponds to a directory within your Go workspace's src directory.
- Packages promote modularity, reusability, and maintainability of code.

By understanding the concept of packages and how they relate to directories, you can start structuring your Go code in a more organized and scalable way.

Creating and Using Packages

Creating a Package

Creating a new package in Go is remarkably straightforward. It involves creating a directory within your Go workspace's `src` directory and placing your Go source code files within it. The name of the directory becomes the name of your package.

Steps to Create a Package

1. **Navigate to your Go Workspace's `src` Directory:** Open your terminal or command prompt and navigate to the `src` directory within your Go workspace using the `cd` command.

   ```
   cd $GOPATH/src
   ```

2. **Create a New Directory:** Create a new directory with the name you want to give your package. Let's say we want to create a package named `myutils`.

   ```
   mkdir myutils
   ```

3. **Create Go Source Files:** Inside the `myutils` directory, create one or more Go source files (`.go` files) that will contain the code for your package. For example, you might create a file named `helpers.go`.
4. **Declare the Package Name:** At the beginning of each Go source file within the `myutils` directory, add the following line to declare the package name:

   ```
   package myutils
   ```

   This line tells the Go compiler that the code in this file belongs to the `myutils` package.

Example

```
$GOPATH/src/
└── myutils/
    └── helpers.go
```

Contents of `helpers.go`:

```go
package myutils

import "fmt"

func PrintGreeting(name string) {
    fmt.Println("Hello,", name, "from the myutils package!")
}
```

Key Points

- A package is created by creating a directory within the `src` directory of your Go workspace.
- The directory name becomes the package name.
- Each Go source file within the package directory must declare the package name using the `package` keyword.

- You can have multiple Go source files within a single package, allowing you to organize your code into logical units.

By following these simple steps, you can create your own Go packages to organize your code, promote reusability, and prevent naming conflicts.

Using a Package

Once you have created or installed packages, you can leverage their functionalities in your Go programs by importing them. The `import` statement acts as the gateway to access the code defined within other packages, enabling you to reuse existing code and build upon the work of others.

Importing a Package

To import a package, you use the `import` keyword followed by the package's import path enclosed in double quotes.

Syntax

```
import "importPath"
```

- **importPath**: This is the unique identifier for the package you want to import. It can be either:
    - A path relative to your $GOPATH/src directory for packages within your workspace.
    - A remote repository URL for packages hosted on platforms like GitHub.

Accessing Exported Identifiers

Once a package is imported, you can access its *exported* identifiers (functions, variables, types, etc.) using the package name as a prefix. In Go, identifiers that start with a capital letter are considered exported and are accessible from other packages.

Syntax

```
packageName.Identifier
```

Examples

1. **Importing and Using a Function**

```
package main

import (
    "fmt"
    "math"
)

func main() {
    fmt.Println(math.Sqrt(16)) // Output: 4
}
```

In this example, we import the `fmt` and `math` packages from the standard library. We then use the `math.Sqrt` function to calculate the square root of 16.

2. **Importing and Using a Variable**

```
package main

import (
```

```
    "fmt"
    "math/rand"
)

func main() {
    fmt.Println(rand.Intn(100)) // Output: a random integer between 0 and 99
}
```

Here, we import the `rand` package and use the `rand.Intn` function to generate a random integer.

3. **Importing and Using a Type**

```
package main

import (
    "fmt"
    "time"
)

func main() {
    now := time.Now()
    fmt.Println(now) // Output: the current time
}
```

In this case, we import the `time` package and use the `time.Now` function to get the current time, which is of type `time.Time`.

Key Points

- Use the `import` statement to import packages.
- Access exported identifiers from imported packages using the package name as a prefix.
- You can import multiple packages within a single `import` block using parentheses.

By understanding how to import and use packages, you can leverage the vast ecosystem of Go code available in the standard library and third-party repositories. This enables you to build upon existing solutions, avoid reinventing the wheel, and accelerate your development process.

Importing Packages

Import Paths

In the realm of Go programming, import paths serve as the guiding stars that lead the Go toolchain to the packages you want to incorporate into your projects. They are unique identifiers that pinpoint the exact location of a package, whether it resides within your local Go workspace or in a remote repository like GitHub.

Structure of Import Paths

- **Local Packages:** For packages located within your Go workspace, the import path is based on their relative path within the `src` directory.
    - **Example:** If you have a package named `myutils` located at `$GOPATH/src/myproject/myutils`, its import path would be `"myproject/myutils"`
- **Remote Packages:** For packages hosted on remote repositories, the import path typically includes the repository URL and the package's path within that repository
    - **Example:** The popular Gin web framework is hosted on GitHub at `github.com/gin-gonic/gin`. So, its import path is `"github.com/gin-gonic/gin"`.

Key Points

- Import paths are unique identifiers for Go packages
- They specify the location of the package, either within your workspace or in a remote repository
- Local import paths are based on the package's relative path within the `src` directory
- Remote import paths usually include the repository URL and the package's path within the repository
- The `go get` command automatically downloads and installs packages based on their import paths

Illustrative Examples

- **Local Package:**

  ```
  import "myproject/myutils"
  ```

- **Remote Package (GitHub):**

  ```
  import "github.com/stretchr/testify/assert"
  ```

The Role of `go get`

The `go get` command is instrumental in fetching and installing packages based on their import paths. When you execute `go get <importPath>`, Go automatically:

1. **Resolves the Import Path:** It determines the location of the package based on the import path.
2. **Downloads the Package:** It downloads the package's source code and any required dependencies.
3. **Installs the Package:** It installs the package in your Go workspace, making it available for use in your projects.

Conclusion

Import paths act as the crucial link between your Go programs and the packages they rely on. By understanding how import paths work and how to use them effectively, you can seamlessly integrate external code into your projects, leverage the vast Go ecosystem, and build upon the work of others to create powerful and efficient applications.

Aliasing Imports

In the realm of Go programming, where clarity and conciseness reign supreme, import aliases emerge as a valuable tool for enhancing code readability and resolving potential naming conflicts. They offer a way to provide alternative, more convenient names for imported packages, making your code more expressive and easier to understand.

The Need for Aliases

- **Naming Conflicts:** When you import multiple packages, there's a chance that they might contain identifiers (functions, variables, types) with the same name. This can lead to naming conflicts, where the compiler wouldn't know which identifier you're referring to.
- **Readability:** Sometimes, the full package name might be long or cumbersome to use repeatedly in your code. Aliases can provide shorter and more descriptive names, improving code readability.

Creating Import Aliases

You create an import alias in Go by adding the alias name before the import path within the `import` statement.

Syntax

```
import (
    aliasName "importPath"
)
```

- **aliasName**: The alternative name you want to use for the imported package.
- **importPath**: The original import path of the package.

Example:

```
import (
    "fmt"
    m "math" // Alias 'math' as 'm'
)

func main() {
    fmt.Println(m.Sqrt(16)) // Use the alias 'm' to access the Sqrt function
}
```

In this example, we import the math package and assign it the alias m. We can then use m.Sqrt to access the Sqrt function from the math package, making the code slightly more concise.

Benefits of Import Aliases

- **Resolving Naming Conflicts:** Aliases prevent naming collisions when multiple packages have identifiers with the same name.
- **Improved Readability:** Aliases can provide shorter and more descriptive names for frequently used packages, making your code easier to read and understand.
- **Clarity and Context:** Aliases can convey the purpose or context of an imported package, making your code more self-documenting.

Key Points

- Use import aliases to provide alternative names for imported packages
- Aliases help resolve naming conflicts and improve code readability
- Choose descriptive alias names that convey the purpose or context of the imported package

By leveraging import aliases judiciously, you can write Go code that is not only functional but also elegant, clear, and maintainable. Aliases enhance the expressiveness of your code, making it easier to read, understand, and collaborate on with other developers.

Blank Imports

In Go, you can import a package without directly using any of its exported identifiers by using the blank identifier (_) as the alias in the import statement. This is known as a *blank import*.

Syntax

```
import _ "importPath"
```

Purpose of Blank Imports

Blank imports are primarily used to trigger the package's *init* function, which is automatically executed when the package is imported. The init function is often used to perform package-level initialization, such as:

- **Registering functions or types:** Some packages might register functions or types with other parts of your program during initialization.
- **Initializing global variables:** Packages might initialize global variables or data structures that are needed by other parts of your program.
- **Setting up database connections or network services:** Some packages might establish connections to external resources during initialization.

Example:

```
import (
    "fmt"
    _ "image/png" // Import the png package for its image decoding side effects
)

func main() {
    // ... (code that uses image decoding, even though we didn't directly import any identifiers from the png package)
}
```

In this example, we import the `image/png` package using a blank import. This triggers the package's `init` function, which registers the PNG image decoder with Go's `image` package. Now, even though we haven't directly imported any identifiers from the png package, we can still use functions from the `image` package to decode PNG images.

Key Points

- Blank imports are used to import a package solely for its side effects (typically its `init` function).
- They do not allow you to directly access any of the package's exported identifiers.
- Use blank imports sparingly and only when necessary, as they can make your code less explicit and harder to understand.

Blank imports can be a useful tool in specific situations where you need to trigger a package's initialization without directly using its exported identifiers. However, it's important to use them judiciously and document their purpose clearly to maintain code readability and avoid confusion.

Exported vs. Unexported Identifiers

In Go, the distinction between exported and unexported identifiers is a cornerstone of its design philosophy, promoting encapsulation and providing a clear mechanism for controlling access to the internal workings of your packages. This convention, based on the capitalization of the first letter of an identifier, plays a crucial role in maintaining code organization, modularity, and preventing unintended dependencies between different parts of your program.

Exported Identifiers

- **Capitalization:** Identifiers (variables, functions, types, constants, etc.) that start with a capital letter are considered exported.
- **Public Access:** Exported identifiers are accessible from other packages that import the package where they are defined. They form the public API of your package, allowing other parts of your program to interact with its functionality in a controlled manner.
- **Example:**

    ```
    package mymath

    func Add(x, y int) int {
        return x + y
    ```

}

In this example, the Add function is exported because it starts with a capital letter. It can be accessed from other packages that import the `mymath` package.

Unexported Identifiers

- **Capitalization:** Identifiers that start with a lowercase letter are considered unexported.
- **Private Access:** Unexported identifiers are only accessible within the same package where they are defined. They are hidden from other packages, preventing accidental or unintended usage.
- **Example:**

```
package mymath

func add(x, y int) int { // Unexported function
    return x + y
}
```

In this example, the `add` function is unexported because it starts with a lowercase letter. It can only be used within the `mymath` package itself.

Encapsulation and Access Control

The distinction between exported and unexported identifiers enforces encapsulation, a key principle in software engineering. Encapsulation promotes modularity by hiding the internal implementation details of a package and exposing only a well-defined public interface. This allows you to modify the internals of a package without affecting other parts of your program that depend on it, as long as the public interface remains unchanged.

Key Points:

- Exported identifiers start with a capital letter and are accessible from other packages.
- Unexported identifiers start with a lowercase letter and are only accessible within the same package.
- This convention helps enforce encapsulation and control access to package internals.
- Use exported identifiers to define the public API of your packages.
- Use unexported identifiers for internal implementation details that should not be exposed to other packages.

By understanding and adhering to this convention, you can create Go packages that are well-organized, modular, and maintainable. This contributes to the overall robustness and scalability of your Go projects, enabling you to build complex systems with clear boundaries and controlled dependencies between different components.

The `main` Package and Executable Programs

In the world of Go, the `main` package holds a distinguished position. It is the designated package for creating executable programs, the kind of programs you can run directly from your terminal or command prompt. The `main` package serves as the starting point for your Go application, and within it resides the crucial `main` function, which acts as the program's entry point.

The `main` Function: The Starting Gate

Every executable Go program must have a `main` function defined within the `main` package. This function serves as the gateway to your program's execution. When you run your compiled Go program, the Go runtime looks for the `main` function within the `main` package and starts executing the code within it.

- **Syntax:**

    ```
    package main

    func main() {
        // Your program's logic goes here
    }
    ```

- **No Parameters or Return Values:** The `main` function does not take any parameters and does not return any values. Its purpose is to initiate the execution of your program's logic.

The `main` Package: The Container

The `main` package acts as the container for your `main` function and any other code that is directly involved in the core functionality of your executable program. While you can import and use other packages within your `main` package, the `main` function itself must reside within the `main` package.

Key Points

- The `main` package is used to create executable Go programs
- Every executable Go program must have a `main` function within the `main` package
- The `main` function is the entry point of the program
- The `main` function does not take any parameters or return any values

By understanding the special role of the `main` package and the `main` function, you can create Go programs that can be compiled into standalone executables and run independently. This capability is crucial for building command-line tools, servers, and other applications that need to be executed directly by the user or the operating system.

Organizing Code with Packages

As your Go projects grow in size and complexity, maintaining a well-structured and organized codebase becomes paramount. Packages in Go provide a powerful mechanism for achieving this organization, enabling you to group related code, promote modularity and reusability, and achieve separation of concerns.

Grouping Related Code

The first principle of package organization is to group together code that shares a common functionality or purpose. This creates cohesive units that are easier to understand, maintain, and test.

- **Example:**
    - You might have a package named `math` that contains functions for performing mathematical operations, a `database` package that handles database interactions, and a web package that deals with web-related functionality.

Modularity and Reusability

Packages encapsulate code into self-contained units, fostering modularity and reusability.

- **Modularity:** Each package focuses on a specific aspect of your application's functionality, making it easier to reason about and modify individual components without affecting the entire system.
- **Reusability:** Well-designed packages can be reused across different projects, saving development time and effort.

Separation of Concerns

Packages help you achieve separation of concerns, a fundamental principle in software engineering. By dividing your code into logical components with distinct responsibilities, you create a more maintainable and adaptable codebase.

- **Example:**
    - In a web application, you might have separate packages for handling user authentication, data access, business logic, and presentation. This separation makes it easier to modify or replace individual components without impacting the entire application.

Key Strategies for Package Organization

- **Functionality-Based Packages:** Group code based on the functionality it provides. For example, a `utils` package might contain various helper functions, while a `logging` package handles logging-related tasks.
- **Feature-Based Packages:** Organize code based on the features or modules of your application. For instance, in an e-commerce system, you might have packages for `products`, `orders`, `payments`, and `users`.
- **Layer-Based Packages:** Structure your code into layers, such as data access, business logic, and presentation. This promotes separation of concerns and makes it easier to test and maintain each layer independently.
- **Avoid Circular Dependencies:** Ensure that your packages don't have circular dependencies, where package A depends on package B, which in turn depends on package A. This can lead to complex build processes and make your code harder to understand and modify.

Benefits of Organized Code

- **Improved Readability:** Organized code is easier to read and understand, as related functionalities are grouped together and dependencies are clear.
- **Enhanced Maintainability:** Changes and updates are easier to implement in well-organized code, as you can focus on specific packages without affecting the entire system.
- **Facilitated Collaboration:** A clear and consistent package structure makes it easier for multiple developers to work on the same project, minimizing conflicts and promoting efficient collaboration.
- **Increased Reusability:** Well-designed packages can be reused across different projects, saving development time and effort.
- **Better Testability:** Organized code lends itself to better testing, as you can write targeted unit tests for individual packages and functions.

By embracing these strategies and leveraging the power of packages, you can create Go projects that are not only functional but also well-structured, maintainable, and scalable. Remember that code organization is an ongoing process. As your project grows, you might need to refactor and reorganize your packages to ensure that they remain cohesive and aligned with the evolving needs of your application.

Standard Library Packages

The Go standard library stands as a testament to the language's philosophy of practicality and efficiency. It's a treasure trove of pre-built packages that provide solutions for a vast array of common programming tasks, significantly reducing the need to rely on external dependencies or reinvent the wheel.

Why the Standard Library Matters:

- **Batteries Included:** Go's "batteries included" approach means that you have a rich set of tools at your disposal right out of the box. This accelerates development and allows you to focus on the core logic of your applications.
- **High Quality and Reliability:** The packages within the standard library are meticulously crafted, well-documented, and thoroughly tested. They adhere to Go's idiomatic style and best practices, making them reliable and easy to integrate into your projects.
- **Consistency:** By using standard library packages, you ensure consistency and familiarity across your Go codebase. This simplifies collaboration and makes it easier for other developers to understand and contribute to your projects.

Commonly Used Standard Library Packages:

- `fmt`: This package provides functions for formatted I/O (input/output), including printing to the console, formatting strings, and scanning input from the user. It's a staple for interacting with the user and displaying information.
- `os`: This package offers functions for interacting with the operating system, such as file operations, directory manipulation, environment variables, and process management. It's essential for any Go program that needs to interact with the underlying system.
- `io`: This package provides basic interfaces and functionalities for reading and writing data, abstracting away the specifics of different input/output sources like files, network connections, or in-memory buffers. It forms the foundation for many other I/O-related packages in the standard library.
- `net/http`: This package is the cornerstone of Go's web development capabilities. It provides a powerful and flexible HTTP server and client implementation, allowing you to build web applications, APIs, and network services with ease.
- `encoding/json`: This package handles the encoding and decoding of JSON (JavaScript Object Notation) data, a popular format for data exchange over the web. It enables seamless communication with web APIs and facilitates data serialization and deserialization in your Go programs.

Additional Notable Packages:

- `strings`: Provides functions for string manipulation, such as searching, replacing, splitting, and joining strings
- `time`: Handles time and date operations, including formatting, parsing, and time zone conversions
- `math`: Offers mathematical functions and constants
- `crypto`: Provides cryptographic algorithms and protocols for data security
- `testing`: Enables unit testing and benchmarking of your Go code

Key Points

- The Go standard library offers a rich collection of packages for various tasks
- These packages are well-designed, reliable, and promote consistency across your codebase
- Leverage the standard library to accelerate development, avoid reinventing the wheel, and build robust and efficient Go programs

By familiarizing yourself with the standard library and its commonly used packages, you'll be equipped with a powerful set of tools to tackle a wide range of programming challenges in Go. The standard library is a testament to Go's commitment to practicality and efficiency, providing you with the building blocks to create sophisticated and high-performing applications.

Third-Party Packages

While Go's standard library offers a comprehensive set of tools, the vibrant Go community has contributed a vast ecosystem of third-party packages that extend the language's capabilities and accelerate development. These packages, often hosted on platforms like GitHub, provide solutions for a wide range of tasks, from web development and database access to logging, testing, and much more.

Leveraging Third-Party Packages

- **Extended Functionality:** Third-party packages fill gaps in the standard library, offering specialized functionalities or alternative implementations for specific tasks.
- **Accelerated Development:** By leveraging pre-built solutions, you can save time and effort, focusing on the core logic of your application instead of reinventing the wheel.
- **Community-Driven Innovation:** The Go community is constantly creating and improving packages, fostering innovation and providing a wealth of options to choose from.

Using `go get` to Install Packages

The `go get` command is your gateway to the world of third-party Go packages. It simplifies the process of downloading and installing packages from remote repositories, handling dependencies automatically.

Syntax

```
go get <importPath>
```

- **importPath:** The import path of the package you want to install. This usually includes the repository URL and the package's path within the repository.

Example:

```
go get github.com/gin-gonic/gin
```

This command downloads and installs the Gin web framework, placing its source code and dependencies within your Go workspace.

Popular Third-Party Packages

- **Web Development**
    - **Gin:** A high-performance web framework known for its simplicity and speed.
    - **Echo:** Another popular web framework offering a minimalist and extensible design
    - **Gorilla Mux:** A powerful HTTP router and URL matcher.
- **Database Access**
    - **GORM:** An ORM (Object-Relational Mapping) library that simplifies database interactions.
    - **sqlx:** Extends the standard `database/sql` package with powerful features and conveniences
    - **pgx:** A PostgreSQL driver offering high performance and flexibility
- **Logging**
    - **logrus:** A structured logging library that makes it easier to manage and analyze logs.
    - **zap:** A high-performance logging library focused on speed and efficiency
    - **zerolog:** A zero-allocation JSON logger designed for performance-critical applications

Key Points:

- Third-party packages extend Go's capabilities and accelerate development
- Use the `go get` command to download and install packages from remote repositories
- Explore the vast ecosystem of Go packages to find solutions for various tasks

By embracing the power of third-party packages, you can tap into the collective wisdom and innovation of the Go community. These packages can significantly enhance your productivity, allowing you to build feature-rich and efficient applications while focusing on the unique aspects of your projects. Remember to choose packages carefully, considering their popularity, documentation, and community support to ensure a smooth and successful integration into your Go codebase.

Best Practices for Package Design

Designing well-structured and maintainable packages is crucial for creating Go projects that are easy to understand, modify, and collaborate on. By adhering to best practices and adopting a thoughtful approach to package design, you can ensure that your codebase remains organized, reusable, and adaptable as it grows.

Clear and Descriptive Names

- **Reflect Purpose and Functionality:** Choose package names that clearly convey the purpose and functionality of the code within the package. Avoid generic or ambiguous names that might lead to confusion.
- **Use Lowercase:** Package names should be all lowercase, with no underscores or mixed caps.
- **Short and Concise:** Strive for short and concise names that are easy to remember and type.

Concise and Focused

- **Single Responsibility Principle:** Each package should ideally have a single, well-defined responsibility or area of concern. This promotes modularity and makes it easier to understand and test individual packages.
- **Avoid Bloated Packages:** Large, monolithic packages can become difficult to manage and understand. Break down complex functionalities into smaller, more focused packages.

Well-Documented

- **Godoc Comments:** Use Godoc comments to document your packages and their exported identifiers. Provide clear and concise descriptions of their purpose, usage, and any potential side effects.
- **Examples:** Include examples in your documentation to demonstrate how to use the package's functionalities.
- **Clarity and Completeness:** Strive for clear, complete, and up-to-date documentation that helps other developers understand and use your packages effectively.

Versioning

- **Semantic Versioning:** Consider using semantic versioning (e.g., v1.2.3) for your packages, especially if you plan to share them publicly or use them in multiple projects. Semantic versioning provides a clear way to communicate changes and manage compatibility between different versions of your packages.
- **Go Modules:** Go modules, introduced in Go 1.11, provide built-in support for versioning and dependency management, making it easier to track and update package versions in your projects.

Conclusion: The Power of Packages

Packages are the cornerstone of code organization, reusability, and maintainability in Go. By grouping related code into well-designed packages, you create a modular and scalable architecture that facilitates collaboration, simplifies testing, and promotes long-term project health. Remember, investing time and effort in thoughtful package design pays off in the long run, leading to Go projects that are not only functional but also elegant, adaptable, and enjoyable to work with.

Chapter Summary

In this chapter, we explored the vital role of packages in organizing and managing Go code. You've learned:

- **The Importance of Code Organization:** We discussed how well-organized code enhances readability, maintainability, and collaboration in Go projects.
- **Understanding Packages:** You gained insights into packages as containers for grouping related code, creating namespaces, and preventing naming conflicts.
- **Creating and Using Packages:** You learned how to create packages by organizing code into directories and how to use code from other packages through imports.
- **Importing Packages:** We explored import paths, aliases, and blank imports, providing flexibility and control over how you incorporate external code into your projects.
- **Exported vs. Unexported Identifiers:** You understood the distinction between exported and unexported identifiers and how they contribute to encapsulation and access control.
- **The `main` Package:** You learned about the special role of the `main` package in creating executable Go programs.
- **Organizing Code with Packages:** We discussed strategies for organizing code into packages, promoting modularity, reusability, and separation of concerns.
- **Standard Library Packages:** You were introduced to the wealth of functionalities available in the Go standard library through its collection of well-designed packages.
- **Third-Party Packages:** You learned how to leverage third-party packages to extend Go's capabilities and accelerate development using the `go get` command.
- **Best Practices:** We provided guidance on best practices for designing and naming packages, emphasizing clarity, conciseness, documentation, and versioning.

By mastering the art of package organization, you can create Go projects that are not only functional but also well-structured, maintainable, and scalable. Remember, a well-organized codebase is a joy to work with, facilitating collaboration, promoting reusability, and ensuring the long-term health of your Go projects.

In the next chapter, we will explore interfaces, a powerful concept in Go that enables polymorphism and code flexibility. You'll learn how interfaces define contracts for behavior and how they can be used to create loosely coupled and adaptable code.

Interfaces: Achieving Polymorphism and Code Flexibility

Outline

- Understanding Interfaces
- Defining Interfaces
- Implementing Interfaces
- Polymorphism with Interfaces
- Empty Interface
- Type Assertions and Type Switches
- Interfaces and Composition
- Best Practices for Interface Design
- Chapter Summary

Understanding Interfaces

In the world of Go programming, where adaptability and modularity are prized, interfaces emerge as a cornerstone for achieving code flexibility and decoupling. Think of an interface as a contract that outlines a set of behaviors or capabilities that a type must possess. It defines a collection of method signatures, specifying the names, parameters, and return types of methods that any type implementing the interface must provide.

Interfaces as Contracts

- **Behavioral Agreement**: An interface establishes a behavioral agreement between different parts of your code. It says, "If you want to work with me, you must provide these specific methods." This allows you to write code that interacts with values of different types, as long as those types adhere to the interface's contract.
- **Loose Coupling**: Interfaces promote loose coupling between different components of your system. Instead of relying on concrete types, your code can interact with interfaces, making it easier to swap out different implementations or add new ones without affecting the rest of the codebase.
- **Abstraction**: Interfaces provide a layer of abstraction, allowing you to focus on the essential behavior of a type rather than its specific implementation details. This makes your code more adaptable and easier to reason about.
- **Code Flexibility**: By programming to interfaces, you create code that is more flexible and resilient to change. You can introduce new types that implement the same interface without modifying the existing code that interacts with that interface.

Analogy

Imagine you're building a music player application. You want to be able to play different types of audio files, such as MP3s, WAVs, and OGGs. Instead of writing separate code for each file type, you can define a `Player` interface that specifies the methods required for playing audio (e.g., `Play`, `Pause`, `Stop`). Then, you can create different types (e.g., `MP3Player`, `WAVPlayer`, `OGGPlayer`) that implement this interface, providing specific implementations for each file format. Your music player application can then work with any type that implements the `Player` interface, allowing you to seamlessly add support for new file formats in the future without changing the core logic of your player.

Key Points

- Interfaces define contracts for behavior, specifying method signatures.
- Types implement interfaces by providing concrete implementations for the interface's methods.
- Interfaces promote loose coupling, abstraction, and code flexibility.
- They allow you to write code that can work with values of different types as long as they implement the same interface.

In the following sections, we'll delve deeper into the mechanics of defining and implementing interfaces in Go. You'll learn how to create interfaces, implement them with different types, and leverage their power to achieve polymorphism and build more adaptable and maintainable code.

Defining Interfaces

Defining interfaces in Go involves outlining a blueprint for behavior that types can adhere to. You use the `type` and `interface` keywords to establish this contract, specifying the method signatures that any type implementing the interface must fulfill.

Syntax

```
type interfaceName interface {
    methodName1(parameterTypes...) returnTypes
    methodName2(parameterTypes...) returnTypes
    // ... more method signatures
}
```

- `type`: The keyword used to introduce a new type definition
- `interfaceName`: The name you choose for your interface
- `interface`: The keyword indicating the definition of an interface type
- `methodName(parameterTypes...) returnTypes`: Method signatures, each specifying:
  - `methodName`: The name of the method
  - `parameterTypes...`: The types of parameters the method accepts (if any)
  - `returnTypes`: The types of values the method returns (if any)

Examples

1. **Shape Interface**

   ```
   type Shape interface {
       Area() float64
       Perimeter() float64
   }
   ```

   This interface defines the behavior of a geometric shape, requiring any type that implements it to provide methods for calculating its area and perimeter.

2. **Reader Interface**

   ```
   type Reader interface {
       Read(p []byte) (n int, err error)
   }
   ```

   This interface, from the standard library's `io` package, defines the behavior of a type that can read data into a byte slice.

3. **Logger Interface**

```go
type Logger interface {
    Print(v ...interface{})
    Printf(format string, v ...interface{})
    Println(v ...interface{})
}
```

This interface defines the behavior of a logger, requiring implementations to provide methods for logging messages at different levels of verbosity.

Key Points

- Interfaces define a contract for behavior, not implementation
- Method signatures within an interface specify the required methods, their parameters, and return types
- Any type that provides concrete implementations for all the methods in an interface is said to implement that interface
- Interfaces promote loose coupling and code flexibility by allowing different types to exhibit the same behavior

By defining interfaces, you establish clear expectations for the behavior of types that interact with your code. This enables you to write code that is adaptable and can work with a variety of types, as long as they fulfill the interface's contract.

Implementing Interfaces

In the world of Go, implementing an interface is like fulfilling a contract. A type (such as a struct or a custom type) implements an interface by providing concrete implementations for all the methods declared within that interface. This act of implementation signifies that the type adheres to the interface's behavioral contract and can be used wherever that interface is expected.

The Implicit Implementation

One of the elegant aspects of Go's interface implementation is its implicit nature. There's no need for an explicit declaration that a type implements a particular interface. If a type provides definitions for all the methods specified in an interface, it is automatically considered to implement that interface. This promotes a more flexible and less verbose coding style.

Defining Methods on Structs

Let's illustrate how to implement an interface using a struct:

```go
type Shape interface {
    Area() float64
    Perimeter() float64
}

type Rectangle struct {
    Width  float64
    Height float64
}

// Implement the Area method for Rectangle
func (r Rectangle) Area() float64 {
    return r.Width * r.Height
}
```

```go
// Implement the Perimeter method for Rectangle
func (r Rectangle) Perimeter() float64 {
    return 2 * (r.Width + r.Height)
}
```

In this example, we define a Shape interface that requires two methods: `Area()` and `Perimeter()`. We then create a `Rectangle` struct and define methods on it that match the signatures of the methods in the Shape interface. Because the `Rectangle` struct provides implementations for both `Area()` and `Perimeter()`, it implicitly implements the Shape interface.

Key Points

- Types implement interfaces by providing concrete implementations for all the methods defined in the interface
- There's no need for an explicit declaration of interface implementation
- You can define methods on structs (or other types) to satisfy the requirements of an interface
- A type implicitly implements an interface if it has all the required methods

By implementing interfaces, you create a powerful mechanism for code flexibility and adaptability. Next, we will explore how interfaces enable polymorphism, allowing you to write code that can work with values of different types as long as they adhere to the same interface contract.

Polymorphism with Interfaces

Polymorphism, a cornerstone of object-oriented programming, empowers you to write code that can operate on values of different types in a uniform way. In Go, interfaces serve as the conduit for achieving polymorphism, allowing you to create flexible and adaptable code that can work with a variety of types as long as they adhere to a common behavioral contract.

The Essence of Polymorphism

- **Many Forms:** The word "polymorphism" stems from the Greek words "poly" (meaning "many") and "morph" (meaning "form"). It signifies the ability of code to take on many forms or work with objects of different types.
- **Interface as the Contract:** In Go, interfaces act as the contract that defines the common behavior expected from different types. Any type that implements the interface's methods is considered polymorphic with respect to that interface.
- **Flexibility and Adaptability:** Polymorphism enables you to write functions and data structures that can operate on values of different types without needing to know their specific concrete types at compile time. This promotes code flexibility and adaptability, as you can introduce new types that implement the same interface without modifying the existing code that interacts with that interface.

Decoupling from Concrete Types

Interfaces decouple your code from specific concrete types, allowing you to write code that is more generic and reusable.

- **Example:**

```go
type Shape interface {
    Area() float64
}

func printArea(s Shape) {
    fmt.Println("Area:", s.Area())
```

```go
}

func main() {
    circle := Circle{Radius: 5}
    rectangle := Rectangle{Width: 4, Height: 3}

    printArea(circle)     // Output: Area: 78.53981633974483
    printArea(rectangle)  // Output: Area: 12
}
```

In this example, the `printArea` function takes a value of type Shape as its argument. It doesn't care about the specific type of shape it receives; it only cares that the shape implements the `Area()` method defined in the Shape interface. This allows the `printArea` function to work with both `Circle` and `Rectangle` instances, demonstrating the power of polymorphism.

Key Points

- Interfaces enable polymorphism in Go by defining a contract for behavior.
- Types that implement the same interface are considered polymorphic with respect to that interface.
- Polymorphism promotes code flexibility and adaptability by decoupling code from specific concrete types.
- You can write functions and data structures that can work with values of different types as long as they implement the same interface.

By leveraging the power of interfaces and polymorphism, you can create Go code that is more generic, reusable, and adaptable to change. This leads to cleaner, more maintainable, and more extensible software systems.

Empty Interface

The empty interface, denoted by `interface{}`, holds a special place in Go's type system. It's an interface that doesn't declare any methods. This might seem counterintuitive at first, but its lack of constraints makes it incredibly versatile and powerful for handling values of unknown or dynamic types.

The Universal Type

- **Implicit Implementation:** In Go, every type automatically implements the empty interface because it has no methods to satisfy. This means you can assign a value of any type to a variable of type `interface{}`.
- **Dynamic Typing:** The empty interface essentially enables a form of dynamic typing in Go, where you can store and manipulate values of different types within the same variable.

Use Cases

The empty interface is particularly useful in scenarios where:

1. **Storing Values of Unknown Types**

```go
var data interface{}
data = 42        // int
data = "Hello"   // string
data = []float64{3.14, 2.71} // slice of float64
```

In this example, the `data` variable can hold values of various types because it's declared as an empty interface.

2. **Processing Values of Different Types**

```
func printValue(v interface{}) {
    switch v.(type) {
    case int:
        fmt.Println("Integer:", v)
    case string:
        fmt.Println("String:", v)
    default:
        fmt.Println("Unknown type")
    }
}
```

The `printValue` function uses a type switch to determine the concrete type of the v argument (which is of type `interface{}`) and performs different actions based on the type.

3. **Functions with Flexible Arguments:**

```
func printValues(values ...interface{}) {
    for _, v := range values {
        fmt.Println(v)
    }
}
```

The `printValues` function uses a variadic parameter of type `interface{}` to accept any number of arguments of different types.

Key Points

- The empty interface (`interface{}`) has no methods.
- Any type in Go implicitly implements the empty interface
- It allows you to store and process values of unknown or dynamic types
- Use type assertions or type switches to work with the concrete values stored in an empty interface variable

The empty interface provides a powerful mechanism for handling data whose type is not known at compile time or might change during program execution. It enables you to write more flexible and adaptable code that can work with a variety of types, promoting code reusability and dynamic behavior. However it's crucial to use type assertions or type switches to safely access and manipulate the concrete values stored within an empty interface variable.

Type Assertions and Type Switches

Type Assertions

When working with interface values, you often need to access the underlying concrete value stored within them. Type assertions in Go provide a way to achieve this, allowing you to "assert" that an interface value holds a specific concrete type and extract that value for further use.

Syntax

The syntax for a type assertion is as follows:

```
concreteValue, ok := interfaceValue.(concreteType)
```

- `interfaceValue`: The interface value you want to perform the type assertion on

- `concreteType`: The concrete type you believe the interface value holds
- `concreteValue`: A variable to store the extracted concrete value (if the assertion succeeds)
- `ok`: A boolean variable that indicates whether the type assertion was successful

Handling Type Assertion Failures: The Comma-ok Idiom

Type assertions can fail if the interface value doesn't hold the asserted concrete type. To handle these potential failures gracefully, Go provides the "comma-ok idiom."

- **ok Check:** The ok variable in the type assertion syntax will be `true` if the assertion succeeds and `false` if it fails. You should always check the value of ok before using the extracted `concreteValue`.

Example

```go
func main() {
    var data interface{} = 42

    // Successful type assertion
    intValue, ok := data.(int)
    if ok {
        fmt.Println("Integer value:", intValue)
    }

    // Unsuccessful type assertion
    stringValue, ok := data.(string)
    if ok {
        fmt.Println("String value:", stringValue)
    } else {
        fmt.Println("Type assertion failed: data is not a string")
    }
}
```

In this example, the first type assertion succeeds because `data` holds an integer value. The second type assertion fails because `data` is not a string, and the `else` block handles the failure gracefully.

Key Points

- Type assertions allow you to extract the underlying concrete value from an interface value
- Use the comma-ok idiom (`value, ok := i.(T)`) to handle potential type assertion failures
- Always check the ok value before using the extracted concrete value
- Type assertions are useful when you need to perform operations that are specific to a particular concrete type

By understanding how to use type assertions and the comma-ok idiom, you can safely and effectively work with interface values, extracting their underlying concrete values when needed and handling potential type mismatches gracefully. This empowers you to write more flexible and adaptable Go code that can handle values of dynamic or unknown types.

Type Switches

While type assertions allow you to check and extract the concrete type of an interface value, type switches offer a more structured and expressive way to handle multiple type assertions and perform different actions based on the concrete type. They provide a concise mechanism for branching your code's execution based on the type of the value stored within an interface variable.

Syntax

The syntax for a type switch is as follows:

```
switch concreteType := interfaceValue.(type) {
case type1:
    // Code to execute if the concrete type is type1
case type2:
    // Code to execute if the concrete type is type2
// ... (more cases)
default:
    // Code to execute if the concrete type doesn't match any of the cases
}
```

- `concreteType := interfaceValue.(type)`: This is the type switch expression. It assigns the concrete type of the `interfaceValue` to the `concreteType` variable and compares it against the types listed in the `case` clauses
- `case type1`, `case type2`, etc.: These are the cases that specify the possible concrete types that the `interfaceValue` might hold
- `default`: This is an optional case that is executed if the concrete type doesn't match any of the explicitly listed cases

How Type Switches Work:

1. **Type Assertion:** The type switch expression performs a type assertion on the `interfaceValue`.
2. **Case Matching:** The concrete type extracted from the `interfaceValue` is compared against the types specified in the `case` clauses.
3. **Code Execution:** If a match is found, the code block associated with the matching `case` is executed. If no match is found, the `default` case (if present) is executed.

Examples

```
func printValue(v interface{}) {
    switch v.(type) {
    case int:
        fmt.Println("Integer:", v)
    case string:
        fmt.Println("String:", v)
    case []int:
        fmt.Println("Slice of integers:", v)
    default:
        fmt.Println("Unknown type")
    }
}

func main() {
    printValue(42)              // Output: Integer: 42
    printValue("Hello, Go!")    // Output: String: Hello, Go!
    printValue([]int{1, 2, 3})  // Output: Slice of integers: [1 2 3]
    printValue(true)            // Output: Unknown type
}
```

In this example, the `printValue` function uses a type switch to handle different types of values passed to it through the `interface{}` parameter.

Key Points

- Type switches provide a structured way to handle multiple type assertions
- They allow you to perform different actions based on the concrete type of an interface value

- The `default` case handles scenarios where no other case matches
- Type switches enhance code readability and maintainability when dealing with interface values of varying types

Type switches are a valuable tool for working with interface values in a type-safe and organized manner. They enable you to write flexible code that can handle different concrete types, promoting code reusability and adaptability.

Interfaces and Composition

In the realm of software design, the principles of composition and interfaces intertwine to create a powerful synergy that fosters flexibility, modularity, and adaptability. Composition allows you to build complex systems by combining smaller, self-contained components. Interfaces, on the other hand, define contracts for behavior, enabling these components to interact seamlessly even if their internal implementations differ.

Interfaces as the Glue

- **Defining Component Behavior**: Interfaces act as the glue that binds components together in a loosely coupled manner. They define the essential methods that a component must provide to interact with other parts of the system.
- **Swapping Implementations**: By programming to interfaces, you gain the freedom to swap out different implementations of a component as long as they adhere to the same interface. This enables you to experiment with different algorithms, data structures, or external services without affecting the overall structure of your system.
- **Modularity and Maintainability**: Composition and interfaces promote modularity by encapsulating functionality within self-contained components. This modularity makes your code easier to understand, test, and maintain, as changes to one component are less likely to ripple through the entire system.

Example: A Pluggable Logging System

```go
type Logger interface {
    Log(message string)
}

type FileLogger struct {
    filename string
}

func (fl *FileLogger) Log(message string) {
    // ... (write message to a file)
}

type ConsoleLogger struct{}

func (cl *ConsoleLogger) Log(message string) {
    fmt.Println(message)
}

func main() {
    var logger Logger // Use an interface to represent the logger

    // Choose a specific logger implementation
    if useFileLogging {
        logger = &FileLogger{filename: "log.txt"}
    } else {
```

```
        logger = &ConsoleLogger{}
    }

    logger.Log("This is a log message")
}
```

In this example, we define a `Logger` interface that specifies a single method Log. We then create two different implementations of this interface: `FileLogger` (logs messages to a file) and `ConsoleLogger` (prints messages to the console). The main function uses the `Logger` interface to represent the logger component, and based on a configuration setting, it can choose to use either the `FileLogger` or the `ConsoleLogger`. This demonstrates how interfaces allow you to swap out different implementations of a component seamlessly.

Key Points:

- Interfaces define contracts for behavior, enabling loose coupling between components
- Composition allows you to build complex systems by combining smaller, self-contained components
- Interfaces and composition promote modularity, flexibility, and maintainability
- You can swap out different implementations of a component as long as they adhere to the same interface

By combining the principles of composition and interfaces, you can create Go programs that are adaptable, extensible, and resilient to change. This approach empowers you to build complex systems with clear boundaries between components, making your code easier to understand, test, and evolve over time.

Best Practices for Interface Design

Designing effective interfaces in Go involves striking a balance between capturing essential behaviors and maintaining flexibility. By adhering to best practices, you can create interfaces that promote loose coupling, enhance code readability, and facilitate maintainable and adaptable designs.

1. Small and Focused

- **Interface Segregation Principle:** Strive to keep interfaces small and focused on a specific set of related behaviors. Avoid creating large interfaces that encompass a wide range of unrelated functionalities.
- **Single Responsibility:** Each interface should ideally represent a single, well-defined responsibility or concept within your application. This promotes modularity and makes it easier to reason about and implement different types that adhere to the interface.

2. Clear Naming

- **Descriptive Names:** Choose interface names that clearly convey the purpose and behavior they represent. Avoid generic or ambiguous names that might lead to confusion.
- **Suffix "er":** It's a common convention in Go to name interfaces with a suffix "er" to indicate that they represent a set of actions or capabilities (e.g., `Reader`, `Writer`, `Formatter`).

3. Avoid Large Interfaces

- **Tight Coupling:** Large interfaces with numerous methods can lead to tight coupling between types that implement them. This can make your code less flexible and harder to modify, as changes to the interface might necessitate changes in multiple implementations.

- **Interface Pollution:** Large interfaces can also lead to "interface pollution," where types are forced to implement methods they don't actually need, cluttering their code and potentially violating the Interface Segregation Principle.

4. Composition over Inheritance

- **Flexibility and Reusability:** Go favors composition over inheritance as a means of achieving code reuse and flexibility. Instead of creating complex inheritance hierarchies, compose your types from smaller, more focused components that implement specific interfaces
- **Loose Coupling:** Composition with interfaces promotes loose coupling, allowing you to swap out different implementations of components without affecting the overall structure of your system.

Conclusion: The Power of Interfaces

Interfaces lie at the heart of Go's approach to polymorphism, code flexibility, and maintainable designs. By defining contracts for behavior, they enable you to write code that can work with values of different types seamlessly. They promote loose coupling, abstraction, and adaptability, making your code more resilient to change and easier to maintain.

By following these best practices and designing your interfaces thoughtfully, you can harness the full potential of interfaces in your Go projects. Remember to keep them small, focused, and well-documented, and favor composition over inheritance to create flexible and modular designs. By mastering the art of interface design, you'll be well on your way to writing clean, efficient, and adaptable Go code that stands the test of time.

Chapter Summary

In this chapter, you embarked on a journey to explore the powerful world of interfaces in Go. We covered the following essential concepts:

- **Understanding Interfaces:** We introduced interfaces as collections of method signatures that define contracts for behavior, promoting loose coupling, abstraction, and code flexibility.
- **Defining Interfaces:** You learned the syntax for defining interfaces using the `type` and `interface` keywords and how to declare method signatures within an interface.
- **Implementing Interfaces:** We discussed how types can implement interfaces by providing concrete implementations for the interface's methods, emphasizing the implicit nature of interface implementation in Go.
- **Polymorphism with Interfaces:** You explored how interfaces enable polymorphism, allowing you to write code that can work with values of different types as long as they adhere to the same interface contract.
- **Empty Interface:** We introduced the empty interface (`interface{}`) as a versatile tool for handling values of unknown or dynamic types.
- **Type Assertions and Type Switches:** You learned how to use type assertions to extract concrete values from interface values and how to handle potential type assertion failures using the comma-ok idiom. We also discussed type switches as a way to perform different actions based on the concrete type of an interface value.
- **Interfaces and Composition:** We explored how interfaces and composition work together to create flexible and modular designs, allowing you to swap out different implementations of components that adhere to the same interface.
- **Best Practices:** We provided guidance on best practices for designing interfaces, emphasizing small, focused interfaces with clear names, and promoting composition over inheritance.

By mastering these concepts, you've unlocked the potential of interfaces to create adaptable, maintainable, and expressive Go code. Interfaces empower you to write code that is decoupled from specific concrete types, enabling you to build systems that are more flexible, testable, and resilient to change.

In the next chapter, we will delve into the realm of concurrency in Go, exploring goroutines and channels, which are fundamental tools for building concurrent and high-performance applications. Get ready to harness the true power of Go's concurrency model and unleash the full potential of your multi-core processors!

Section IV:
Concurrency in Go

Introduction to Concurrency and Goroutines

Outline

- Concurrency vs. Parallelism
- The Need for Concurrency
- Go's Concurrency Model
- Goroutines: Lightweight Threads
- Creating and Running Goroutines
- The main Goroutine and Program Termination
- Goroutine Communication and Synchronization (Brief Overview)
- Chapter Summary

Concurrency vs. Parallelism

In the realm of programming, concurrency and parallelism are often used interchangeably, but they represent distinct concepts with subtle yet important differences. Understanding these differences is crucial for harnessing the full power of Go's concurrency model and building efficient applications that leverage modern hardware.

Concurrency

- **Juggling Multiple Tasks:** Concurrency is the ability of a program to handle multiple tasks or events seemingly at the same time. It's like a chef juggling multiple dishes on the stove, switching between them to ensure they all cook properly. Even though the chef might not be actively working on all the dishes simultaneously, they are making progress on each one concurrently.
- **Interleaved Execution:** Concurrency often involves interleaving the execution of different tasks, switching between them rapidly to give the illusion of simultaneous progress. This is particularly useful when dealing with tasks that involve waiting, such as network requests or user input. While one task is waiting, the program can switch to another task and make progress on it.

Parallelism

- **True Simultaneity:** Parallelism, on the other hand, is the actual simultaneous execution of multiple tasks on separate processing units, such as multiple cores in a CPU or multiple threads within a process. It's like having multiple chefs working on different dishes at the same time, each with their own dedicated stove.
- **Hardware Utilization:** Parallelism allows you to fully utilize the available processing power of your hardware, potentially leading to significant performance gains for tasks that can be divided into independent subtasks.

Go's Concurrency Model: The Best of Both Worlds

Go's concurrency model, built on goroutines and channels, elegantly bridges the gap between concurrency and parallelism, enabling you to write programs that:

- **Achieve Concurrency:** Goroutines are lightweight threads managed by the Go runtime. They allow you to express concurrent tasks in a natural and intuitive way. The Go runtime efficiently schedules these goroutines, interleaving their execution to achieve concurrency even on a single processor core.
- **Exploit Parallelism:** When your program runs on a multi-core machine, the Go runtime can distribute goroutines across multiple cores, achieving true parallelism and maximizing hardware utilization.

Illustrative Example

Consider a web server that needs to handle multiple incoming requests concurrently. Using Go's concurrency model, you can create a goroutine for each request, allowing the server to process multiple requests simultaneously. If the server is running on a multi-core machine, these goroutines can be executed in parallel on different cores, further enhancing the server's throughput and responsiveness.

Key Takeaways

- Concurrency is about handling multiple tasks seemingly at the same time, even if they are not executed simultaneously.
- Parallelism is about the actual simultaneous execution of multiple tasks on separate processing units.
- Go's concurrency model enables both concurrency and parallelism, allowing you to write efficient and scalable programs that leverage modern hardware.

By understanding the distinction between concurrency and parallelism and how Go's concurrency model supports both, you'll be well-equipped to design and implement concurrent programs that are both performant and maintainable.

The Need for Concurrency

In the landscape of modern software development, where applications are expected to handle a multitude of tasks, interact with various resources, and scale to meet growing demands, concurrency has emerged as an indispensable tool. It empowers developers to create responsive, efficient, and scalable programs that can harness the power of today's multi-core processors and distributed systems.

Why Concurrency Matters

1. **Responsiveness:** Concurrency allows your programs to remain responsive even when performing time-consuming operations. By delegating tasks to separate execution units (goroutines), your application can continue to process user input, handle events, and update the user interface while background tasks are running. This leads to a smoother and more interactive user experience.
2. **Efficiency and Resource Utilization:** Concurrency enables your programs to make the most of available hardware resources. By distributing tasks across multiple cores or threads, you can achieve parallelism and speed up computations or data processing. This is particularly beneficial for tasks that can be broken down into independent subtasks, such as image processing, data analysis, or simulations.
3. **Scalability:** Concurrency is essential for building scalable systems that can handle increasing workloads and user demands. By leveraging concurrency, your applications can efficiently manage multiple network connections, process concurrent requests, and distribute tasks across multiple machines in a distributed environment.
4. **Handling Multiple Network Connections:** In network-centric applications like web servers, chat applications, or gaming servers, concurrency is crucial for handling multiple client connections or requests simultaneously. Each connection or request can be processed by a separate goroutine, ensuring that the server remains responsive and can handle a large number of clients efficiently.

5. **Performing Background Tasks:** Many applications need to perform background tasks, such as data synchronization, file uploads/downloads, or scheduled jobs. Concurrency allows you to execute these tasks in the background without blocking the main application thread, keeping the user interface responsive and interactive.
6. **Speeding Up Computations:** For computationally intensive tasks, concurrency can lead to significant performance improvements. By breaking down a large task into smaller subtasks that can be executed concurrently on multiple cores, you can leverage the full power of your hardware and achieve faster results.
7. **Building Distributed Systems:** Concurrency is fundamental for building distributed systems that span multiple machines. By using goroutines and channels, you can create components that communicate and collaborate across a network, enabling you to build scalable and fault-tolerant systems.

Key Points

- Concurrency is crucial for building responsive, efficient, and scalable applications
- It enables you to handle multiple tasks or events seemingly simultaneously
- Concurrency promotes efficient resource utilization and parallelism on multi-core systems
- It's essential for building network services, performing background tasks, speeding up computations, and creating distributed systems

By understanding the need for concurrency and how it can benefit your Go programs, you'll be well-prepared to leverage Go's powerful concurrency model to create high-performance, scalable, and responsive applications that meet the demands of modern software development.

Go's Concurrency Model

Go's concurrency model, often hailed as one of its most distinctive and powerful features, is built upon two fundamental concepts: **goroutines** and **channels**. This model empowers developers to express concurrent execution of tasks in a natural and intuitive manner, while also providing mechanisms for safe communication and synchronization between those tasks.

Goroutines: The Lightweight Threads

- **Lightweight Powerhouses:** Goroutines are the heart of Go's concurrency model. They are functions or methods that execute concurrently with other goroutines, managed efficiently by the Go runtime. Unlike traditional operating system threads, which can be heavyweight and resource-intensive, goroutines are incredibly lightweight, allowing you to create thousands or even millions of them within a single program without overwhelming your system.
- **Effortless Concurrency:** Creating a goroutine is as simple as adding the go keyword before a function call. This instructs the Go runtime to execute that function in a separate goroutine, allowing it to run concurrently with the rest of your code.
- **Efficient Scheduling:** The Go runtime intelligently schedules goroutines across the available processor cores, maximizing parallelism and ensuring that your program utilizes the full potential of your hardware.

Channels: The Communication Conduits

- **Typed Communication:** Channels are the communication pipelines that connect goroutines, enabling them to safely exchange data and synchronize their actions. They are typed conduits, meaning they can only carry values of a specific data type, ensuring type safety and preventing errors.
- **Synchronization and Coordination:** Channels provide a built-in mechanism for synchronization. Sending or receiving values on a channel is a blocking operation. This means that if a goroutine tries to send a value to a full channel or receive a value from an empty channel, it will wait until the

operation can be completed. This blocking behavior helps prevent race conditions and ensures that goroutines coordinate their activities correctly.

Simplicity, Efficiency, and Safety

Go's concurrency model is designed with these principles in mind:

- **Simplicity:** The syntax for creating and using goroutines and channels is remarkably straightforward, making concurrent programming in Go accessible and intuitive.
- **Efficiency:** Goroutines are lightweight and efficiently scheduled by the Go runtime, allowing you to create highly concurrent programs without sacrificing performance.
- **Safety:** Channels provide a safe and reliable way for goroutines to communicate and synchronize, helping you avoid common concurrency pitfalls like data races and deadlocks.

By combining goroutines and channels, you can build concurrent Go programs that are not only powerful and performant but also maintainable and less prone to errors.

Goroutines: Lightweight Threads

Goroutines are the fundamental building blocks of concurrency in Go. They are often described as lightweight threads, but they offer a level of efficiency and scalability that traditional operating system threads can't match. Let's delve into the characteristics that make goroutines so special:

Lightweight

- **Minimal Memory Footprint:** Goroutines are incredibly lightweight, typically requiring only a few kilobytes of stack space. This allows you to create thousands or even millions of them within a single program without worrying about exhausting system resources.
- **Efficient Creation and Destruction:** Creating and destroying goroutines is a relatively inexpensive operation compared to creating and destroying operating system threads. This enables you to dynamically spawn goroutines as needed to handle concurrent tasks, without incurring significant overhead.

Efficiently Scheduled

- **Go Scheduler:** The Go runtime employs a sophisticated scheduler that intelligently manages the execution of goroutines. It distributes goroutines across the available processor cores, maximizing parallelism and ensuring that your program efficiently utilizes the underlying hardware.
- **Cooperative Scheduling:** Goroutines cooperate with the scheduler by yielding control at specific points, such as when they are waiting for I/O operations or communicating on channels. This cooperative approach allows the scheduler to seamlessly switch between goroutines, ensuring that all goroutines make progress even on a single-core machine.
- **Work Stealing:** The Go scheduler also employs work-stealing techniques to balance the workload across multiple processor cores. If one core is idle while others are busy, the scheduler can "steal" work from a busy core and assign it to the idle core, further improving performance.

Multiplexed onto Threads

- **M:N Threading Model:** Go's concurrency model uses an M:N threading model, where a small number of operating system threads (M) are used to execute a larger number of goroutines (N). This multiplexing of goroutines onto threads reduces the overhead associated with context switching, as switching between goroutines within the same thread is much faster than switching between operating system threads.

Key Takeaways

- Goroutines are lightweight threads managed by the Go runtime.
- They have a small memory footprint, allowing you to create many of them efficiently.
- The Go scheduler intelligently schedules goroutines, maximizing parallelism and utilizing hardware resources effectively.
- Goroutines are multiplexed onto a smaller number of operating system threads, reducing context switching overhead and improving performance.

By leveraging the power of goroutines, you can write concurrent Go programs that are both efficient and scalable. The lightweight nature of goroutines, combined with Go's intelligent scheduler, empowers you to create highly concurrent applications that can handle massive workloads and leverage the full potential of modern multi-core processors.

In the next section, we'll explore how to create and run goroutines in your Go code, bringing concurrency to life in your programs.

Creating and Running Goroutines

Creating and running goroutines in Go is remarkably simple and intuitive. The go keyword is the magic wand that brings concurrency to life in your programs. By placing go before a function call, you instruct the Go runtime to execute that function in a separate goroutine, allowing it to run concurrently with the rest of your code.

Syntax

```
go functionName(arguments...)
```

- go: The keyword that spawns a new goroutine.
- functionName: The name of the function you want to execute in the goroutine.
- arguments...: The arguments to be passed to the function (if any).

Example: A Simple Goroutine

```go
func greet(name string) {
    fmt.Println("Hello,", name, "from a goroutine!")
}

func main() {
    go greet("Alice")
    fmt.Println("Main goroutine continues...")
}
```

In this example, the greet function is executed in a separate goroutine. The main function, which runs in the main goroutine, continues to execute concurrently with the greet goroutine.

Example: Multiple Goroutines

```go
func printNumbers() {
    for i := 1; i <= 5; i++ {
        fmt.Println(i)
        time.Sleep(time.Second)
    }
}

func printLetters() {
    for char := 'a'; char <= 'e'; char++ {
        fmt.Println(string(char))
        time.Sleep(500 * time.Millisecond)
```

```go
    }
}

func main() {
    go printNumbers()
    go printLetters()

    time.Sleep(6 * time.Second) // Keep the main goroutine alive to allow others to finish
    fmt.Println("Done!")
}
```

This example demonstrates how multiple goroutines can execute concurrently, performing different tasks. The `printNumbers` and `printLetters` functions are executed in separate goroutines, leading to interleaved output of numbers and letters. The `time.Sleep` calls are used to introduce delays and make the concurrent execution more visible.

Key Points

- Use the go keyword before a function call to create a goroutine
- Goroutines execute concurrently with the current goroutine
- You can create multiple goroutines to perform different tasks simultaneously
- The `main` goroutine continues to execute even after spawning other goroutines

By mastering the creation and execution of goroutines, you unlock the power of concurrency in your Go programs. This enables you to build responsive, efficient, and scalable applications that can handle multiple tasks simultaneously and leverage the full potential of modern hardware.

The `main` Goroutine and Program Termination

Every Go program embarks on its journey with a single, distinguished goroutine known as the **main goroutine**. This main goroutine is responsible for executing the `main` function, which serves as the entry point for your program's logic. As the conductor of your program's symphony, the main goroutine plays a pivotal role in its lifecycle, particularly when it comes to termination.

The Main Goroutine's Reign

- **The Beginning:** When you run a Go program, the Go runtime automatically creates the main goroutine and starts executing the `main` function within it.
- **The End:** The program's execution continues as long as the main goroutine is running. However, once the `main` function completes and the main goroutine exits, the program terminates, regardless of whether other goroutines are still actively running.

The Challenge of Premature Termination

This behavior can pose a challenge in concurrent programs where you have spawned additional goroutines to perform background tasks or handle long-running operations. If the main goroutine finishes before these other goroutines complete their work, the program might terminate prematurely, leaving those tasks unfinished.

Synchronization to the Rescue

To ensure that all goroutines have a chance to complete their tasks before the program terminates, you need to employ synchronization techniques. Synchronization mechanisms in Go, such as channels and sync packages, allow goroutines to coordinate their activities and signal when they have finished their work.

- **Channels as Signals:** You can use channels to send signals between goroutines, indicating when a task is complete or when it's safe to proceed. The main goroutine can wait to receive signals from all other goroutines before exiting, ensuring that they have a chance to finish.
- **sync Package:** The sync package provides additional synchronization primitives, such as WaitGroup and Mutex, which can be used to coordinate the execution of goroutines and protect shared data.

Key Points

- Every Go program starts with a single main goroutine that executes the main function.
- The program terminates when the main goroutine exits, even if other goroutines are still running.
- Synchronization techniques, such as channels and the sync package, are essential for ensuring that all goroutines complete their tasks before the program terminates.

By understanding the relationship between the main goroutine and program termination, you can design your concurrent Go programs to execute reliably and predictably.

Goroutine Communication and Synchronization (Brief Overview)

In the world of concurrent Go programming, where multiple goroutines dance and weave, performing their tasks independently, the need for communication and synchronization arises. How do these goroutines exchange data? How do they coordinate their actions to ensure a harmonious execution? The answer lies in **channels**, the elegant conduits that facilitate seamless communication and synchronization between goroutines.

Channels: The Typed Pipelines

Think of channels as typed pipelines that connect goroutines. They allow goroutines to send and receive values of a specific data type, ensuring type safety and preventing errors. You can create a channel using the make function, specifying the type of data it will carry.

- **Example**

```
ch := make(chan int) // Create a channel to send and receive integers
```

Sending and Receiving on Channels

Goroutines can send values to a channel using the channel send operator (<-) and receive values from a channel using the channel receive operator (<-).

- **Example**

```
ch <- 42    // Send the value 42 to the channel
value := <-ch // Receive a value from the channel and store it in 'value'
```

Blocking Behavior: The Key to Synchronization

One of the most crucial aspects of channels is their inherent blocking nature.

- **Sending on a Full Channel:** If a goroutine tries to send a value to a channel that's already full (its buffer is full), the goroutine will block (pause its execution) until another goroutine receives a value from the channel, creating space for the new value.

- **Receiving from an Empty Channel:** Similarly, if a goroutine tries to receive a value from an empty channel, it will block until another goroutine sends a value to the channel.

This blocking behavior acts as a natural synchronization mechanism. It ensures that goroutines wait for each other at critical points, preventing race conditions and data corruption.

Looking Ahead: Deeper into Channels

In the next chapter, we will explore channels in depth, delving into their creation, usage, buffering, and advanced patterns. You'll learn how to leverage channels to build robust and well-coordinated concurrent programs that communicate effectively and synchronize their actions seamlessly.

Key Takeaways

- Channels are typed conduits for sending and receiving values between goroutines
- They facilitate communication and synchronization
- Channels are inherently blocking, ensuring data synchronization and preventing race conditions
- The next chapter will provide a comprehensive exploration of channels and their usage in Go's concurrency model

By understanding the fundamental concepts of channels, you're taking a significant step toward mastering Go's concurrency model. Channels empower you to build concurrent programs that communicate effectively, coordinate their actions, and achieve safe and efficient parallel execution.

Chapter Summary

In this chapter, we took the first steps into the exciting world of concurrency in Go. We've covered:

- The distinction between concurrency (handling multiple tasks seemingly at the same time) and parallelism (true simultaneous execution on multiple processing units).
- The importance of concurrency in modern software development, enabling responsiveness, efficiency, scalability, and the ability to handle multiple network connections, perform background tasks, speed up computations, and build distributed systems
- Go's built-in concurrency model based on goroutines and channels, designed for simplicity, efficiency, and safety
- Goroutines as lightweight threads managed by the Go runtime, offering efficient creation, scheduling, and multiplexing onto a smaller number of operating system threads
- How to create and run goroutines using the go keyword, enabling concurrent execution of functions
- The role of the main goroutine and how program termination is tied to its completion
- A brief overview of how goroutines communicate and synchronize using channels, setting the stage for a deeper exploration in the next chapter.

By understanding the fundamentals of concurrency and goroutines, you're now equipped to start writing concurrent Go programs. You can leverage goroutines to express concurrent tasks in a natural and intuitive way, harnessing the power of your multi-core processors and creating responsive and efficient applications.

In the next chapter, we will delve into the intricacies of channels, exploring how they facilitate communication and synchronization between goroutines, empowering you to build sophisticated and well-coordinated concurrent programs.

Synchronization: Channels and Select Statements

Outline

- The Need for Synchronization
- Channels: The Communication Conduits
- Creating and Using Channels
- Sending and Receiving on Channels
- Blocking Behavior and Synchronization
- Buffered Channels
- The `close` Function and Channel Closing
- The `for-range` Loop with Channels
- The `select` Statement
- Common Channel Patterns
- Deadlocks and How to Avoid Them
- Chapter Summary

The Need for Synchronization

In the realm of concurrent programming, where multiple goroutines dance and interact, the potential for chaos lurks. Without proper coordination, these independent entities can step on each other's toes, leading to a phenomenon known as a **race condition**. In a race condition, the program's output becomes unpredictable and depends on the capricious timing of goroutine execution. Data can be corrupted, calculations can go awry, and your once-harmonious program can descend into disarray.

The Perils of Race Conditions

Imagine a shared bank account accessed by multiple goroutines representing different transactions. Without synchronization, two goroutines might attempt to update the account balance simultaneously. One goroutine might read the balance, perform a calculation, and then write the updated balance back to memory. However, in the meantime, another goroutine might have already read the same initial balance, performed its own calculation, and overwritten the first goroutine's update. The result? An incorrect account balance and a frustrated customer.

Enter Synchronization

Synchronization is the key to taming the wild dance of goroutines. It provides mechanisms for goroutines to coordinate their actions, ensuring that they access shared data in a controlled and predictable manner. Synchronization prevents race conditions and guarantees data integrity, making your concurrent programs reliable and deterministic.

Channels as Synchronization Superheroes

In Go, channels emerge as the primary tool for achieving synchronization between goroutines. They are not merely communication conduits; they also possess inherent synchronization properties that make them ideal for coordinating concurrent activities.

- **Blocking Behavior:** The blocking nature of channel operations acts as a natural synchronization mechanism. When a goroutine attempts to send a value on a full channel or receive a value from an empty channel, it blocks, waiting for another goroutine to either receive or send a value. This ensures that goroutines wait for each other at critical points, preventing data races and maintaining data consistency.

- **Explicit Communication:** Channels facilitate explicit communication between goroutines. By sending and receiving values on channels, goroutines can signal each other, exchange data, and coordinate their actions in a clear and structured way.
- **Safety and Simplicity:** Go's channel-based synchronization is designed to be safe and easy to use. The language handles much of the complexity of low-level synchronization primitives, allowing you to focus on the logic of your concurrent program.

Key Points

- Synchronization is crucial for coordinating the actions of multiple goroutines and preventing race conditions
- Race conditions lead to unpredictable program behavior and data corruption
- Channels provide a safe and efficient mechanism for achieving synchronization in Go
- Their blocking behavior ensures that goroutines wait for each other, preventing data races
- Channels facilitate explicit communication and coordination between goroutines

By understanding the need for synchronization and how channels provide a powerful solution, you're well on your way to mastering Go's concurrency model. In the following sections, we'll delve deeper into the mechanics of creating and using channels, exploring their various forms and patterns for building robust and well-coordinated concurrent programs.

Channels: The Communication Conduits

In the intricate ballet of goroutines, where multiple dancers perform their routines concurrently, channels emerge as the essential communication lines that ensure harmonious coordination. They serve as the typed conduits through which goroutines exchange data, synchronize their actions, and orchestrate the flow of information in your Go programs.

Typed Communication

Think of channels as pipes that connect goroutines. Each channel is associated with a specific data type, allowing it to carry only values of that type. This enforces type safety, preventing you from accidentally sending or receiving incompatible data.

- **Example:**

```
ch := make(chan int) // Create a channel to send and receive integers
```

Sending and Receiving Values

Goroutines can send values to a channel using the channel send operator (<-) and receive values from a channel using the channel receive operator (<-).

- **Example:**

```
ch <- 42    // Send the value 42 to the channel
value := <-ch // Receive a value from the channel and store it in 'value'
```

Blocking Behavior: The Synchronization Key

One of the most powerful aspects of channels is their inherent blocking behavior.

- **Sending on a Full Channel:** If a goroutine attempts to send a value to a channel that is already full (its buffer is full, if it's a buffered channel), the sending goroutine will block (pause its execution) until another goroutine receives a value from the channel, creating space for the new value.

- **Receiving from an Empty Channel:** Similarly, if a goroutine tries to receive a value from an empty channel, it will block until another goroutine sends a value to the channel.

This blocking behavior acts as a natural synchronization point, ensuring that goroutines wait for each other at critical moments. This prevents data races, where multiple goroutines try to access or modify the same data simultaneously, leading to unpredictable and potentially disastrous results.

Key Takeaways

- Channels are the primary means of communication and synchronization between goroutines in Go.
- They are typed conduits for sending and receiving values.
- Channels have inherent blocking behavior, which ensures synchronization and prevents data races.
- By using channels, you can create concurrent programs that are safe, efficient, and well-coordinated.

Creating and Using Channels

Creating Channels

In Go, you create channels using the make function, specifying the data type of the values that will be sent and received on the channel. The make function allocates the necessary resources for the channel and returns a reference to it.

Syntax

```
ch := make(chan dataType)
```

- ch: The name of the channel variable
- dataType: The type of values the channel will carry (e.g., int, string, struct, etc.)

Unbuffered Channels

- **Zero Capacity:** Unbuffered channels have a capacity of zero, meaning they cannot hold any values internally.
- **Synchronous Communication:** Sending a value on an unbuffered channel blocks the sending goroutine until another goroutine receives the value. Similarly, receiving from an unbuffered channel blocks the receiving goroutine until another goroutine sends a value.
- **Tight Coupling:** Unbuffered channels create a tight coupling between sender and receiver goroutines, as they must synchronize directly for every communication.

Example:

```
ch := make(chan int)

go func() {
    ch <- 42 // Send a value; blocks until received
}()

value := <-ch // Receive a value; blocks until sent
fmt.Println(value)
```

Buffered Channels

- **Finite Capacity:** Buffered channels have a specified capacity, allowing them to store a certain number of values before blocking the sender.

- **Asynchronous Communication (Up to Capacity):** Sending a value on a buffered channel only blocks if the channel is full. Similarly, receiving from a buffered channel only blocks if the channel is empty.
- **Decoupling:** Buffered channels provide some decoupling between sender and receiver goroutines, as the sender can continue sending values until the buffer is full, even if the receiver is not ready to receive them immediately.

Example:

```
ch := make(chan int, 2) // Buffered channel with capacity 2

ch <- 10 // Send without blocking
ch <- 20 // Send without blocking

// The next send will block until a value is received
ch <- 30

value1 := <-ch // Receive without blocking
value2 := <-ch // Receive without blocking

// The next receive will block until a value is sent
value3 := <-ch
```

Choosing Between Unbuffered and Buffered Channels

- **Unbuffered Channels:** Use them when you need strict synchronization between goroutines, ensuring that a value is sent only when another goroutine is ready to receive it.
- **Buffered Channels:** Use them when you want to allow some buffering of values, potentially improving throughput by decoupling the sender and receiver to some extent.

By understanding the distinction between unbuffered and buffered channels and how to create them using the make function, you gain the ability to choose the right type of channel for your specific concurrency needs.

Using Channels

Once you've created a channel, you can use it to send and receive values between goroutines. Go provides intuitive operators for these operations, making channel-based communication feel natural and seamless.

Sending Values to a Channel

You send a value to a channel using the channel send operator (<-). The syntax is:

```
channel <- value
```

- `channel`: The channel you want to send the value to.
- `value`: The value you want to send. The value's type must match the channel's data type.

Example:

```
ch := make(chan string)
go func() {
    ch <- "Hello, channel!"
}()

message := <-ch
fmt.Println(message) // Output: Hello, channel!
```

In this example, we create a channel ch to send and receive strings. A goroutine is spawned to send the string "Hello, channel!" to the channel. The main goroutine then receives the message from the channel and prints it.

Receiving Values from a Channel

You receive a value from a channel using the channel receive operator (<-). The syntax is:

```
value := <-channel
```

- channel: The channel you want to receive a value from
- value: A variable to store the received value

Example:

```
ch := make(chan int)
go func() {
    ch <- 42
}()

result := <-ch
fmt.Println(result) // Output: 42
```

In this example, a goroutine sends the integer 42 to the channel ch. The main goroutine then receives the value from the channel and stores it in the result variable.

Sending and Receiving Different Data Types

Channels can carry values of various data types, including basic types, structs, pointers, and even other channels.

```
type Person struct {
    Name string
    Age  int
}

ch := make(chan Person)
go func() {
    p := Person{Name: "Alice", Age: 30}
    ch <- p
}()

person := <-ch
fmt.Println(person.Name, person.Age) // Output: Alice 30
```

Key Points

- Use the channel send operator (<-) to send values to a channel.
- Use the channel receive operator (<-) to receive values from a channel
- The sent and received values must match the channel's data type
- Both sending and receiving operations are blocking by default

By understanding how to send and receive values on channels, you have the fundamental tools to enable communication between goroutines.

Sending and Receiving on Channels

Channels in Go provide a straightforward and intuitive syntax for sending and receiving values between goroutines. The channel send and receive operators (<-) make these operations feel like natural assignments, enhancing the readability of your concurrent code. However, it's crucial to understand their blocking behavior, which is key to achieving synchronization in your Go programs.

Sending Values: `ch <- value`

- **Syntax:** The channel send operator (<-) is used to send a value to a channel. The value is placed on the right side of the operator, and the channel is placed on the left side.
- **Behavior:**
  - **Unbuffered Channels:** Sending on an unbuffered channel blocks the sending goroutine until another goroutine receives the value from the channel. This ensures that the value is not lost and that the sender and receiver are synchronized.
  - **Buffered Channels:** Sending on a buffered channel blocks only if the channel's buffer is full. If there's space in the buffer, the value is added to the buffer, and the sending goroutine continues execution without blocking.

Receiving Values: `value := <-ch`

- **Syntax:** The channel receive operator (<-) is used to receive a value from a channel. The channel is placed on the right side of the operator, and a variable to store the received value is placed on the left side.
- **Behavior:**
  - **Unbuffered Channels:** Receiving from an unbuffered channel blocks the receiving goroutine until another goroutine sends a value to the channel. This ensures that the receiver waits for the data to become available.
  - **Buffered Channels:** Receiving from a buffered channel blocks only if the channel is empty. If there are values in the buffer, the receiver gets the oldest value from the buffer, and the receiving goroutine continues execution without blocking.

Blocking Behavior and Synchronization

The inherent blocking behavior of channel operations is fundamental to achieving synchronization in Go's concurrency model.

- **Sender-Receiver Coordination:** The blocking nature ensures that the sender and receiver goroutines are coordinated. The sender cannot proceed until the receiver is ready, and the receiver cannot proceed until the sender has provided data.
- **Data Integrity:** By enforcing synchronization, channels prevent race conditions, where multiple goroutines might try to access or modify the same data simultaneously, leading to unpredictable results.

Key Points:

- Use the channel send operator (<-) to send values to a channel
- Use the channel receive operator (<-) to receive values from a channel
- Both sending and receiving operations are blocking by default
- The blocking behavior ensures synchronization between goroutines and prevents data races

By understanding the syntax and behavior of channel send and receive operations, you can start building concurrent Go programs that communicate effectively and safely.

Blocking Behavior and Synchronization

The inherent blocking behavior of channel operations in Go is the cornerstone of its synchronization mechanism. It ensures that goroutines wait for each other at critical points, preventing data races and ensuring the orderly flow of information.

Sending on a Full Channel

- **Scenario:** When a goroutine attempts to send a value on a channel that is already full (its buffer is full, if it's a buffered channel), the sending goroutine is blocked. It's like trying to put a letter into a mailbox that's already overflowing – you have to wait until someone collects some mail to make space.
- **Synchronization:** This blocking behavior enforces synchronization between the sender and receiver goroutines. The sender cannot proceed until the receiver is ready to accept the value. This prevents the sender from overwriting data or creating inconsistencies.

Receiving from an Empty Channel

- **Scenario:** When a goroutine tries to receive a value from an empty channel, it is blocked. It's akin to waiting at a bus stop for a bus that hasn't arrived yet – you have to patiently wait until the bus shows up.
- **Synchronization:** This blocking behavior again ensures synchronization. The receiver goroutine cannot proceed until a sender goroutine provides the data it's waiting for. This prevents the receiver from accessing invalid or incomplete data.

Illustrative Examples

```go
func worker(id int, tasks <-chan int, results chan<- int) {
    for task := range tasks {
        fmt.Println("Worker", id, "started task", task)
        time.Sleep(time.Second) // Simulate some work
        fmt.Println("Worker", id, "finished task", task)
        results <- task * 2
    }
}

func main() {
    tasks := make(chan int, 10)
    results := make(chan int, 10)

    // Create worker goroutines
    for i := 0; i < 3; i++ {
        go worker(i, tasks, results)
    }

    // Send tasks to the workers
    for i := 1; i <= 5; i++ {
        tasks <- i
    }
    close(tasks)

    // Collect results from the workers
    for i := 0; i < 5; i++ {
        result := <-results
        fmt.Println("Result:", result)
    }
}
```

In this example, we have a pool of worker goroutines that receive tasks from the `tasks` channel and send results to the `results` channel. The blocking behavior of channel operations ensures that:

- **Workers wait for tasks:** Worker goroutines block on the `tasks` channel until a task is available.
- **Main goroutine waits for results:** The main goroutine blocks on the `results` channel until a worker sends a result.
- **Task distribution:** Tasks are distributed among the workers in a coordinated manner, preventing race conditions and ensuring that each task is processed by a single worker.

Key Takeaways

- The blocking nature of channel operations is fundamental for synchronization in Go.
- Sending on a full channel or receiving from an empty channel causes the goroutine to block until the operation can be completed.
- This blocking behavior ensures that goroutines wait for each other, preventing data races and maintaining data integrity.
- Channels facilitate coordination and communication between goroutines, leading to safe and efficient concurrent programs.

By understanding and leveraging the blocking behavior of channels, you can create concurrent Go programs that execute reliably and predictably, even in the face of complex interactions between multiple goroutines.

Buffered Channels

While unbuffered channels provide strict synchronization between goroutines, buffered channels introduce a layer of flexibility by allowing a certain number of values to be stored within the channel itself before blocking the sender. This buffering capability can improve throughput and decouple the sender and receiver goroutines to some extent, enabling them to operate at slightly different paces.

Understanding Buffered Channels

- **Finite Capacity**: When you create a buffered channel using the `make` function, you specify its capacity, which determines how many values it can hold internally.
- **Non-Blocking Sends (Up to Capacity):** Sending a value on a buffered channel will not block the sender as long as there is space available in the buffer. The value is simply added to the buffer, and the sender goroutine can continue its execution.
- **Blocking Sends (When Full):** If the buffer is full, the sender goroutine will block until a receiver goroutine retrieves a value from the channel, creating space in the buffer.
- **Non-Blocking Receives (If Data Available):** Receiving from a buffered channel will not block if there are values available in the buffer. The receiver goroutine will retrieve the oldest value from the buffer and continue its execution.
- **Blocking Receives (When Empty):** If the buffer is empty, the receiver goroutine will block until a sender goroutine sends a value to the channel.

Creating Buffered Channels

You create a buffered channel by specifying its capacity as the second argument to the `make` function

Syntax

```
ch := make(chan dataType, bufferSize)
```

- `bufferSize`: The number of values the channel can hold before blocking the sender

Example

```
ch := make(chan int, 3) // Buffered channel with capacity 3
```

Using Buffered Channels

```
ch <- 10 // Send without blocking (buffer has space)
ch <- 20 // Send without blocking
ch <- 30 // Send without blocking (buffer is now full)

// The next send will block until a value is received
ch <- 40

value1 := <-ch // Receive without blocking
value2 := <-ch // Receive without blocking
```

Benefits of Buffered Channels

- **Improved Throughput**: Buffered channels can improve throughput in scenarios where the sender might produce values faster than the receiver can consume them. The buffer acts as a temporary storage, allowing the sender to continue working even if the receiver is momentarily busy.
- **Decoupling**: Buffered channels provide some level of decoupling between sender and receiver goroutines. They don't need to be perfectly synchronized for every communication, as the buffer can absorb some fluctuations in their execution speeds

Key Points

- Buffered channels have a finite capacity to store values.
- Sending on a buffered channel blocks only if the buffer is full
- Receiving from a buffered channel blocks only if the buffer is empty
- Buffered channels can improve throughput and provide some decoupling between sender and receiver goroutines

By understanding the concept of buffered channels and their behavior, you can fine-tune your concurrent Go programs to achieve better performance and flexibility. Choose the appropriate channel capacity based on your application's requirements and the expected communication patterns between goroutines.

The `close` Function and Channel Closing

In the world of Go concurrency, channels not only facilitate communication but also serve as signals of completion. The `close` function provides a way to indicate that no more values will be sent on a channel, allowing receiver goroutines to gracefully handle the end of data transmission and avoid potential deadlocks.

The `close` Function

- **Purpose:** The `close` function is used to close a channel, signaling that no further values will be sent on it.
- **Syntax:** `close(ch)`
- **Behavior:**
    - After a channel is closed, any attempts to send values on it will result in a panic.
    - Receiver goroutines can continue to receive values from the channel until it's empty.

- Once the channel is closed and empty, subsequent receive operations will return the zero value for the channel's type and a `false` value for the second return value (the "ok" value) in the comma-ok idiom.

Detecting Channel Closure: The Comma-ok Idiom

The comma-ok idiom is a common pattern in Go for receiving values from a channel and simultaneously checking if the channel has been closed.

- **Syntax:** `value, ok := <-ch`
- **Behavior:**
    - If the channel is open and contains a value, the receive operation succeeds, `value` receives the value, and ok is `true`.
    - If the channel is closed and empty, the receive operation returns the zero value for the channel's type, and ok is `false`.

Importance of Closing Channels

1. **Preventing Deadlocks:** If a receiver goroutine is waiting to receive from a channel that will never send any more values, it will be blocked indefinitely, leading to a deadlock. Closing the channel signals to the receiver that no more values are coming, allowing it to exit gracefully.
2. **Signaling Completion:** Closing a channel can be used to signal the completion of a task or the end of a data stream. Receiver goroutines can use the comma-ok idiom to detect channel closure and take appropriate actions, such as terminating their own execution or performing final cleanup operations.

Example

```go
func producer(ch chan<- int) {
    for i := 1; i <= 5; i++ {
        ch <- i
    }
    close(ch) // Signal completion
}

func consumer(ch <-chan int) {
    for {
        value, ok := <-ch
        if !ok {
            fmt.Println("Channel closed")
            break // Exit the loop
        }
        fmt.Println("Received:", value)
    }
}

func main() {
    ch := make(chan int)
    go producer(ch)
    consumer(ch)
}
```

In this example, the `producer` goroutine sends values to the channel and then closes it. The `consumer` goroutine receives values from the channel until it's closed, at which point it prints a message and exits the loop.

Key Points:

- Use the `close` function to signal that no more values will be sent on a channel
- Use the comma-ok idiom (`value, ok := <-ch`) to detect channel closure
- Closing channels is important for preventing deadlocks and signaling completion

By understanding how to close channels and detect their closure, you can write concurrent Go programs that communicate effectively, handle completion gracefully, and avoid potential deadlocks.

The `for-range` Loop with Channels

The `for-range` loop, a versatile construct for iterating over collections in Go, seamlessly extends its capabilities to channels. It provides an elegant and concise way to receive and process values from a channel until the channel is closed. This synergy between `for-range` and channels simplifies the handling of data streams and concurrent communication in your Go programs.

Automatic Termination on Channel Closure

When you use a `for-range` loop with a channel, the loop continues to execute as long as the channel is open and values are being sent. However, once the channel is closed, the loop automatically terminates, eliminating the need for manual checks or complex termination logic.

Syntax

```go
for value := range channel {
    // Process the received value
}
```

- `value`: A variable to store each value received from the channel
- `channel`: The channel you want to receive values from

Examples

- **Processing Numbers from a Channel**

    ```go
    func generateNumbers(ch chan<- int) {
        for i := 1; i <= 5; i++ {
            ch <- i
        }
        close(ch)
    }

    func main() {
        ch := make(chan int)
        go generateNumbers(ch)

        for num := range ch {
            fmt.Println("Received:", num)
        }
    }
    ```

    In this example, the `generateNumbers` goroutine sends numbers to the channel `ch` and then closes it. The `main` goroutine uses a `for-range` loop to receive and print the numbers until the channel is closed.

- **Processing Strings from a Channel**

```
func processStrings(ch <-chan string) {
    for str := range ch {
        fmt.Println("Processed:", str)
    }
}
```

This `processStrings` function uses a `for-range` loop to receive and process strings from the ch channel until it's closed.

Key Points:

- The `for-range` loop provides a convenient way to iterate over values received from a channel
- The loop automatically terminates when the channel is closed
- You can use `for-range` loops to process data received from channels in a sequential and organized manner

By combining the power of `for-range` loops with channels, you can create elegant and efficient code for handling data streams and concurrent communication in your Go programs. The automatic termination on channel closure simplifies your code and eliminates the need for manual checks, leading to more readable and maintainable solutions.

The `select` Statement

In the realm of Go's concurrency model, where multiple channels orchestrate the flow of data and synchronization between goroutines, the `select` statement emerges as a powerful conductor. It allows you to multiplex operations on multiple channels, enabling your code to react to events or messages arriving on different channels concurrently. Think of `select` as a vigilant traffic controller, directing the flow of data through various channels and ensuring that your program responds promptly to the first available communication.

The Essence of `select`

- **Multiplexing:** The `select` statement provides a way to wait on multiple channel operations simultaneously. It blocks until one of its cases can proceed, allowing you to write code that can react to events on different channels without getting stuck waiting on a single channel.
- **Non-Blocking Behavior (with `default`):** If you include a `default` case in your `select` statement, it becomes non-blocking. If none of the other cases are ready to proceed, the `default` case is executed immediately.

Syntax

```
select {
case <-channel1:
    // Code to execute if a value is received from channel1
case channel2 <- value:
    // Code to execute if a value can be sent to channel2
// ... (more cases)
default:
    // Code to execute if no other case is ready
}
```

- `case <-channel`: This case is selected if a value can be received from the specified channel.

- `case channel <- value`: This case is selected if a value can be sent to the specified channel.
- `default`: This optional case is selected if none of the other cases are ready to proceed.

Use Cases

1. **Receiving from Multiple Channels**

```
func main() {
    ch1 := make(chan string)
    ch2 := make(chan int)

    go func() {
        time.Sleep(2 * time.Second)
        ch1 <- "Hello from goroutine 1"
    }()

    go func() {
        time.Sleep(1 * time.Second)
        ch2 <- 42
    }()

    select {
    case msg := <-ch1:
        fmt.Println("Received message:", msg)
    case num := <-ch2:
        fmt.Println("Received number:", num)
    }
}
```

In this example, the `select` statement waits for a value to be available on either ch1 or ch2. The first goroutine to send a value will have its corresponding `case` selected, and the received value will be printed.

2. **Sending to Multiple Channels**

```
func main() {
    ch1 := make(chan string)
    ch2 := make(chan string)

    select {
    case ch1 <- "Hello":
        fmt.Println("Sent to channel 1")
    case ch2 <- "World":
        fmt.Println("Sent to channel 2")
    }
}
```

This example demonstrates how to use `select` to send a value to the first available channel among multiple channels.

3. **Timeouts**

```
func main() {
    ch := make(chan string)

    select {
    case msg := <-ch:
        fmt.Println("Received message:", msg)
```

```go
        case <-time.After(3 * time.Second):
            fmt.Println("Timeout!")
        }
}
```

Here, the `select` statement waits for a value on the `ch` channel or a timeout after 3 seconds. If no value is received within the timeout period, the "Timeout!" message is printed.

4. **Default Case**

```go
func main() {
    ch := make(chan string)

    select {
    case msg := <-ch:
        fmt.Println("Received message:", msg)
    default:
        fmt.Println("No message received")
    }
}
```

In this case, the `select` statement has a `default` case. If no value is available on the `ch` channel, the "No message received" message is printed immediately without blocking.

Key Points:

- The `select` statement multiplexes operations on multiple channels
- It blocks until one of its cases can proceed
- You can use `select` to receive from multiple channels, send to multiple channels, implement timeouts, and handle scenarios where no other case is ready

The `select` statement is a powerful tool for building concurrent Go programs that need to react to events on multiple channels. By mastering its usage, you can create responsive and efficient applications that handle concurrent communication gracefully.

Common Channel Patterns

Channels, with their ability to facilitate communication and synchronization, lend themselves to various powerful patterns in Go's concurrency model. These patterns provide elegant solutions for common concurrency challenges, enabling you to build efficient and scalable applications. Let's explore some of the most prevalent channel patterns:

1. Worker Pools

- **Scenario:** You have a set of tasks to perform, and you want to distribute these tasks among a pool of worker goroutines to achieve concurrency and parallelism.
- **Pattern:**
    1. Create a channel to represent the tasks.
    2. Spawn multiple worker goroutines that receive tasks from the channel and process them.
    3. Send tasks to the channel from the main goroutine or other parts of your program.
    4. Optionally, create another channel for the workers to send results back.
- **Example:**

```go
func worker(id int, tasks <-chan int, results chan<- int) {
    for task := range tasks {
        // ... process the task
```

```go
            results <- task * 2 // Send the result back
    }
}

func main() {
    tasks := make(chan int, 100)
    results := make(chan int, 100)

    // Create worker pool
    for i := 0; i < 3; i++ {
        go worker(i, tasks, results)
    }

    // Send tasks
    for i := 1; i <= 5; i++ {
        tasks <- i
    }
    close(tasks)

    // Collect results
    for i := 0; i < 5; i++ {
        result := <-results
        fmt.Println("Result:", result)
    }
}
```

2. Pipelines

- **Scenario:** You need to perform a series of transformations or computations on data, and you want to chain multiple goroutines together to create a processing pipeline.
- **Pattern:**
    1. Create a series of channels to represent the stages of the pipeline
    2. Spawn goroutines that read from one channel, process the data and send the results to the next channel
    3. The final goroutine collects the processed data from the last channel
- **Example:**

```go
func generateData(out chan<- int) {
    for i := 1; i <= 5; i++ {
        out <- i
    }
    close(out)
}

func square(in <-chan int, out chan<- int) {
    for num := range in {
        out <- num * num
    }
    close(out)
}

func main() {
    naturals := make(chan int)
    squares := make(chan int)

    go generateData(naturals)
    go square(naturals, squares)

    for num := range squares {
```

```
        fmt.Println(num)
    }
}
```

3. Fan-in and Fan-out

- **Scenario:** You need to merge data from multiple channels (fan-in) or distribute data to multiple channels (fan-out)
- **Pattern:** Use the `select` statement to wait on multiple channel operations simultaneously.
- **Fan-in Example:**

```go
func merge(channels ...<-chan int) <-chan int {
    out := make(chan int)
    go func() {
        defer close(out)
        for _, ch := range channels {
            for val := range ch {
                out <- val
            }
        }
    }()
    return out
}
```

- **Fan-out Example:**

```go
func distribute(in <-chan int, outs ...chan<- int) {
    for val := range in {
        for _, out := range outs {
            out <- val
        }
    }

    for _, out := range outs {
        close(out)
    }
}
```

Key Takeaways

- Channels enable various powerful patterns for concurrent programming in Go.
- Worker pools distribute tasks among multiple goroutines for parallel execution
- Pipelines chain goroutines together to process data in stages.
- Fan-in and fan-out allow merging or distributing data from multiple channels

These patterns, combined with other concurrency tools in Go, provide you with the building blocks to design and implement sophisticated concurrent applications that are efficient, scalable, and maintainable.

Deadlocks and How to Avoid Them

In the intricate choreography of concurrent Go programs, where goroutines interact through channels, a potential pitfall lurks: the dreaded deadlock. A deadlock is a standstill, a frozen state where two or more goroutines are locked in an eternal embrace, each waiting for the other to perform an action that will never happen. It's like two dancers caught in an unbreakable hold, unable to continue their routine.

Understanding Deadlocks

- **Mutual Waiting:** A deadlock occurs when two or more goroutines are blocked, each waiting for a resource or a signal from another goroutine that is also blocked, creating a circular dependency.
- **Program Freeze:** When a deadlock occurs, the affected goroutines are stuck indefinitely, and the program essentially freezes, unable to make any further progress.

Common Causes of Deadlocks

1. **Sending on an Unbuffered Channel without a Receiver**
   - **Scenario:** A goroutine attempts to send a value on an unbuffered channel, but no other goroutine is ready to receive it. The sending goroutine blocks, waiting for a receiver, but no receiver ever arrives.
2. **Receiving from a Channel without a Sender**
   - **Scenario:** A goroutine tries to receive a value from a channel, but no other goroutine is sending any values to it. The receiving goroutine blocks, waiting for a sender, but no sender ever appears.
3. **Circular Dependencies**
   - **Scenario:** Multiple goroutines are interconnected in a way that creates a circular dependency. Goroutine A is waiting for Goroutine B, which is waiting for Goroutine C, which, in turn, is waiting for Goroutine A. This circular chain of dependencies leads to a deadlock.

Tips to Avoid Deadlocks

1. **Use Buffered Channels When Appropriate**
   - Buffered channels can act as a buffer between sender and receiver goroutines, allowing the sender to continue sending values even if the receiver is not immediately ready. This can help prevent deadlocks in scenarios where there might be temporary mismatches in the timing of send and receive operations.
2. **Close Channels When No More Values Will Be Sent**
   - Closing a channel signals to receiver goroutines that no more values will be sent. This allows them to exit gracefully instead of waiting indefinitely for values that will never arrive.
3. **Carefully Design Goroutine Interactions**
   - Analyze the communication and synchronization patterns between your goroutines. Avoid creating circular dependencies where goroutines are waiting for each other in a circular chain.
   - Use tools like the Go race detector (`go run -race myprogram.go`) to help identify potential race conditions and deadlocks during development.

Key Takeaways

- Deadlocks occur when goroutines are blocked forever, waiting for each other.
- Common causes include sending on unbuffered channels without receivers, receiving from channels without senders, and circular dependencies.
- Use buffered channels, close channels when done, and carefully design goroutine interactions to avoid deadlocks

By understanding the causes of deadlocks and adopting these preventive measures, you can create concurrent Go programs that are not only efficient and powerful but also robust and free from the perils of deadlocks. Remember that careful design and thoughtful use of channels are key to ensuring the smooth and harmonious execution of your concurrent Go programs.

Chapter Summary

In this chapter, we delved into the heart of Go's concurrency model, exploring the mechanisms for synchronization and communication between goroutines. Here's a recap of the key takeaways:

- **The Need for Synchronization:** We discussed the importance of synchronization in concurrent programs to avoid race conditions and ensure data integrity.
- **Channels as Communication Conduits:** We reiterated the role of channels as typed conduits for sending and receiving values between goroutines.
- **Creating and Using Channels:** You learned how to create channels using the `make` function and how to send and receive values on them using the channel operators (`<-`).
- **Blocking Behavior and Synchronization:** We explored the inherent blocking nature of channel operations and how it contributes to synchronization between goroutines.
- **Buffered Channels:** You learned about buffered channels, their capacity, and how they can improve throughput and provide some decoupling between sender and receiver goroutines.
- **Channel Closing:** You were introduced to the `close` function and the comma-ok idiom for detecting channel closure, preventing deadlocks, and signaling completion.
- **`for-range` Loop with Channels:** You saw how to use the `for-range` loop to iterate over values received from a channel until it's closed.
- **The `select` Statement:** We explored the `select` statement as a way to multiplex operations on multiple channels, enabling your code to react to events on different channels concurrently.
- **Common Channel Patterns:** You learned about common patterns for using channels, such as worker pools, pipelines, and fan-in/fan-out.
- **Deadlocks:** We discussed the concept of deadlocks, their common causes, and how to prevent them through careful design and the use of buffered channels and channel closing.

By mastering these concepts, you've gained a solid understanding of how to use channels for communication and synchronization in your concurrent Go programs. You can now leverage the power of channels to build sophisticated applications that handle multiple tasks concurrently, exchange data safely, and coordinate their actions effectively.

In the next chapter, we will explore advanced concurrency patterns in Go, delving into worker pools, wait groups, and mutexes. These patterns will equip you with even more tools to tackle complex concurrency challenges and build high-performance, scalable, and reliable Go applications.

Advanced Concurrency Patterns: Worker Pools, WaitGroups, and Mutexes

Outline

- Beyond Basic Concurrency
- Worker Pools
- WaitGroups
- Mutexes
- Choosing the Right Synchronization Tool
- Chapter Summary

Beyond Basic Concurrency

In the previous chapters, we embarked on a journey into the world of concurrency in Go, exploring the fundamental concepts of goroutines and channels. We learned that goroutines are lightweight threads that enable concurrent execution of tasks, while channels serve as the communication and synchronization conduits between these goroutines.

Goroutines and channels form the bedrock of Go's concurrency model, providing a powerful and elegant way to express parallelism and handle asynchronous operations. However, as your concurrent programs grow in complexity, you'll encounter scenarios that demand more sophisticated synchronization and coordination mechanisms.

Go's standard library comes to the rescue with a set of additional tools and patterns that complement goroutines and channels, allowing you to tackle intricate concurrency challenges with finesse. In this chapter, we'll delve into three essential tools:

1. **Worker Pools**: A worker pool is a collection of goroutines that stand ready to process tasks concurrently. It provides an efficient way to manage and distribute work, ensuring that tasks are executed in parallel without overwhelming system resources.
2. **WaitGroups**: A `WaitGroup` is a synchronization primitive that helps you wait for a collection of goroutines to complete their execution. It acts as a counter, keeping track of the number of active goroutines, and allows you to block until all goroutines in a group have finished their work.
3. **Mutexes**: A `Mutex` (mutual exclusion lock) is a synchronization primitive that provides exclusive access to shared data, preventing data races and ensuring data integrity in concurrent programs. It acts as a gatekeeper, allowing only one goroutine to access the protected data at a time.

These tools, along with goroutines and channels, form a comprehensive toolkit for managing concurrent tasks and shared data in your Go programs. By understanding their purpose and how to use them effectively, you can build robust, scalable, and high-performance applications that harness the full power of modern multi-core processors and distributed systems. So, let's dive deeper into these advanced concurrency patterns and unlock the next level of Go programming mastery!

Worker Pools

The Worker Pool Pattern

In the realm of concurrent programming, where efficiency and resource management are paramount, the worker pool pattern shines as a beacon of optimized task execution. It provides a structured approach to managing and distributing a collection of tasks among a pool of worker goroutines, ensuring that tasks are processed concurrently and efficiently.

Imagine a bustling factory floor with various workstations (worker goroutines) and a conveyor belt (task queue) carrying tasks to be completed. As tasks arrive on the conveyor belt, workers pick them up, process them at their workstations, and potentially place the finished products on another conveyor belt (result channel). The worker pool pattern emulates this scenario, allowing you to distribute work among multiple goroutines and achieve parallelism, especially when running on multi-core systems.

Key Components

1. **Task Queue:** The task queue is typically implemented as a buffered channel that holds the tasks waiting to be processed. The buffer allows for some decoupling between the goroutines that generate tasks (producers) and the worker goroutines that consume them.
2. **Worker Goroutines:** The worker pool consists of multiple goroutines that continuously listen for tasks on the task queue. When a task becomes available, a worker goroutine picks it up, processes it, and optionally sends the result back on a separate result channel.
3. **Dynamic Scaling:** A well-designed worker pool can dynamically adjust the number of worker goroutines based on the workload or available system resources. This ensures that the pool can handle varying levels of demand without becoming overwhelmed or underutilized.

Advantages of Worker Pools

- **Concurrency and Parallelism:** Worker pools enable concurrent execution of tasks, allowing your program to leverage the full power of multi-core processors and achieve parallelism.
- **Resource Management:** By controlling the number of worker goroutines, you can prevent your program from creating too many goroutines and overwhelming system resources.
- **Task Distribution:** The task queue ensures that tasks are distributed fairly among the worker goroutines, preventing any single goroutine from becoming a bottleneck.
- **Scalability:** Worker pools can be scaled up or down dynamically to adapt to changing workloads, ensuring that your program remains responsive and efficient even under heavy load.

Next, we'll dive into the implementation details of worker pools in Go, demonstrating how to create the task queue, spawn worker goroutines, distribute tasks, and collect results.

Implementing Worker Pools

Let's dive into the practical implementation of a worker pool in Go. We'll break down the process into clear steps, accompanied by code examples and explanations to solidify your understanding.

1. Creating the Task Queue and Result Channel

- **Task Queue:** We'll use a buffered channel to represent the task queue. The buffer size determines how many tasks can be queued before the sender blocks.

    ```go
    tasks := make(chan int, 100) // Channel to hold tasks (integers in this example)
    ```

- **Result Channel (Optional):** If your worker goroutines need to send results back, create another buffered channel to collect them.

    ```go
    results := make(chan int, 100) // Channel to collect results
    ```

2. Spawning Worker Goroutines

- **Worker Function:** Define a function that represents the behavior of a worker goroutine. It should receive tasks from the task queue, process them, and optionally send results back on the result channel.

    ```
    func worker(id int, tasks <-chan int, results chan<- int) {
        for task := range tasks {
            fmt.Println("Worker", id, "processing task", task)
            time.Sleep(time.Second) // Simulate some work
            results <- task * 2
        }
    }
    ```

- **Spawning Goroutines:** Use a `for` loop to create multiple worker goroutines, each executing the `worker` function.

    ```
    for i := 0; i < numWorkers; i++ {
        go worker(i, tasks, results)
    }
    ```

3. Sending Tasks

- **Send to Task Queue:** From the main goroutine or other parts of your program, send tasks to the `tasks` channel using the channel send operator (`<-`).

    ```
    for i := 1; i <= 5; i++ {
        tasks <- i
    }
    ```

- **Close the Task Queue:** Once all tasks have been sent, close the `tasks` channel to signal to the worker goroutines that there's no more work.

    ```
    close(tasks)
    ```

4. Collecting Results (Optional)

- **Receive from Result Channel:** If your worker goroutines send results back, use a `for-range` loop or other mechanisms to receive and process the results from the `results` channel.

    ```
    for i := 0; i < 5; i++ {
        result := <-results
        fmt.Println("Received result:", result)
    }
    ```

5. Graceful Shutdown

- **Wait for Workers:** If you need to ensure that all worker goroutines have finished processing their tasks before the program terminates, you can use a `sync.WaitGroup`.

    ```
    var wg sync.WaitGroup
    wg.Add(numWorkers)

    for i := 0; i < numWorkers; i++ {
        go func(id int) {
            defer wg.Done()
            worker(id, tasks, results)
        }(i)
    }

    // ... send tasks ...
    ```

```
    close(tasks)

wg.Wait() // Wait for all workers to finish
```

In this enhanced example, we use a `WaitGroup` to wait for all worker goroutines to complete before the `main` goroutine exits.

By implementing these steps, you can create a worker pool that efficiently distributes tasks among multiple goroutines, allowing you to leverage concurrency and parallelism in your Go programs. Remember to choose an appropriate buffer size for your task queue and consider dynamic scaling mechanisms to optimize performance based on your workload and system resources.

WaitGroups

Synchronizing Goroutine Completion

In the dynamic world of concurrent Go programs, where goroutines operate independently, it's often crucial to ensure that a collection of goroutines has completed their tasks before proceeding further in your code. This synchronization point is where the `sync.WaitGroup` steps in, acting as a vigilant coordinator that patiently waits for all its assigned goroutines to finish their work.

The `sync.WaitGroup` is a synchronization primitive from Go's sync package that helps you manage and coordinate the execution of groups of goroutines. It functions as a counter, keeping track of the number of active goroutines within a group. By incrementing the counter before starting a goroutine and decrementing it when the goroutine finishes, you can use the `WaitGroup` to block the main goroutine (or any other coordinating goroutine) until all the goroutines in the group have completed their tasks.

This synchronization mechanism is vital in scenarios where:

- **Data Dependency:** You need to ensure that certain data processing or computations performed by goroutines are complete before using the results in subsequent parts of your program
- **Resource Cleanup:** You want to guarantee that all goroutines have finished using shared resources before releasing or cleaning them up
- **Orderly Termination:** You need to ensure that all goroutines have finished their work before the program terminates, preventing premature termination and potential data inconsistencies

In essence, the `sync.WaitGroup` acts as a reliable signal, ensuring that your program waits patiently at a designated point until all the goroutines within a group have crossed the finish line. This synchronization mechanism promotes code clarity, prevents race conditions, and ensures the correctness and reliability of your concurrent Go programs.

Using `WaitGroup`

Let's bring the concept of `WaitGroup` to life with a practical example and a breakdown of its essential methods.

Example: Downloading Multiple Files Concurrently

```
func downloadFile(url string, wg *sync.WaitGroup) {
    defer wg.Done() // Decrement the counter when the goroutine completes

    // ... (download the file from the URL)
    fmt.Println("Downloaded:", url)
}
```

```go
func main() {
    var wg sync.WaitGroup
    urls := []string{
        "https://example.com/file1.txt",
        "https://example.com/file2.jpg",
        "https://example.com/file3.pdf",
    }

    for _, url := range urls {
        wg.Add(1)          // Increment the counter for each goroutine
        go downloadFile(url, &wg)
    }

    wg.Wait() // Wait for all downloads to complete
    fmt.Println("All downloads finished!")
}
```

Explanation:

1. **Creating a `WaitGroup` Instance:**
   - We declare a variable wg of type sync.WaitGroup. This instance will keep track of the active goroutines.
2. **Incrementing the Counter: `wg.Add(1)`**
   - Before starting each goroutine (in this case, the downloadFile function), we call wg.Add(1) to increment the WaitGroup's internal counter. This signals that a new goroutine is joining the group.
3. **Decrementing the Counter: `wg.Done()`**
   - Within each goroutine, we use defer wg.Done() to ensure that the counter is decremented when the goroutine completes, regardless of how it exits (normal return or panic). The defer statement guarantees that wg.Done() is called even if an error occurs during the download.
4. **Waiting for Completion: `wg.Wait()`**
   - In the main function, we call wg.Wait(). This causes the main goroutine to block (pause its execution) until the WaitGroup's counter reaches zero, indicating that all the download goroutines have finished.

Key Points

- Create a sync.WaitGroup instance to manage a group of goroutines.
- Call wg.Add(delta) to increment the counter before starting each goroutine.
- Use defer wg.Done() within each goroutine to decrement the counter when it completes.
- Call wg.Wait() to block until all goroutines in the group have finished.

By employing the sync.WaitGroup, you can ensure that your program waits for all concurrent tasks to complete before proceeding, preventing premature termination and potential data inconsistencies. This synchronization mechanism enhances the reliability and predictability of your concurrent Go programs.

In the next section, we will explore another powerful synchronization primitive: mutexes. Mutexes provide a way to protect shared data from concurrent access, preventing data races and ensuring data integrity in your Go programs.

Mutexes

Protecting Shared Data

In the intricate dance of concurrent Go programs, where multiple goroutines waltz around shared data, the potential for collisions and missteps is ever-present. Without proper safeguards, these goroutines might trample on each other's toes, leading to a phenomenon known as a **data race**. In a data race, multiple goroutines attempt to access or modify the same data simultaneously, resulting in unpredictable behavior and potentially corrupting the shared data.

Mutexes: The Guardians of Shared Data

To prevent such chaotic scenarios and ensure the integrity of shared data, Go provides a powerful synchronization primitive called a **mutex** (short for "mutual exclusion"). A mutex acts as a lock that grants exclusive access to a critical section of your code, where shared data is accessed or modified. Only one goroutine can hold the lock at any given time, forcing other goroutines to wait patiently until the lock is released.

How Mutexes Work

1. **Lock Acquisition:** When a goroutine wants to access the shared data, it first attempts to acquire the mutex lock using the Lock() method.
2. **Exclusive Access:** If the lock is available (not held by any other goroutine), the goroutine acquires the lock and proceeds to access or modify the shared data.
3. **Blocking:** If the lock is already held by another goroutine, the attempting goroutine blocks (pauses its execution) until the lock is released.
4. **Lock Release:** Once the goroutine is done working with the shared data, it releases the lock using the Unlock() method, allowing other waiting goroutines to acquire the lock and proceed.

The Dance of Synchronization

Imagine a dance floor where only one couple is allowed to dance at a time. The mutex acts as the dance floor, and goroutines are the eager couples waiting for their turn. When a couple acquires the lock (steps onto the dance floor), they have exclusive access to dance (modify the shared data). Other couples must wait patiently until the current couple releases the lock (leaves the dance floor) before they can take their turn.

Key Points

- Mutexes provide exclusive access to shared data, preventing data races.
- Only one goroutine can hold the mutex lock at a time.
- Goroutines that attempt to acquire a locked mutex will block until it's released
- Always remember to release the lock using Unlock() after you're done with the shared data to avoid deadlocks

Using `Mutex`

Let's solidify your understanding of mutexes with a practical example and a breakdown of their usage in Go.

Example: Concurrent Counter

```go
package main

import (
    "fmt"
    "sync"
    "time"
)

func incrementCounter(counter *int, wg *sync.WaitGroup, mutex *sync.Mutex) {
```

```go
    defer wg.Done()

    for i := 0; i < 1000; i++ {
        mutex.Lock()    // Acquire the lock
        *counter++
        mutex.Unlock()  // Release the lock
    }
}

func main() {
    var counter int
    var wg sync.WaitGroup
    var mutex sync.Mutex

    wg.Add(2)
    go incrementCounter(&counter, &wg, &mutex)
    go incrementCounter(&counter, &wg, &mutex)

    wg.Wait()
    fmt.Println("Final counter value:", counter)
}
```

Explanation:

1. **Creating a Mutex Instance:**
   - We declare a variable `mutex` of type `sync.Mutex`. This instance will act as our lock.
2. **Acquiring the Lock: `mutex.Lock()`**
   - Inside the `incrementCounter` function, before accessing the shared `counter` variable, we call `mutex.Lock()`. This attempts to acquire the lock. If the lock is available, the goroutine proceeds. If not, it blocks until the lock is released by another goroutine.
3. **Releasing the Lock: `mutex.Unlock()`**
   - After modifying the `counter`, we call `mutex.Unlock()` to release the lock. This allows other goroutines that are waiting on the lock to acquire it and proceed with their operations.
   - **Crucial:** It is imperative to always release the lock using `Unlock()` after you're done with the shared data. Failing to do so will result in a deadlock, where other goroutines will be blocked indefinitely, waiting for a lock that will never be released.

Key Points

- Create a `sync.Mutex` instance to protect shared data
- Call `mutex.Lock()` before accessing or modifying shared data within a critical section
- Call `mutex.Unlock()` after you're done with the shared data to release the lock
- Always ensure that the lock is released to prevent deadlocks

The Perils of Deadlocks

If you forget to release the lock using `Unlock()`, or if there's a logical error in your code that prevents the lock from being released, your program can enter a deadlock state. In a deadlock, multiple goroutines are blocked, each waiting for a lock held by another goroutine, creating a circular dependency that halts the program's execution.

In Summary

Mutexes are indispensable tools for ensuring data integrity and preventing race conditions in concurrent Go programs. By using mutexes to protect critical sections of your code, you can orchestrate the harmonious interaction of goroutines and ensure that shared data is accessed and modified in a safe and predictable manner. Remember, the key to avoiding deadlocks is to always release the lock after you're done working with the shared data.

Choosing the Right Synchronization Tool

In the realm of concurrent Go programming, where goroutines dance and interact, the choice of the right synchronization tool can be the difference between a graceful performance and a chaotic deadlock. Worker pools, wait groups, and mutexes each serve distinct purposes, and understanding their strengths and use cases is essential for building robust and efficient concurrent applications.

Worker Pools

- **Ideal for:** Distributing and managing a collection of independent tasks that can be executed concurrently.
- **When to Use:**
    - You have a set of tasks that can be processed independently, without requiring shared data access.
    - You want to control the number of goroutines to avoid overwhelming system resources.
    - You need to dynamically scale the number of workers based on the workload.

WaitGroups

- **Ideal for:** Waiting for a group of goroutines to complete their execution before proceeding further in your program.
- **When to Use:**
    - You have a set of goroutines that need to finish before you can continue with the main logic of your program.
    - You don't need to collect specific results from the goroutines, just ensure their completion.

Mutexes

- **Ideal for:** Protecting shared data from concurrent access and preventing data races.
- **When to Use:**
    - You have multiple goroutines that need to access or modify the same shared data.
    - You need to ensure that only one goroutine can access the shared data at a time to maintain data integrity.

Choosing the Right Tool: A Decision Tree

1. **Do you need to distribute and manage a collection of independent tasks?**
    - **Yes:** Consider using a worker pool.
    - **No:** Proceed to the next question
2. **Do you need to wait for a group of goroutines to complete before proceeding?**
    - **Yes:** Use a `WaitGroup`.
    - **No:** Proceed to the next question
3. **Do you have shared data that needs protection from concurrent access?**
    - **Yes:** Use a `Mutex`.
    - **No:** You might not need any additional synchronization mechanisms beyond basic channels.

Remember, these are just guidelines, and the best choice often depends on the specific requirements and complexities of your concurrent program. In some cases, you might need to combine multiple synchronization tools to achieve the desired behavior.

Conclusion

By mastering advanced concurrency patterns like worker pools, wait groups, and mutexes, you empower yourself to build robust and efficient Go programs that can tackle complex synchronization and coordination challenges. These patterns, along with the fundamental concepts of goroutines and channels, provide a comprehensive toolkit for harnessing the full potential of concurrency in Go.

With these tools at your disposal, you can create high-performance, scalable, and reliable applications that leverage the power of modern multi-core processors and distributed systems. Remember, concurrency is a powerful tool, but it requires careful design and thoughtful application of synchronization mechanisms to ensure the correctness and stability of your programs. As you continue your Go programming journey, keep exploring, experimenting, and refining your concurrency skills to build the next generation of innovative and efficient software.

Chapter Summary

In this chapter, we ventured beyond the fundamentals of concurrency in Go, exploring advanced patterns that empower you to tackle more complex synchronization and coordination challenges. We covered the following key topics:

- **Worker Pools:** We discussed the worker pool pattern, which efficiently manages and distributes tasks among a pool of goroutines, promoting concurrency and parallelism.
- **WaitGroups:** We introduced the `sync.WaitGroup` as a synchronization primitive that helps you wait for a collection of goroutines to complete their execution, ensuring orderly program termination and preventing premature exits.
- **Mutexes:** We explored mutexes (`sync.Mutex`) as a way to protect shared data from concurrent access, preventing data races and ensuring data integrity.
- **Choosing the Right Tool:** We provided guidance on how to choose the appropriate synchronization tool (worker pools, wait groups, or mutexes) based on the specific requirements of your concurrent program.

By understanding and applying these advanced concurrency patterns, you can create Go programs that are not only concurrent but also well-structured, maintainable, and efficient. You can now leverage worker pools to distribute tasks, use wait groups to synchronize goroutine completion, and employ mutexes to protect shared data. These tools, along with goroutines and channels, provide a comprehensive toolkit for mastering concurrency in Go.

As you continue your Go programming journey, remember that concurrency is a powerful but nuanced concept. Careful design, thoughtful application of synchronization mechanisms, and thorough testing are crucial for building robust and reliable concurrent applications. With practice and experience, you'll gain the confidence and expertise to harness the full potential of Go's concurrency model and create high-performance, scalable, and fault-tolerant software.

In the next chapter, we will shift our focus to working with files and the web. You'll learn how to read from and write to files, interact with the file system, and build web applications using Go's powerful `net/http` package. Get ready to expand your Go skills and explore the world of file I/O and web development!

Section V:
Working with Files and the Web

File I/O in Go: Reading and Writing to Files

Outline

- Introduction to File I/O
- Opening and Closing Files
- Reading from Files
- Writing to Files
- Working with File Paths
- File Permissions and Error Handling
- Best Practices for File I/O
- Chapter Summary

Introduction to File I/O

In the realm of programming, where data is the lifeblood of applications, **file I/O (input/output)** emerges as a crucial bridge between your code and the persistent storage offered by the file system. It encompasses the essential operations of reading data from files, writing data to files, and performing various other file-related tasks.

At its core, file I/O enables your Go programs to interact with the external world, storing and retrieving information that persists beyond the program's execution. This capability opens doors to a multitude of use cases, making file I/O an indispensable tool in your Go programming arsenal.

The Significance of File I/O

- **Persistent Data Storage and Retrieval**: File I/O allows you to save data to files, ensuring that it remains available even after your program terminates. This is crucial for applications that need to store user preferences, configuration settings, game progress, or any other information that needs to be preserved across sessions.
- **Configuration Management**: Many applications rely on configuration files to store settings and parameters that influence their behavior. File I/O enables you to read and write these configuration files, allowing users to customize the application's behavior or for the application to adapt to different environments.
- **Logging**: Logging is a vital practice for monitoring and troubleshooting applications. File I/O allows you to write log messages to files, creating a historical record of events, errors, and other relevant information that can be analyzed later.
- **Communication with External Systems:** File I/O can be used to exchange data with external systems or processes. For example, you might read data from a CSV file generated by another program, or write results to a file that will be consumed by a different application.

Key Points

- File I/O enables interaction with files on the file system
- It involves reading data from files, writing data to files, and performing other file-related operations.

- File I/O is essential for persistent data storage, configuration management, logging, and communication with external systems.

In the following sections, we'll dive into the specifics of file I/O in Go. You'll learn how to open and close files, read and write data using various techniques, work with file paths, handle file permissions, and implement best practices for efficient and reliable file I/O operations. By mastering these concepts, you'll be well-equipped to leverage the power of file I/O to build Go programs that interact seamlessly with the file system and manage persistent data effectively.

Opening and Closing Files

The `os.Open` and `os.Create` Functions

Before you can read from or write to a file in Go, you need to establish a connection to it. This connection is represented by an `*os.File` value, which acts as a handle to the open file. The os package in the Go standard library provides two essential functions for opening and creating files: `os.Open` and `os.Create`.

- **os.Open**
  - **Purpose:** Opens an existing file for reading.
  - **Syntax:** `file, err := os.Open("filename")`
  - **Return Values:**
    - `file`: A pointer to an `os.File` value representing the open file.
    - `err`: An `error` value indicating any errors that occurred during the opening process (e.g., file not found, permission denied).
- **os.Create**
  - **Purpose:** Creates a new file or truncates an existing file (empties its contents) and opens it for writing.
  - **Syntax:** `file, err := os.Create("filename")`
  - **Return Values:**
    - `file`: A pointer to an `os.File` value representing the newly created or truncated file, open for writing
    - `err`: An `error` value indicating any errors that occurred during the creation or truncation process

Error Handling is Crucial

Both `os.Open` and `os.Create` can return errors, so it's essential to always check the `err` value after calling these functions

```
file, err := os.Open("data.txt")
if err != nil {
    // Handle the error (e.g., log it, return it to the caller)
}
// ... (work with the open file)
```

Key Points

- Use `os.Open` to open an existing file for reading.
- Use `os.Create` to create a new file or truncate an existing file and open it for writing
- Both functions return an `*os.File` value representing the open file and an `error` value
- Always check for errors after calling these functions

By understanding how to use `os.Open` and `os.Create`, you can establish connections to files, paving the way for reading and writing operations.

The `File.Close` Method

Once you've finished working with a file, it's crucial to close it using the `File.Close` method. Closing a file serves two important purposes:

1. **Releasing System Resources:** When you open a file, the operating system allocates resources to manage the file handle and associated buffers. Closing the file releases these resources, ensuring that your program doesn't consume unnecessary system resources, especially when dealing with multiple files.
2. **Ensuring Data Integrity:** In some cases, data written to a file might be buffered in memory before being flushed to the disk. Closing the file guarantees that any buffered data is written to the file, ensuring that your changes are persistent and the file's contents are consistent.

Using `File.Close`

The `File.Close` method is called on an `*os.File` value to close the associated file.

```go
file, err := os.Open("data.txt")
if err != nil {
    // Handle the error
}
// ... (work with the open file)

err = file.Close()
if err != nil {
    // Handle the error (e.g., log it)
}
```

The `defer` Statement: A Safety Net

The `defer` statement provides a convenient way to ensure that a file is always closed, even if an error occurs or the function panics. When you use `defer` before a function call, that function call is scheduled to be executed at the end of the current function's execution, regardless of how the function exits.

```go
func processFile(filename string) error {
    file, err := os.Open(filename)
    if err != nil {
        return err
    }
    defer file.Close() // Close the file when the function exits

    // ... (read or write to the file)
}
```

In this example, the `defer file.Close()` statement ensures that the `file.Close()` method is called when the `processFile` function returns, even if an error occurs within the function or if it panics. This guarantees that the file is always closed properly, preventing resource leaks and potential data corruption.

Key Points

- Always close files using the `File.Close` method after you're done using them.
- Closing files releases system resources and ensures data integrity

- Use the `defer` statement to guarantee that files are always closed, even in the presence of errors or panics

By diligently closing files and utilizing the `defer` statement, you can write Go code that interacts with the file system responsibly and maintains the integrity of your data.

Reading from Files

The `io.Reader` Interface

In the world of Go's input/output (I/O) operations, the `io.Reader` interface reigns supreme as the fundamental abstraction for reading data. It acts as a versatile contract, defining a single method, Read, that any type aspiring to be a "reader" must implement. This interface-driven approach empowers you to read data from various sources, such as files, network connections, or even in-memory buffers, in a unified and streamlined manner.

The `io.Reader` Contract

```
type Reader interface {
    Read(p []byte) (n int, err error)
}
```

- `Read(p []byte) (n int, err error)`: This method attempts to read up to `len(p)` bytes into the byte slice p. It returns the number of bytes read (n) and an error value (`err`). If the read operation encounters an end-of-file (EOF) condition, `err` will be set to `io.EOF`.

The Power of Abstraction

The beauty of the `io.Reader` interface lies in its abstraction. By programming to this interface, your code becomes decoupled from the specific source of the data. Whether you're reading from a file, a network socket, or a string in memory, you can use the same Read method to access the data, promoting code reusability and flexibility.

Key Points

- The `io.Reader` interface defines a single method, Read, for reading data into a byte slice
- Any type that implements the Read method can be used as a reader.
- The `io.Reader` interface provides a powerful abstraction for reading data from various sources in a unified way

Reading with `bufio.NewReader`

While you can directly read from a file using the `*os.File`'s Read method, it's often more efficient to use a buffered reader. The `bufio.NewReader` type from the `bufio` package provides a buffered reader that wraps an `*os.File`, optimizing read operations by reading data in chunks and storing them in an internal buffer.

Benefits of Buffered Readers

- **Reduced System Calls:** Reading data directly from a file often involves making system calls to the operating system for each read operation. Buffered readers minimize these system calls by reading larger chunks of data at once and storing them in a buffer, reducing the overhead of frequent system interactions.

- **Improved Performance:** By buffering data in memory, buffered readers can provide faster read access, especially for sequential reads. The data can be accessed directly from the buffer, avoiding the need to make additional system calls until the buffer is empty.

Creating a Buffered Reader

You create a buffered reader by wrapping an `*os.File` using the `bufio.NewReader` function.

```go
file, err := os.Open("data.txt")
if err != nil {
    // Handle the error
}
defer file.Close()

reader := bufio.NewReader(file)
```

Reading Data with `bufio.NewReader`

The `bufio.NewReader` provides several methods for reading data from the file:

1. **Read(p []byte) (n int, err error):**
   - Reads up to `len(p)` bytes into the byte slice p.
   - Returns the number of bytes read (n) and an error value (err).
   - If the read operation encounters an end-of-file (EOF) condition, err will be set to `io.EOF`.
2. **ReadLine() (line []byte, isPrefix bool, err error):**
   - Reads a single line of text from the file, including the newline character (\n).
   - Returns the line as a byte slice (line), a boolean indicating if the line is longer than the buffer (isPrefix), and an error value (err).
3. **ReadBytes(delim byte) (line []byte, err error):**
   - Reads bytes from the file until the specified delimiter (delim) is encountered.
   - Returns the bytes read (including the delimiter) as a byte slice (line) and an error value (err).

Examples

```go
// Read a single byte
b, err := reader.ReadByte()

// Read a line of text
line, _, err := reader.ReadLine()
text := string(line)

// Read until a specific delimiter
data, err := reader.ReadBytes('\n') // Read until a newline character
```

Key Points

- Use `bufio.NewReader` to create a buffered reader that wraps an `*os.File`
- Buffered readers improve performance by reading data in chunks and buffering it in memory.
- Use the Read, ReadLine, and ReadBytes methods to read data from a file using a buffered reader

By utilizing buffered readers, you can optimize your file reading operations in Go, achieving faster and more efficient data access, especially when dealing with large files or sequential read patterns.

Reading the Entire File at Once

While buffered readers offer efficiency for sequential reads and large files, there are scenarios where you might want to read the entire contents of a file into memory in a single operation. Go provides the convenient `os.ReadFile` function for this purpose.

The `os.ReadFile` Function

- **Purpose:** Reads the entire contents of a file into a byte slice
- **Syntax:** `data, err := os.ReadFile("filename")`
- **Return Values:**
  - `data`: A byte slice containing the file's contents
  - `err`: An error value indicating any errors that occurred during the reading process

Example

```
data, err := os.ReadFile("data.txt")
if err != nil {
    // Handle the error
}

content := string(data) // Convert the byte slice to a string
fmt.Println(content)
```

Trade-offs: Buffered Readers vs. Reading the Entire File

- **File Size:**
  - **Small Files:** For small files, reading the entire file at once using `os.ReadFile` can be simpler and more convenient
  - **Large Files:** For large files, using a buffered reader (`bufio.NewReader`) is generally more memory-efficient, as it reads data in chunks instead of loading the entire file into memory at once
- **Read Patterns:**
  - **Sequential Reads:** If you need to process the entire file sequentially, a buffered reader can be more performant, as it optimizes for sequential access
  - **Random Access:** If you need to access specific parts of the file randomly, reading the entire file into memory might be more convenient, as you can then use indexing or other techniques to access specific portions
- **Simplicity vs. Control:**
  - `os.ReadFile`: Offers a simple and concise way to read the entire file
  - `bufio.NewReader`: Provides more control over the reading process, allowing you to read data in chunks, handle lines or delimiters, and potentially improve performance for large files

Key Points:

- Use `os.ReadFile` to read the entire contents of a file into a byte slice
- Consider file size and read patterns when choosing between buffered readers and reading the entire file
- `os.ReadFile` is convenient for small files or random access scenarios
- Buffered readers are generally more efficient for large files and sequential reads

By understanding the trade-offs between these approaches, you can make informed decisions about how to read data from files in your Go programs, balancing simplicity, performance, and memory efficiency based on your specific requirements.

Writing to Files

The `io.Writer` Interface

In the realm of Go's file I/O operations, the `io.Writer` interface stands as the counterpart to `io.Reader`, providing a fundamental abstraction for writing data. It acts as a versatile contract, stipulating a single method, `Write`, that any type aspiring to be a "writer" must implement. This interface-driven approach allows you to write data to various destinations, such as files, network connections, or even in-memory buffers, in a unified and streamlined fashion.

The `io.Writer` Contract

```go
type Writer interface {
    Write(p []byte) (n int, err error)
}
```

- `Write(p []byte) (n int, err error)`: This method attempts to write the byte slice p to the underlying data stream. It returns the number of bytes written (n) and an error value (`err`). If the write operation encounters an error, `err` will be set to the corresponding error value.

The Power of Abstraction

The beauty of the `io.Writer` interface, much like its counterpart `io.Reader`, lies in its abstraction. By programming to this interface, your code becomes decoupled from the specific destination of the data. Whether you're writing to a file, a network socket, or a string builder in memory, you can use the same `Write` method to send the data, promoting code reusability and flexibility.

Key Points

- The `io.Writer` interface defines a single method, `Write`, for writing data from a byte slice
- Any type that implements the `Write` method can be used as a writer
- The `io.Writer` interface provides a powerful abstraction for writing data to various destinations in a unified way

Writing with `bufio.NewWriter`

While you can directly write to a file using the `*os.File`'s `Write` method, employing a buffered writer can significantly enhance performance, especially when dealing with frequent or large write operations. The `bufio.NewWriter` type from the `bufio` package steps in to provide this buffering capability, wrapping an `*os.File` and optimizing write operations by temporarily storing data in memory before flushing it to the file system in larger, more efficient chunks.

Benefits of Buffered Writers:

- **Reduced System Calls:** Writing data directly to a file often necessitates making system calls to the operating system for each write operation. Buffered writers mitigate these system calls by accumulating data in a buffer and periodically flushing the buffer's contents to the file system, minimizing the overhead of frequent system interactions.
- **Enhanced Performance:** By buffering write operations in memory, buffered writers can achieve faster write speeds, particularly when dealing with numerous small writes. The data is written to the buffer first, and then the buffer is flushed to the file system in a single, optimized operation.

Creating a Buffered Writer

You create a buffered writer by wrapping an *os.File using the bufio.NewWriter function

```
file, err := os.Create("output.txt")
if err != nil {
    // Handle the error
}
defer file.Close()

writer := bufio.NewWriter(file)
```

Writing Data with bufio.NewWriter

The bufio.NewWriter type offers a couple of methods for writing data to the file

1. **Write(p []byte) (n int, err error):**
   - Writes the contents of the byte slice p to the buffer
   - Returns the number of bytes written (n) and an error value (err)
   - If the buffer becomes full, it's automatically flushed to the file system
2. **WriteString(s string) (int, error):**
   - A convenience method that writes a string s to the buffer
   - Returns the number of bytes written and an error value

The Crucial Flush Method:

- **Purpose:** The Flush method forces any buffered data to be written to the underlying file immediately.
- **Importance:** It's essential to call Flush before closing the file or when you want to ensure that all buffered data is written to the file system without delay.

Illustrative Examples

```
// Write a byte slice
data := []byte("Hello, buffered writer!")
_, err = writer.Write(data)

// Write a string
_, err = writer.WriteString("\nThis is another line.")

// Flush the buffer to ensure data is written to the file
err = writer.Flush()
```

Key Points

- Use bufio.NewWriter to create a buffered writer that wraps an *os.File
- Buffered writers improve performance by buffering write operations in memory
- Use the Write and WriteString methods to write data to a file
- Always call the Flush method before closing the file to ensure all buffered data is written

By utilizing buffered writers, you can optimize your file writing operations in Go, leading to faster and more efficient data transfer to the file system. Remember to call Flush at appropriate times to guarantee that your data is persistently stored.

Writing the Entire File at Once

While buffered writers excel at handling frequent or large write operations, there are scenarios where you might prefer to write the entire contents of a byte slice to a file in a single, atomic operation. The `os.WriteFile` function in Go's standard library provides a convenient way to achieve this.

The `os.WriteFile` Function

- **Purpose:** Writes the entire contents of a byte slice to a file, creating the file if it doesn't exist or truncating it if it does
- **Syntax:** `err := os.WriteFile("filename", data, perm)`
- **Arguments:**
    - `filename`: The name of the file to write to
    - `data`: The byte slice containing the data to be written
    - `perm`: The file permissions (mode) to set for the file (e.g., `0644` for read/write by owner, read by group and others)

Example

```go
data := []byte("This is the entire content of the file.\n")
err := os.WriteFile("output.txt", data, 0644)
if err != nil {
    // Handle the error
}
```

Scenarios Where `os.WriteFile` is Appropriate

- **Small Files:** When dealing with small files, writing the entire content at once can be simpler and more convenient than using a buffered writer
- **Atomic Writes:** `os.WriteFile` provides an atomic write operation, meaning that either the entire content is written successfully, or the file remains unchanged. This can be important in scenarios where you need to ensure data integrity and prevent partial writes

Key Points

- Use `os.WriteFile` to write the entire contents of a byte slice to a file in a single operation
- Specify file permissions using the `perm` argument
- `os.WriteFile` is suitable for small files or when you need atomic writes

By understanding how to use `os.WriteFile`, you have another tool in your Go file I/O toolkit. You can now choose between buffered writers and `os.WriteFile` based on your specific needs, balancing performance, convenience, and data integrity considerations.

Working with File Paths

The `filepath` Package

File paths are the addresses that guide your Go programs to specific files within the intricate structure of your file system. However, different operating systems have varying conventions for representing file paths. Windows uses backslashes (\), while macOS and Linux use forward slashes (/). To ensure that your Go code works seamlessly across different platforms, the `filepath` package comes to the rescue, providing a collection of functions for working with file paths in a platform-independent way.

Key Functions in the `filepath` Package

- `filepath.Join(elem ...string) string`

- Purpose: Joins multiple path elements into a single path, using the appropriate separator for the current operating system
- Example:

```
path := filepath.Join("documents", "reports", "summary.txt")
fmt.Println(path) // Output: documents/reports/summary.txt (on macOS/Linux)
                  // Output: documents\reports\summary.txt (on Windows)
```

- **filepath.Abs(path string) (string, error)**
  - Purpose: Converts a relative path to an absolute path
  - Example:

```
absPath, err := filepath.Abs("documents/reports")
if err != nil {
    // Handle the error
}
fmt.Println(absPath) // Output: /Users/username/documents/reports (on macOS)
                     // Output: C:\Users\username\documents\reports (on Windows)
```

- **filepath.Dir(path string) string**
  - Purpose: Extracts the directory portion of a file path
  - Example:

```
dir := filepath.Dir("/Users/username/documents/reports/summary.txt")
fmt.Println(dir) // Output: /Users/username/documents/reports
```

- **filepath.Base(path string) string**
  - Purpose: Extracts the base filename (including the extension) from a file path.
  - Example:

```
base := filepath.Base("/Users/username/documents/reports/summary.txt")
fmt.Println(base) // Output: summary.txt
```

Benefits of Using the `filepath` Package

- **Platform Independence:** The `filepath` package ensures that your file path manipulations work correctly across different operating systems, eliminating the need to write platform-specific code.
- **Clarity and Readability:** The functions in the `filepath` package provide a clear and expressive way to work with file paths, making your code more readable and maintainable
- **Error Handling:** Many `filepath` functions return an `error` value, allowing you to handle potential errors gracefully, such as invalid paths or permission issues

Key Takeaways

- The `filepath` package provides platform-independent functions for working with file paths
- Use `filepath.Join` to construct file paths correctly
- Use `filepath.Abs` to convert relative paths to absolute paths
- Use `filepath.Dir` and `filepath.Base` to extract directory and filename components from a path

By leveraging the `filepath` package, you can write Go code that interacts with the file system in a portable and reliable manner. This ensures that your programs work seamlessly across different platforms and simplifies the handling of file paths, leading to more robust and maintainable code.

File Permissions and Error Handling

File Permissions

In the world of file systems, permissions act as the gatekeepers, controlling who can access a file and what actions they can perform on it. They determine whether a file can be read, written, or executed by the owner, the group, or others. Understanding and managing file permissions is crucial for ensuring data security and controlling access to sensitive information.

File Permissions in Go:

- **Read, Write, Execute:** Go, like most Unix-like systems, uses a combination of read (r), write (w), and execute (x) permissions to define access levels for files.
- **Owner, Group, Others:** Permissions are typically set for three categories of users:
    - **Owner:** The user who owns the file.
    - **Group:** A group of users associated with the file
    - **Others:** All other users on the system

The os.Chmod Function:

The os.Chmod function in Go allows you to change the permissions of a file.

- **Syntax:** `err := os.Chmod("filename", mode)`
    - `filename`: The name of the file whose permissions you want to change
    - `mode`: An integer representing the new permissions, typically expressed in octal notation (e.g., 0644)
- **Octal Notation:**
    - The first digit represents special permissions (rarely used in basic scenarios).
    - The next three digits represent permissions for the owner:
        - 4: Read permission
        - 2: Write permission
        - 1: Execute permission
    - The following three digits represent permissions for the group
    - The last three digits represent permissions for others
- **Example:**

```go
err := os.Chmod("myfile.txt", 0644)
if err != nil {
    // Handle the error
}
```

This example sets the permissions for myfile.txt to:

- Owner: Read and write (rw-)
- Group: Read only (r--)
- Others: Read only (r--)

Key Points:

- File permissions control access to files
- Go uses read, write, and execute permissions for owner, group, and others
- Use the os.Chmod function to change file permissions
- Express permissions using octal notation

By understanding file permissions and using the os.Chmod function, you can control access to your files and ensure data security in your Go programs. Remember to set appropriate permissions based on the sensitivity of your data and the intended use of the files.

Error Handling

In the world of file I/O, where interactions with the file system are prone to unexpected hiccups, error handling emerges as a guardian of robustness and reliability. Files might be missing, permissions might be denied, disks might be full, or a myriad of other unforeseen circumstances could arise. Failing to handle these errors gracefully can lead to crashes, data corruption, and frustrated users. Therefore, incorporating meticulous error handling into your file I/O operations is not just a best practice; it's an imperative.

The error Value: Your Guiding Light

- **Error as a Return Value**: Virtually every function in Go's os and io packages that deals with file I/O returns an error value as its last return value. This error value acts as a signal, indicating whether the operation succeeded or encountered an issue.
- **The nil Check**: After every file I/O operation, diligently check if the returned error value is nil. If it's not nil, it means an error occurred, and you need to handle it appropriately.

Handling Errors: A Multifaceted Approach

The specific way you handle an error depends on the context and the nature of the error. Here are some common strategies:

1. **Logging the Error**

```go
data, err := os.ReadFile("myfile.txt")
if err != nil {
    log.Println("Error reading file:", err)
}
```

Logging the error provides a record of the issue for later analysis and debugging.

2. **Returning the Error to the Caller**

```go
func processFile(filename string) error {
    // ... (file operations)
    if err != nil {
        return fmt.Errorf("error processing file: %w", err) // Wrap the error with context
    }
    return nil
}
```

Returning the error allows higher-level functions in your call stack to handle the error or propagate it further up if necessary.

3. **Taking Corrective Action**

```go
if err != nil {
    if errors.Is(err, os.ErrNotExist) {
        // File doesn't exist, create a new one
        file, err := os.Create(filename)
        // ...
    } else if errors.Is(err, os.ErrPermission) {
```

```
        // Permission denied, prompt the user or try a different action
    } else {
        // Handle other unexpected errors
    }
}
```

In some cases, you might be able to take corrective action based on the specific error encountered. For example, if a file doesn't exist, you might create a new one, or if permission is denied, you might prompt the user or try a different operation

Key Points

- Always check for errors returned by file I/O operations
- Handle errors promptly and appropriately
- Use logging, error propagation, or corrective actions based on the context
- Consider using error wrapping to provide more informative error messages

By incorporating robust error handling into your file I/O code, you create Go programs that are resilient, reliable, and provide a smooth user experience even in the face of unexpected file-related issues. Remember, error handling is not an optional add-on; it's an integral part of writing production-ready Go code that can gracefully handle the complexities of the file system

Best Practices for File I/O

File I/O operations, while fundamental to many Go programs, can be fraught with potential pitfalls if not handled with care. Adhering to best practices ensures that your code interacts with the file system responsibly, efficiently, and reliably, leading to robust and maintainable applications.

1. Always Close Files

- **Resource Leaks:** Leaving files open can lead to resource leaks, where your program consumes system resources unnecessarily.
- **Data Integrity:** Unclosed files might retain buffered data in memory, potentially leading to data inconsistencies or loss if the program crashes or terminates unexpectedly.
- `defer file.Close()`: The `defer` statement provides a convenient and reliable way to ensure that files are always closed, even if an error occurs or the function panics. It schedules the `file.Close()` call to be executed at the end of the function, guaranteeing proper cleanup.

2. Use Buffered I/O for Performance

- **Reduced System Calls:** Buffered I/O, using `bufio.NewReader` and `bufio.NewWriter`, minimizes the number of system calls required for reading and writing, especially when dealing with large files. This can lead to significant performance improvements.
- **Optimized Data Transfer:** Buffered I/O reads and writes data in chunks, optimizing data transfer between your program and the file system.

3. Handle Errors Gracefully

- **Check for Errors:** Always check for errors returned by file I/O operations. Don't assume that every operation will succeed.
- **Informative Error Messages:** Use error wrapping to provide context and details about the error, making it easier to diagnose and fix issues.
- **Appropriate Actions:** Handle errors gracefully by logging them, returning them to the caller, or taking corrective actions based on the specific error encountered.

4. Use the `filepath` Package

- **Platform Independence:** Leverage the `filepath` package to work with file paths in a platform-independent way. This ensures that your code functions correctly across different operating systems.
- **Path Manipulation:** Use functions like `filepath.Join`, `filepath.Abs`, `filepath.Dir`, and `filepath.Base` to construct, manipulate, and extract components from file paths.

5. Consider File Permissions

- **Data Security:** Be mindful of file permissions and set appropriate permissions using `os.Chmod` to control access to your files. This helps protect sensitive data and prevent unauthorized modifications.
- **User Experience:** If your program needs to create or modify files, ensure that it has the necessary permissions to do so. Otherwise, handle permission errors gracefully and provide informative feedback to the user.

By adhering to these best practices, you can write Go code that interacts with the file system responsibly, efficiently, and reliably. Remember, proper file I/O handling is not just about functionality; it's about creating robust and user-friendly applications that can gracefully handle the complexities of the file system and ensure the integrity of your data.

Chapter Summary

In this chapter, we embarked on an exploration of file I/O in Go, learning how to interact with the file system, read data from files, write data to files, and handle file-related operations effectively.

We covered the following key aspects:

- **Introduction to File I/O:** We discussed the concept of file I/O and its importance for persistent data storage, configuration management, logging, and communication with external systems.
- **Opening and Closing Files:** You learned how to open existing files using `os.Open` and create new files using `os.Create`. We also emphasized the importance of closing files using `File.Close` and the convenience of the `defer` statement for ensuring proper file closure.
- **Reading from Files:** You were introduced to the `io.Reader` interface and how to use `bufio.NewReader` to create buffered readers for efficient file reading. We also demonstrated how to read the entire contents of a file at once using `os.ReadFile` and discussed the trade-offs between these approaches.
- **Writing to Files:** You learned about the `io.Writer` interface and how to use `bufio.NewWriter` to create buffered writers for optimized file writing. We also showed how to write the entire contents of a byte slice to a file using `os.WriteFile` and discussed scenarios where this approach is appropriate.
- **Working with File Paths:** You were introduced to the `filepath` package and its functions for platform-independent file path manipulation.
- **File Permissions and Error Handling:** We briefly discussed file permissions and how to change them using `os.Chmod`. We also emphasized the importance of error handling in file I/O operations and demonstrated how to check for and handle errors gracefully.
- **Best Practices:** We provided guidance on best practices for file I/O, including always closing files, using buffered I/O for performance, handling errors gracefully, using the `filepath` package, and considering file permissions.

By mastering these concepts and techniques, you've gained the ability to interact with the file system confidently and efficiently in your Go programs. You can now read data from files, write data to files, manipulate file paths, and handle errors gracefully, opening up a world of possibilities for persistent data storage, configuration management, logging, and communication with external systems.

In the next chapter, we will shift our focus to the web, exploring how to build web applications and APIs using Go's powerful `net/http` package.

Building Web Applications with Go's `net/http` Package

Outline

- Introduction to Web Applications
- The `net/http` Package
- Creating a Basic Web Server
- Handling HTTP Requests
- Serving Static Files
- Routing and Handlers
- HTML Templates
- Working with Forms and User Input
- Middleware
- Building RESTful APIs
- Security Considerations
- Advanced Web Development with Go
- Chapter Summary

Introduction to Web Applications

Web applications have become an integral part of our digital lives, powering everything from social media platforms and e-commerce websites to online banking systems and collaborative tools. At their core, web applications operate on a client-server model, where a client (typically a web browser) communicates with a server to request and receive information.

The Client-Server Model

- **Client:** The client is the user-facing part of the web application, usually a web browser like Chrome, Firefox, or Safari. It's responsible for rendering the user interface, handling user interactions, and sending requests to the server.
- **Server:** The server is the backend component of the web application, running on a remote machine. It receives requests from clients, processes them, interacts with databases or other data sources, and generates responses to send back to the clients.
- **Communication:** The client and server communicate with each other over a network using the Hypertext Transfer Protocol (HTTP).

The Role of HTTP

HTTP is the foundation of web communication. It defines the format and rules for the messages exchanged between clients and servers.

- **Requests:** Clients send HTTP requests to the server, specifying the desired action (e.g., GET, POST), the resource they want to access (e.g., a webpage, an image, or data from an API), and additional information in headers.
- **Responses:** The server processes the request and sends back an HTTP response, containing the requested resource (if available), a status code indicating the outcome of the request (e.g., 200 OK, 404 Not Found), and additional information in headers.

Fundamental Components

A typical web application consists of several fundamental components:

1. **Client-Side Code:** This includes HTML (Hypertext Markup Language) for structuring the content, CSS (Cascading Style Sheets) for styling the appearance, and JavaScript for adding interactivity and dynamic behavior to the user interface.
2. **Server-Side Code:** This is the core logic of the web application, responsible for handling requests, processing data, interacting with databases, and generating responses. Go's net/http package provides the tools to build this server-side logic.
3. **Database:** Many web applications store and retrieve data from a database. Go offers various database drivers and libraries to connect to and interact with different database systems.
4. **Web APIs:** Web APIs (Application Programming Interfaces) allow different software systems to communicate and exchange data over the web. Go's net/http package can be used to build both clients that consume APIs and servers that expose APIs.

The Web Application Flow

1. **User Interaction:** The user interacts with the web application through the browser.
2. **Request:** The browser sends an HTTP request to the server based on the user's action.
3. **Processing:** The server receives the request, processes it, and interacts with the database or other data sources if necessary.
4. **Response:** The server generates an HTTP response containing the requested data or a status code indicating the outcome of the request
5. **Rendering:** The browser receives the response and renders the content, updating the user interface accordingly

By understanding these fundamental concepts, you can begin to appreciate the dynamics of web applications and how Go's net/http package fits into this landscape. In the following sections, we will delve deeper into the net/http package, exploring how to create web servers, handle requests, serve static files, implement routing, and build dynamic and interactive web applications using Go.

The net/http Package

The net/http package stands as the cornerstone of Go's web development capabilities, providing a robust and flexible toolkit for building web applications, APIs, and network services. It encapsulates the essential functionalities for handling HTTP requests and responses, making it easy to create web servers that can interact with clients over the network.

Key Features

1. **HTTP Server and Client:** The net/http package offers functions and types for creating both HTTP servers and clients. You can use it to build web servers that listen for incoming requests and generate responses, or to create HTTP clients that send requests to external APIs or web services.
2. **Request Handling:** At the heart of web applications lies the ability to handle incoming HTTP requests. The net/http package defines handlers, which are functions that process requests and generate responses. You can register handlers for specific URLs or patterns, allowing your server to respond to different types of requests appropriately.
3. **Routing:** Routing is the mechanism that maps incoming URLs to specific handlers. The net/http package provides a basic routing functionality through the http.HandleFunc function, but you can also use third-party routing libraries like gorilla/mux for more advanced routing capabilities.
4. **Middleware:** Middleware functions act as interceptors in the request/response cycle. They can be used to perform various tasks, such as logging, authentication, authorization, or modifying the request or response before or after it reaches the main handler. Middleware provides a way to add reusable and modular functionality to your web applications.

5. **Static File Serving:** The `net/http` package includes the `http.FileServer` handler, which makes it easy to serve static files like HTML, CSS, JavaScript, and images from a specified directory. This is essential for serving the front-end assets of your web applications.
6. **Other Features:** The `net/http` package also supports other important web development features:
    - **Cookies:** You can use cookies to store small pieces of data on the client-side, enabling features like user sessions and personalization.
    - **Sessions:** You can build session management mechanisms on top of cookies to maintain user state and track user activity across multiple requests
    - **Secure Communication (HTTPS):** The `crypto/tls` package, in conjunction with `net/http`, allows you to create secure web servers that use HTTPS for encrypted communication, protecting sensitive data transmitted between the client and the server

In essence

The `net/http` package provides the essential building blocks for creating web applications and APIs in Go. Its comprehensive feature set, combined with its simplicity and performance, makes it a popular choice for web development in Go.

Creating a Basic Web Server

Let's embark on our web development journey by crafting a rudimentary web server using Go's `net/http` package. We'll guide you through the essential steps, accompanied by code examples and explanations, to set up a server that can respond to incoming HTTP requests.

1. Importing the net/http Package

The first step is to import the `net/http` package, which provides the core functionalities for creating and managing HTTP servers in Go.

```go
import (
    "fmt"
    "net/http"
)
```

2. Defining a Handler Function

A handler function is the heart of your web server. It processes incoming HTTP requests and generates corresponding responses. Let's define a simple handler that responds with a friendly greeting.

```go
func helloHandler(w http.ResponseWriter, r *http.Request) {
    fmt.Fprintln(w, "Hello, Gopher!")
}
```

- `w http.ResponseWriter`: This interface allows you to write the HTTP response back to the client
- `r *http.Request`: This struct represents the incoming HTTP request, providing access to information like the request method, URL, headers, and body

3. Registering the Handler with a Route

To associate your handler function with a specific URL path (route), you use the `http.HandleFunc` function.

```go
http.HandleFunc("/", helloHandler)
```

This line tells the server to call the `helloHandler` function whenever a request is made to the root path ("/").

4. Starting the Server

Finally, you start the web server using the `http.ListenAndServe` function.

```
err := http.ListenAndServe(":8080", nil)
if err != nil {
    log.Fatal(err)
}
```

- `:8080`: Specifies the port number the server will listen on
- `nil`: Indicates that we're using the default HTTP request multiplexer (we'll explore custom multiplexers later)
- `err`: Captures any errors that might occur while starting the server

Complete Code

```
package main

import (
    "fmt"
    "log"
    "net/http"
)

func helloHandler(w http.ResponseWriter, r *http.Request) {
    fmt.Fprintln(w, "Hello, Gopher!")
}

func main() {
    http.HandleFunc("/", helloHandler)
    fmt.Println("Server listening on :8080...")
    err := http.ListenAndServe(":8080", nil)
    if err != nil {
        log.Fatal(err)
    }
}
```

Running the Server

1. Save the code as `main.go`.
2. Open your terminal and navigate to the directory where you saved the file.
3. Run the following command:

   ```
   go run main.go
   ```

   You should see the message "Server listening on :8080..." in your terminal

4. Open your web browser and visit `http://localhost:8080`.

   You should see the greeting "Hello, Gopher!" displayed in your browser

Congratulations! You've just created your first basic web server in Go. While this server only responds with a static message, it lays the foundation for building more complex and dynamic web applications.

Handling HTTP Requests

The ability to handle incoming HTTP requests and generate appropriate responses lies at the core of web application development. Go's `net/http` package provides the tools to access valuable information from these requests and craft meaningful responses to send back to the client.

Accessing Information from HTTP Requests

The `*http.Request` struct, passed as an argument to your handler functions, encapsulates a wealth of information about the incoming request. Let's explore some key elements:

1. **Request Method: `r.Method`**
    - The HTTP method used for the request (e.g., GET, POST, PUT, DELETE)
    - Useful for determining the intended action (retrieving data, submitting data, updating data, etc.)
2. **URL Path: `r.URL.Path`**
    - The path portion of the requested URL (e.g., /products, /users/123)
    - Used for routing requests to appropriate handlers
3. **Query Parameters: `r.URL.Query()`**
    - Key-value pairs appended to the URL after a question mark (?) (e.g., ?name=Alice&age=30)
    - Useful for passing additional parameters to the server
4. **Headers: `r.Header`**
    - A map-like structure containing the HTTP headers sent with the request
    - Headers provide metadata about the request, such as the user agent, content type, and authentication information
5. **Request Body: `io.ReadAll(r.Body)`**
    - The data sent with the request, typically used in POST or PUT requests
    - You can read the request body using the `io.ReadAll` function from the `io` package

Sending Responses

The `http.ResponseWriter` interface provides methods for constructing and sending HTTP responses back to the client.

1. **`w.WriteHeader(statusCode)`**
    - Sets the HTTP status code for the response (e.g., `http.StatusOK` for 200 OK, `http.StatusNotFound` for 404 Not Found)
    - It's important to set the status code before writing any data to the response body
2. **`w.Write(data)`**
    - Writes the provided byte slice (`data`) to the response body
    - You can convert strings or other data types to byte slices using type conversions or encoding functions

Example:

```
func handleRequest(w http.ResponseWriter, r *http.Request) {
    fmt.Println("Request Method:", r.Method)
    fmt.Println("URL Path:", r.URL.Path)

    if r.Method == http.MethodPost {
        body, err := io.ReadAll(r.Body)
        if err != nil {
```

```go
            http.Error(w, "Error reading request body", http.StatusBadRequest)
            return
        }
        fmt.Println("Request Body:", string(body))
    }

    w.WriteHeader(http.StatusOK)
    fmt.Fprintln(w, "Hello from the server!")
}
```

In this example, the handleRequest function accesses the request method, URL path, and request body (if it's a POST request). It then sends a response with a 200 OK status code and a simple message.

Key Takeaways

- The `*http.Request` struct provides access to various details about the incoming request
- Use the `http.ResponseWriter` interface to construct and send HTTP responses
- Set the status code using `w.WriteHeader` before writing any data to the response body
- Write data to the response body using `w.Write`

By understanding how to access request information and send responses, you lay the groundwork for building dynamic and interactive web applications in Go.

Serving Static Files

Web applications often rely on static files such as HTML, CSS, JavaScript, images, and other assets to create the user interface and provide a rich user experience. Go's `net/http` package makes it straightforward to serve these static files directly from your web server, eliminating the need for a separate web server or complex configuration.

The `http.FileServer` Handler

The `http.FileServer` handler is a specialized handler that serves static files from a specified directory on your file system. It handles requests for files within that directory and its subdirectories, automatically mapping the requested URL paths to the corresponding files on disk.

The `http.Handle` Function

To register the `http.FileServer` handler for a specific route, you use the `http.Handle` function. This function associates a handler with a pattern, allowing you to control which URLs are handled by the file server.

Syntax

```go
http.Handle("/static/", http.StripPrefix("/static/",
http.FileServer(http.Dir("assets"))))
```

- `/static/`: The URL path prefix that will trigger the file server
- `http.StripPrefix("/static/", ...)`: Removes the `/static/` prefix from the URL path before looking for the file on disk
- `http.FileServer(http.Dir("assets"))`: Creates a file server that serves files from the "assets" directory

Example: Serving Files from the "assets" Directory

```go
package main

import (
    "fmt"
    "log"
    "net/http"
)

func main() {
    // Serve static files from the "assets" directory
    fs := http.FileServer(http.Dir("assets"))
    http.Handle("/static/", http.StripPrefix("/static/", fs))

    // Other handlers or routes can be defined here

    fmt.Println("Server listening on :8080...")
    err := http.ListenAndServe(":8080", nil)
    if err != nil {
        log.Fatal(err)
    }
}
```

In this example:

- We create a file server `fs` that serves files from the "assets" directory
- We register the file server with the route `/static/` using `http.Handle`
- The `http.StripPrefix` function removes the `/static/` prefix from the URL path before searching for the file in the "assets" directory

Now, if you have an `index.html` file within the "assets" directory, you can access it in your browser at `http://localhost:8080/static/index.html`

Key Points:

- Use `http.FileServer` to create a handler that serves static files
- Use `http.Handle` to register the file server with a specific route
- Use `http.StripPrefix` to remove a prefix from the URL path before serving the file

By leveraging these functionalities, you can easily incorporate static files into your Go web applications, providing a rich and interactive user experience. Remember to organize your static files in a dedicated directory and configure the file server accordingly to ensure that they are served correctly and securely.

Routing and Handlers

In the intricate world of web applications, where diverse URLs lead to different functionalities, routing emerges as the guiding compass that directs incoming requests to their appropriate destinations. It's the mechanism that maps specific URL patterns or paths to corresponding handler functions, ensuring that each request is processed by the right piece of code.

The Role of Routing

- **URL Mapping:** Routing establishes a connection between the URLs that users access in their browsers and the specific functions within your Go web server that handle those requests
- **Organized Structure:** It provides a structured and organized way to handle different functionalities within your application, making your code more maintainable and easier to navigate

- **Dynamic Content:** Routing enables you to create dynamic web applications where different URLs can lead to personalized content, user-specific data, or tailored responses based on the request parameters

Handlers: The Action Takers

Handlers are the workhorses of your web server. They are functions that receive incoming HTTP requests, process them, and generate appropriate responses. Each handler is responsible for a specific set of URLs or patterns, ensuring that requests are handled by the relevant logic within your application

http.HandleFunc: The Basic Router

The net/http package provides a basic routing mechanism through the http.HandleFunc function. It allows you to register a handler function for a specific URL pattern

Syntax

```
http.HandleFunc(pattern string, handler func(http.ResponseWriter, *http.Request))
```

- pattern: The URL pattern to match (e.g., "/", "/products", "/users/{id}")
- handler: The function that will handle requests matching the pattern

Example

```go
func homeHandler(w http.ResponseWriter, r *http.Request) {
    fmt.Fprintln(w, "Welcome to the homepage!")
}

func aboutHandler(w http.ResponseWriter, r *http.Request) {
    fmt.Fprintln(w, "This is the about page.")
}

func main() {
    http.HandleFunc("/", homeHandler)
    http.HandleFunc("/about", aboutHandler)

    // ... start the server
}
```

In this example, we register two handlers: homeHandler for the root path ("/") and aboutHandler for the "/about" path

Extracting Path Parameters with mux.Vars

For more advanced routing scenarios, where you need to extract dynamic segments or parameters from the URL path, you can use third-party routing libraries like gorilla/mux.

- **Example:**

    ```go
    import "github.com/gorilla/mux"

    func userHandler(w http.ResponseWriter, r *http.Request) {
        vars := mux.Vars(r)
        userID := vars["id"]
        fmt.Fprintln(w, "User ID:", userID)
    }

    func main() {
    ```

```
    r := mux.NewRouter()
    r.HandleFunc("/users/{id}", userHandler)

    // ... start the server with the custom router
    http.ListenAndServe(":8080", r)
}
```

In this example, we use `gorilla/mux` to define a route with a path parameter `{id}`. The `userHandler` function extracts the `id` parameter from the URL using `mux.Vars(r)` and uses it to generate a response.

Key Takeaways

- Routing maps URLs to specific handler functions
- Handlers process requests and generate responses
- Use `http.HandleFunc` for basic routing
- Use third-party libraries like `gorilla/mux` for more advanced routing and path parameter extraction

By understanding routing and handlers, you can build web applications in Go that respond to different URLs with appropriate actions and content. This enables you to create dynamic and interactive web experiences that cater to various user requests and provide tailored responses.

HTML Templates

In the dynamic world of web applications, where content often needs to be tailored to specific user requests or data, HTML templates emerge as a powerful tool for generating dynamic HTML content on the server-side. They allow you to separate the presentation logic (the HTML structure) from the application logic (the Go code), leading to cleaner, more maintainable, and easier-to-update web applications.

The `html/template` Package

Go's standard library provides the `html/template` package, which offers a robust templating engine for creating and parsing HTML templates. Templates are essentially HTML files with placeholders or markers that can be replaced with dynamic content generated by your Go code.

Creating and Parsing Templates

1. **Define the Template:** Create an HTML file (e.g., `template.html`) with placeholders for dynamic content using Go's template syntax (double curly braces `{{ }}`).

   ```
   <!DOCTYPE html>
   <html>
   <head>
       <title>{{.Title}}</title>
   </head>
   <body>
       <h1>{{.Heading}}</h1>
       <p>{{.Message}}</p>
   </body>
   </html>
   ```

2. **Parse the Template:** In your Go code, use the `template.ParseFiles` or `template.New` functions to parse the template file and create a `*template.Template` instance.

```go
tmpl, err := template.ParseFiles("template.html")
if err != nil {
    // Handle the error
}
```

3. **Execute the Template:** Use the `tmpl.Execute` method to execute the template, passing in a data structure (usually a struct) that contains the values to be inserted into the template's placeholders.

```go
data := struct {
    Title    string
    Heading  string
    Message  string
}{
    Title:   "My Webpage",
    Heading: "Welcome!",
    Message: "This is a dynamic webpage generated using Go templates.",
}

err = tmpl.Execute(w, data) // 'w' is the http.ResponseWriter
if err != nil {
    // Handle the error
}
```

Embedding Variables, Logic, and Loops

Go templates support a rich set of features for generating dynamic content:

- **Variables:** Embed variables from your data structure using `{{.FieldName}}`.
- **Conditional Logic:** Use `if`, `else`, and `else if` statements within `{{if pipeline}} T1 {{else}} T0 {{end}}` to control the output based on conditions
- **Loops:** Iterate over arrays, slices, or maps using the `range` action within `{{range pipeline}} T1 {{else}} T0 {{end}}`

Example with Conditional Logic and Loop:

```
{{if .Items}}
    <ul>
        {{range .Items}}
            <li>{{.}}</li>
        {{end}}
    </ul>
{{else}}
    <p>No items found.</p>
{{end}}
```

Key Takeaways

- HTML templates enable you to generate dynamic HTML content on the server-side
- Use the `html/template` package to create and parse templates
- Embed variables, conditional logic, and loops within templates to customize the output
- Templates promote separation of presentation logic from application logic, leading to cleaner and more maintainable code

By mastering HTML templates in Go, you can build web applications that deliver personalized and dynamic content to users, enhancing their experience and making your applications more engaging and interactive.

Working with Forms and User Input

Web applications thrive on interaction, and a significant part of that interaction involves gathering input from users through HTML forms. In Go, handling user input from forms typically involves processing POST requests and parsing the submitted data. Let's explore how to accomplish this using the net/http package.

Handling POST Requests

When a user submits an HTML form using the POST method, the browser sends the form data to the server within the request body. Your Go web server can then access this data and process it accordingly.

Parsing Form Data

The r.ParseForm() method is used to parse the form data from the request body. It populates two values within the *http.Request struct:

1. r.Form: A map-like structure containing the parsed form data, where keys are the field names and values are the submitted values.
2. r.PostForm: Similar to r.Form, but it only contains data from POST requests.

Accessing Form Values

Once the form data is parsed, you can access individual form values using the r.FormValue method.

Syntax

```
value := r.FormValue("fieldName")
```

- fieldName: The name of the form field you want to access.

Example

```
func formHandler(w http.ResponseWriter, r *http.Request) {
    if r.Method == http.MethodPost {
        err := r.ParseForm()
        if err != nil {
            http.Error(w, "Error parsing form", http.StatusBadRequest)
            return
        }

        name := r.FormValue("name")
        email := r.FormValue("email")
        fmt.Fprintf(w, "Hello, %s! Your email is %s\n", name, email)
    } else {
        // Handle GET requests or other methods
    }
}
```

In this example, the formHandler function parses the form data if it's a POST request and then accesses the name and email values using r.FormValue. It then constructs a personalized greeting and sends it as the response.

Validating User Input

It's crucial to validate user input to ensure its correctness and prevent potential security vulnerabilities.

- **Check for Required Fields**: Ensure that all required fields are present and have values
- **Sanitize Input**: Sanitize input to prevent cross-site scripting (XSS) attacks by escaping or removing potentially harmful HTML or JavaScript code
- **Validate Data Types and Formats:** Check if the input values are of the expected data types and adhere to any specific format requirements (e.g., email addresses, phone numbers).

Handling Errors

Always handle potential errors that might occur during form parsing or input validation.

- `r.ParseForm()` **Error:** If `r.ParseForm()` returns an error, it indicates an issue with parsing the form data. You can handle this by sending an appropriate error response to the client.
- **Validation Errors:** If the user input fails validation, provide clear error messages to the user, guiding them on how to correct their input.

Key Takeaways

- Handle user input from HTML forms using POST requests
- Parse form data using `r.ParseForm()`
- Access form values using `r.FormValue("fieldName")`
- Validate user input to ensure correctness and prevent security vulnerabilities
- Handle errors gracefully during form parsing and input validation

By mastering these techniques, you can build Go web applications that interact seamlessly with users, gather their input, and process it securely and reliably.

Middleware

In the realm of web application development, middleware emerges as a versatile tool that empowers you to add reusable and modular functionality to your request/response handling pipeline. Imagine middleware as a series of checkpoints or filters that HTTP requests and responses pass through before or after reaching their final destination, the main handler. These checkpoints can perform a variety of tasks, from logging and authentication to request/response modification and error handling, enhancing the capabilities and maintainability of your web applications.

The Power of Middleware

- **Intercepting Requests and Responses:** Middleware functions intercept incoming HTTP requests and outgoing responses, allowing you to inspect, modify, or process them before or after they reach the main handler.
- **Adding Reusable Functionality:** Middleware promotes code reusability by encapsulating common functionalities into separate functions that can be easily applied to multiple routes or handlers within your application
- **Modular Design:** Middleware encourages a modular design approach, where you can break down complex tasks into smaller, manageable middleware components, making your code more organized and easier to maintain
- **Customization and Flexibility:** Middleware provides a flexible way to customize the behavior of your web server, allowing you to add or remove functionalities without modifying the core handler logic.

Common Use Cases for Middleware

1. **Logging**: Middleware can be used to log incoming requests, including details like the request method, URL, and client information. This helps in tracking user activity, debugging issues, and monitoring the overall health of your application.
2. **Authentication and Authorization:** Middleware can enforce authentication and authorization checks, ensuring that only authorized users can access specific routes or resources within your application.
3. **Request/Response Modification:** Middleware can modify incoming requests or outgoing responses, such as adding headers, compressing data, or transforming the response format
4. **Error Handling**: Middleware can handle errors that occur during request processing, providing a centralized mechanism for error logging, recovery, or graceful degradation.

Creating and Using Middleware in Go

In Go, middleware functions typically have the following signature:

```
type Middleware func(http.Handler) http.Handler
```

They take an `http.Handler` as input and return a new `http.Handler` that wraps the original handler with additional logic

Example: Logging Middleware

```
func loggingMiddleware(next http.Handler) http.Handler {
    return http.HandlerFunc(func(w http.ResponseWriter, r *http.Request) {
        log.Println("Incoming request:", r.Method, r.URL.Path)
        next.ServeHTTP(w, r) // Call the next handler in the chain
    })
}
```

Applying Middleware

You can apply middleware to specific routes or to your entire application using functions like `http.Handle` or `http.HandleFunc` in combination with your middleware functions

Example

```
http.Handle("/", loggingMiddleware(http.HandlerFunc(myHandler)))
```

In this example, the `loggingMiddleware` is applied to the root path ("/"), logging every incoming request before passing it to the `myHandler` function

Key Takeaways

- Middleware functions intercept and process requests and responses
- They add reusable and modular functionality to your web applications
- Common use cases include logging, authentication, request/response modification, and error handling

Middleware empowers you to build more sophisticated and feature-rich web applications in Go. By encapsulating common functionalities into reusable middleware components, you can create a more organized, maintainable, and adaptable codebase that can easily evolve to meet the changing needs of your applications.

Building RESTful APIs

In the interconnected world of modern software, where applications often need to communicate and exchange data seamlessly, RESTful APIs have emerged as the lingua franca of web services. REST, or

Representational State Transfer, is an architectural style that provides a structured and standardized way to design APIs that are scalable, flexible, and easy to consume. Go's `net/http` package, with its robust HTTP handling capabilities, makes it an excellent choice for building RESTful APIs.

Principles of REST

REST is guided by a set of principles that promote a clean and intuitive API design:

1. **Client-Server Architecture:** RESTful APIs adhere to the client-server model, where clients send requests to servers and servers respond with data or actions.
2. **Statelessness:** Each request from the client to the server must contain all the information necessary to understand and process the request. The server does not store any client context between requests.
3. **Cacheability:** Responses from the server can be cached to improve performance and reduce network traffic.
4. **Layered System:** RESTful APIs can be composed of multiple layers, each with its own responsibilities, promoting scalability and flexibility.
5. **Uniform Interface:** RESTful APIs use a uniform interface based on HTTP methods (GET, POST, PUT, DELETE) and resource identifiers (URLs) to perform operations on resources.
6. **Code on Demand (Optional):** Servers can optionally send executable code to clients to extend their functionality.

Mapping HTTP Methods to CRUD Operations

RESTful APIs typically map HTTP methods to CRUD (Create, Read, Update, Delete) operations on resources:

- **GET:** Retrieve a resource or a collection of resources.
- **POST:** Create a new resource.
- **PUT:** Update an existing resource.
- **DELETE:** Delete a resource.

Designing and Implementing RESTful API Endpoints

Let's illustrate how to build RESTful API endpoints using Go's `net/http` package.

```go
package main

import (
    "encoding/json"
    "fmt"
    "log"
    "net/http"
)

type Item struct {
    ID    int    `json:"id"`
    Name  string `json:"name"`
    Price int    `json:"price"`
}

var items []Item

func getItems(w http.ResponseWriter, r *http.Request) {
    json.NewEncoder(w).Encode(items)
}

func addItem(w http.ResponseWriter, r *http.Request) {
```

```go
    var newItem Item
    err := json.NewDecoder(r.Body).Decode(&newItem)
    if err != nil {
        http.Error(w, "Invalid request payload", http.StatusBadRequest)
        return
    }
    newItem.ID = len(items) + 1
    items = append(items, newItem)
    w.WriteHeader(http.StatusCreated)
    json.NewEncoder(w).Encode(newItem)
}

func main() {
    http.HandleFunc("/items", getItems).Methods("GET")
    http.HandleFunc("/items", addItem).Methods("POST")

    fmt.Println("Server is listening on :8080")
    log.Fatal(http.ListenAndServe(":8080", nil))
}
```

In this example:

- We define an `Item` struct to represent a resource
- The `getItems` handler handles GET requests to `/items` and returns a JSON-encoded list of all items
- The `addItem` handler handles POST requests to `/items`, parses the JSON payload from the request body, creates a new `Item`, adds it to the `items` slice and returns the newly created item as a JSON response

Key Points

- RESTful APIs use HTTP methods (GET, POST, PUT, DELETE) to perform CRUD operations on resources
- Use `net/http` package's `HandleFunc` and its `Methods` method to define handlers for specific routes and HTTP methods
- Handle JSON encoding and decoding using the `encoding/json` package
- Consider security aspects like input validation and authentication when building APIs

By adhering to REST principles and utilizing Go's `net/http` package, you can design and implement clean, scalable, and easy-to-consume APIs that facilitate seamless communication and data exchange between different software systems.

Security Considerations

While Go's `net/http` package provides a robust foundation for building web applications, security remains a paramount concern in the online world. Neglecting security best practices can leave your applications vulnerable to attacks, data breaches, and unauthorized access. Let's briefly touch on some crucial security considerations to keep in mind when developing web applications with Go.

1. Input Validation and Sanitization

- **Injection Attacks:** Malicious users can attempt to inject harmful code or commands into your application through user input fields, potentially leading to SQL injection, command injection, or other types of attacks

- **Validation and Sanitization:** Always validate and sanitize user input before processing it. Ensure that input data adheres to expected formats, lengths, and data types. Use appropriate sanitization techniques to remove or escape potentially harmful characters or sequences.

2. Cross-Site Scripting (XSS) Protection

- **XSS Attacks:** XSS attacks occur when malicious scripts are injected into web pages viewed by other users. These scripts can then steal sensitive information, perform actions on behalf of the user, or deface the website
- **Escaping User-Generated Content:** Always escape user-generated content before displaying it on your web pages. This prevents injected scripts from being executed in the context of the user's browser. Go's `html/template` package provides built-in escaping mechanisms to help mitigate XSS vulnerabilities.

3. Cross-Site Request Forgery (CSRF) Protection

- **CSRF Attacks:** CSRF attacks trick users into performing unintended actions on your website, such as changing their password or making a purchase, by exploiting their authenticated session.
- **CSRF Tokens:** Implement CSRF tokens as a defense mechanism. These unique tokens are embedded in forms and verified by the server on submission, ensuring that requests originate from your website and not from a malicious third-party site.

4. Secure Cookies and Sessions

- **HTTPS:** Always use HTTPS (HTTP Secure) to encrypt communication between the client and server, protecting sensitive data like passwords and session IDs from being intercepted during transmission
- **Secure Cookie Flags:** When setting cookies, use the `HttpOnly` and `Secure` flags to prevent client-side scripts from accessing the cookies and ensure that they are only transmitted over HTTPS connections.

Additional Security Considerations

- **Authentication and Authorization:** Implement robust authentication and authorization mechanisms to control access to sensitive parts of your application
- **Secure Password Storage:** Never store passwords in plain text. Use strong hashing algorithms and salting techniques to protect passwords.
- **Regular Updates and Security Audits:** Keep your Go dependencies and libraries up-to-date to address any known security vulnerabilities. Periodically conduct security audits to identify and mitigate potential risks

By prioritizing security and incorporating these best practices into your Go web development workflow, you can build applications that are resilient to attacks, protect user data, and maintain the trust of your users. Remember, security is an ongoing process that requires constant vigilance and adaptation to the ever-evolving threat landscape.

Advanced Web Development with Go

While the foundational concepts and tools we've explored in this chapter equip you to build a wide range of web applications, the ever-evolving landscape of web development demands continuous learning and exploration. As you gain more experience and embark on more ambitious projects, you'll encounter scenarios that require more specialized techniques and frameworks.

Let's briefly touch upon some of these advanced topics and frameworks that can further enhance your Go web development skills:

1. **WebSockets for Real-Time Communication**
   - Traditional HTTP requests and responses follow a request-response cycle, where the client initiates a request and the server responds. However, for applications that require real-time, bidirectional communication, such as chat applications, collaborative tools, or live updates, WebSockets offer a persistent connection between the client and server, enabling efficient and instantaneous data exchange
   - Go provides libraries like `gorilla/websocket` that simplify the implementation of WebSocket-based communication in your web applications
2. **GraphQL for Flexible API Queries**
   - RESTful APIs, while widely adopted, can sometimes lead to over-fetching or under-fetching of data, as clients are often forced to request more or less data than they actually need. GraphQL addresses this by providing a query language that allows clients to specify precisely the data they require, reducing network overhead and improving efficiency.
   - Go has several GraphQL libraries, such as `graphql-go/graphql` and `99designs/gqlgen`, that enable you to build GraphQL servers and handle complex queries in your Go web applications
3. **gRPC for Efficient Communication Between Microservices**
   - In the world of microservices architecture, where applications are composed of multiple independent services that communicate with each other, gRPC emerges as a high-performance and efficient communication protocol. It uses Protocol Buffers for defining service contracts and data serialization, enabling strongly typed and efficient communication between services.
   - Go has excellent support for gRPC through the official `google.golang.org/grpc` library, allowing you to build gRPC servers and clients seamlessly within your Go applications

The Journey Continues

As you continue your Go web development journey, we encourage you to explore these advanced topics and frameworks further. They open doors to exciting possibilities, empowering you to build real-time applications, create flexible APIs, and design scalable microservices architectures. Remember, learning is a continuous process, and the Go ecosystem is constantly evolving with new tools and techniques. Embrace the challenge, stay curious, and continue to expand your Go web development skills to build the next generation of innovative and impactful web applications!

Chapter Summary

In this chapter, we embarked on an exciting journey into the world of web development with Go, exploring the capabilities of the powerful `net/http` package. We covered the following key concepts:

- **Introduction to Web Applications**: We started by understanding the client-server model and the role of HTTP in web communication, laying the groundwork for building web applications in Go.
- **The net/http Package**: We introduced the `net/http` package as the core of Go's web development toolkit, highlighting its key features such as HTTP server and client creation, request handling, routing, middleware, and static file serving.
- **Creating a Basic Web Server**: You learned how to create a simple web server using `http.HandleFunc` and `http.ListenAndServe`, taking the first step towards building web applications in Go.
- **Handling HTTP Requests**: We explored how to access information from HTTP requests, including the request method, URL path, query parameters, headers, and body. You also learned how to send responses to the client using the `http.ResponseWriter` interface.
- **Serving Static Files**: You discovered how to serve static files like HTML, CSS, JavaScript, and images using the `http.FileServer` handler and the `http.Handle` function.

- **Routing and Handlers**: We discussed the importance of routing in web applications and demonstrated how to use `http.HandleFunc` for basic routing and `gorilla/mux` for more advanced routing scenarios.
- **HTML Templates**: You learned how to use HTML templates from the `html/template` package to generate dynamic HTML content on the server-side, separating presentation logic from application logic.
- **Working with Forms and User Input**: We explored how to handle user input from HTML forms using POST requests, parse form data, access form values, and implement input validation and error handling.
- **Middleware**: You were introduced to the concept of middleware as a way to add reusable and modular functionality to your request/response handling pipeline, with common use cases like logging, authentication, and request/response modification.
- **Building RESTful APIs**: We discussed the principles of REST and how to build RESTful APIs in Go using the `net/http` package, mapping HTTP methods to CRUD operations and handling JSON data.
- **Security Considerations**: We touched upon important security aspects like input validation, XSS protection, CSRF protection, and secure cookies and sessions.
- **Advanced Web Development with Go**: We briefly mentioned other advanced topics and frameworks for web development, encouraging you to explore them further as you gain more experience.

By mastering these concepts and techniques, you've laid a strong foundation for building web applications and APIs with Go. You can now create dynamic and interactive web experiences, handle user input, serve static files, implement routing, and leverage the power of middleware and templates.

In the next chapter, we will continue our exploration of web development by delving into web APIs and JSON handling, learning how to interact with external services and exchange data in a structured and efficient manner. Get ready to expand your Go skills and build even more powerful and connected web applications.

Web APIs and JSON Handling in Go

Outline

- Understanding Web APIs
- JSON: The Data Interchange Format
- The encoding/json Package
- Marshaling Go Data into JSON
- Unmarshaling JSON into Go Data
- Making HTTP Requests to Web APIs
- Handling API Responses
- Error Handling and Robustness
- Best Practices for Working with Web APIs
- Chapter Summary

Understanding Web APIs

In the interconnected digital landscape, where software systems often need to collaborate and exchange information, Web APIs (Application Programming Interfaces) emerge as the vital bridges that facilitate communication and data flow. Essentially, Web APIs act as messengers, enabling different software applications to interact and share data over the web, regardless of their underlying technologies or platforms.

Think of a Web API as a restaurant's menu. The menu lists the available dishes (data or functionalities) and how to order them (request formats). Customers (client applications) can browse the menu and place orders (send requests), and the kitchen (the API provider) prepares the dishes (processes the requests) and delivers them to the customers (sends responses).

Benefits of Web APIs

Web APIs offer several key advantages that make them indispensable in modern software development:

1. **Modularity and Reusability**
   - APIs enable you to decompose complex systems into smaller, self-contained components or services. Each component can be developed, deployed, and maintained independently, promoting modularity and code reusability.
   - This modular approach fosters flexibility, as you can update or replace individual components without affecting the entire system. It also encourages collaboration, as different teams can work on different API components concurrently
2. **Integration and Interoperability**
   - APIs provide a standardized way for disparate applications to communicate and exchange data, even if they are written in different programming languages or run on different platforms
   - This interoperability unlocks a world of possibilities for building integrated systems and mashups, where data and functionalities from various sources can be combined to create new and innovative solutions
3. **Data Access and Functionality Exposure**
   - APIs offer a controlled way to expose specific data or functionalities from your application to external clients or services
   - This controlled access allows you to share valuable resources while maintaining security and protecting sensitive information. It also enables you to monetize your data or services by offering them through APIs to third-party developers or businesses

Illustrative Examples

- **Social Media Integrations:** Social media platforms expose APIs that allow other applications to access user data, post updates, or retrieve feeds, enabling seamless integration and social sharing features.
- **Payment Gateways:** E-commerce websites use payment gateway APIs to securely process online payments, abstracting away the complexities of payment processing and fraud prevention
- **Weather Data:** Weather applications leverage weather data APIs to provide real-time weather information and forecasts to users

Key Takeaways

- Web APIs enable communication and data exchange between different software systems over the web
- They promote modularity, reusability, integration, and controlled data access
- Go's `net/http` package provides the tools to build both API clients (to consume APIs) and API servers (to expose APIs)

By understanding the concept of Web APIs and their benefits, you can start leveraging their power to build interconnected applications, access valuable data sources, and create innovative solutions in the Go programming language. In the following sections, we will explore the JSON data format, the `encoding/json` package, and how to make HTTP requests and handle responses when interacting with Web APIs.

JSON: The Data Interchange Format

In the dynamic landscape of web APIs, where data flows seamlessly between diverse systems and applications, a common language is essential. JSON (JavaScript Object Notation) has emerged as that lingua franca, a lightweight and widely adopted data interchange format that facilitates the exchange of structured information over the web.

Key Characteristics of JSON

1. **Human-Readable:**
   - JSON's syntax, based on key-value pairs and arrays, closely resembles the way humans organize and represent data. Its use of familiar structures and formatting makes it easy for developers to read, write, and understand JSON data, even without specialized tools.
2. **Machine-Readable:**
   - While JSON is human-friendly, it's also designed for efficient parsing and generation by machines. Its structured format allows software programs to easily interpret and extract the information encoded within JSON data.
3. **Compact:**
   - JSON's concise syntax, devoid of excessive whitespace or verbose tags, minimizes the amount of data that needs to be transmitted over the network. This compactness is particularly crucial in web environments, where bandwidth and latency can impact performance.
4. **Language-Independent:**
   - JSON's simplicity and widespread adoption have led to its support in virtually every major programming language, including Go. This language independence makes JSON the ideal choice for exchanging data between systems written in different languages or running on different platforms.

JSON's Structure

JSON data is organized into two primary structures:

1. **Objects:** Objects are collections of key-value pairs, where keys are strings and values can be strings, numbers, booleans, null, arrays, or other objects. Objects are enclosed in curly braces { }.
     - Example:

   ```
   {
       "name": "Alice",
       "age": 30,
       "city": "Wonderland"
   }
   ```

2. **Arrays:** Arrays are ordered lists of values, where each value can be of any valid JSON type. Arrays are enclosed in square brackets [ ].
     - Example:

   ```
   [
       "apple",
       "banana",
       "orange"
   ]
   ```

The Prevalence of JSON

JSON's versatility and ease of use have made it the de facto standard for data exchange in web APIs. It's used extensively in various domains, including:

- **Web Services:** RESTful APIs and other web services often use JSON to represent data in requests and responses.
- **Configuration Files:** Many applications use JSON files to store configuration settings.
- **Data Serialization:** JSON is commonly used to serialize and deserialize data structures for storage or transmission.

Key Takeaways

- JSON is a lightweight and widely adopted data interchange format
- It is human-readable, machine-readable, compact, and language-independent
- JSON data is organized into objects (key-value pairs) and arrays
- JSON is the predominant format for data exchange in web APIs

By understanding JSON's structure and characteristics, you're well-prepared to leverage its power in your Go programs.

The `encoding/json` Package

In the realm of Go programming, where seamless interaction with JSON data is often essential, the `encoding/json` package emerges as your trusty companion. This package, nestled within Go's standard library, provides the indispensable tools for converting between Go's native data structures (like structs, maps, and slices) and their JSON representations. It acts as a bridge between your Go code and the world of JSON data, enabling you to effortlessly marshal Go data into JSON format for transmission or storage, and unmarshal JSON data back into Go structures for further processing.

The Dynamic Duo: `Marshal` and `Unmarshal`

- **`Marshal`**: The `json.Marshal` function takes a Go value (typically a struct, map, or slice) and transforms it into a JSON-encoded byte slice. This process is often referred to as *marshaling* or *encoding*. The resulting byte slice can then be sent over a network, written to a file, or used in any other context where JSON data is required.

- **Unmarshal**: The `json.Unmarshal` function performs the reverse operation, taking a JSON-encoded byte slice and converting it into a Go value. This process is known as *unmarshaling* or *decoding*. It allows you to extract structured data from JSON and work with it directly in your Go code.

Beyond the Basics

The `encoding/json` package offers additional functionalities beyond these core functions:

- **Struct Tags:** You can use struct tags (annotations within your struct definitions) to control how your Go structs are mapped to JSON objects. This allows you to customize field names, omit certain fields, or handle nested structures.
- **Streaming Encoding/Decoding:** For large JSON datasets, the package provides streaming encoder and decoder types (`json.Encoder` and `json.Decoder`) that allow you to process JSON data incrementally, reducing memory usage.
- **Custom Marshaling and Unmarshaling:** You can define custom marshaling and unmarshaling behavior for your types by implementing the `json.Marshaler` and `json.Unmarshaler` interfaces.

The Gateway to Web APIs

The `encoding/json` package plays a pivotal role when interacting with web APIs that use JSON for data exchange. You can use `json.Marshal` to encode your Go data structures into JSON payloads for API requests and `json.Unmarshal` to decode JSON responses from APIs into Go structures for further processing.

Key Takeaways:

- The `encoding/json` package is your go-to tool for working with JSON data in Go.
- The `Marshal` function converts Go data into JSON.
- The `Unmarshal` function converts JSON into Go data.
- The package offers additional features like struct tags, streaming encoding/decoding, and custom marshaling/unmarshaling.
- It is essential for interacting with web APIs that use JSON.

In the following sections, we'll dive deeper into the mechanics of marshaling and unmarshaling, exploring how to work with different Go data types, handle struct tags, and gracefully handle errors during the JSON conversion process. By mastering these techniques, you'll be well-equipped to seamlessly integrate your Go programs with the world of JSON data and web APIs.

Marshaling Go Data into JSON

Marshaling, also known as encoding, is the process of transforming Go's native data structures (like structs, maps, and slices) into their equivalent JSON representations. The `json.Marshal` function in Go's `encoding/json` package is your trusty tool for accomplishing this transformation, converting your Go data into a byte slice that adheres to the JSON format. This byte slice can then be readily transmitted over a network, stored in a file, or used in any other context where JSON data is required.

The `json.Marshal` Function

The `json.Marshal` function takes a Go value as input and returns two values:

1. A byte slice containing the JSON encoding of the input value

2. An error value, which will be `nil` if the marshaling operation is successful, or a non-`nil` error if an error occurs during the encoding process

Syntax:

```
data, err := json.Marshal(value)
```

- `value`: The Go value you want to marshal into JSON (e.g., a struct, map, or slice).
- `data`: A byte slice containing the JSON encoding of the value
- `err`: An error value indicating any errors during marshaling

Marshaling Structs

```go
type Person struct {
    Name string `json:"name"`
    Age  int    `json:"age"`
}

func main() {
    p := Person{Name: "Alice", Age: 30}
    jsonData, err := json.Marshal(p)
    if err != nil {
        // Handle the error
    }
    fmt.Println(string(jsonData)) // Output: {"name":"Alice","age":30}
}
```

In this example:

- We define a `Person` struct with `json` struct tags to specify the desired JSON field names
- We create a `Person` instance p
- We use `json.Marshal` to convert p into a JSON-encoded byte slice
- We convert the byte slice to a string and print it, revealing the JSON representation

Marshaling Maps and Slices

```go
func main() {
    myMap := map[string]int{"apple": 1, "banana": 2}
    mapData, _ := json.Marshal(myMap)
    fmt.Println(string(mapData)) // Output: {"apple":1,"banana":2}

    numbers := []int{1, 2, 3, 4, 5}
    sliceData, _ := json.Marshal(numbers)
    fmt.Println(string(sliceData)) // Output: [1,2,3,4,5]
}
```

Handling Struct Tags, Optional Fields, and Nested Structs

- **Struct Tags:** You can use struct tags to control the JSON field names and other aspects of the marshaling process

    ```go
    type Product struct {
        ID          int     `json:"id"`
        Name        string  `json:"name"`
        Price       float64 `json:"price"`
        Description string  `json:",omitempty"` // Omit if empty
    }
    ```

- **Optional Fields:** The `omitempty` tag option omits a field from the JSON output if its value is the zero value for its type
- **Nested Structs:** Nested structs are automatically marshaled into nested JSON objects

Key Takeaways:

- `json.Marshal` converts Go data structures into JSON-encoded byte slices
- Use struct tags to control JSON field names and handle optional fields
- Nested structs are marshaled into nested JSON objects
- Always handle potential errors returned by `json.Marshal`

By mastering the art of marshaling, you can seamlessly transform your Go data into JSON format, ready to be shared with the world through web APIs or stored for later use.

Unmarshaling JSON into Go Data

Unmarshaling, also known as decoding, is the process of converting JSON-encoded data back into Go's native data structures, such as structs, maps, or slices. The `json.Unmarshal` function in the `encoding/json` package is your key to unlocking the structured information hidden within JSON data, allowing you to seamlessly integrate it into your Go programs.

The `json.Unmarshal` Function

The `json.Unmarshal` function takes a JSON-encoded byte slice and a pointer to a Go value as input. It attempts to parse the JSON data and populate the provided Go value with the corresponding data.

Syntax

```
err := json.Unmarshal(jsonData, &destinationValue)
```

- `jsonData`: The byte slice containing the JSON-encoded data.
- `destinationValue`: A pointer to the Go value (struct, map, or slice) where you want to store the unmarshaled data.
- `err`: An error value indicating any errors during unmarshaling.

Unmarshaling into Structs

```go
type Person struct {
    Name string `json:"name"`
    Age  int    `json:"age"`
}

func main() {
    jsonData := []byte(`{"name":"Alice","age":30}`)
    var p Person
    err := json.Unmarshal(jsonData, &p)
    if err != nil {
        // Handle the error
    }
    fmt.Println(p.Name, p.Age) // Output: Alice 30
}
```

In this example:

1. We have a `Person` struct with `json` struct tags to map JSON field names to struct fields

2. We define a byte slice `jsonData` containing JSON-encoded data
3. We create a `Person` variable p
4. We use `json.Unmarshal` to parse the `jsonData` and populate the p struct
5. We print the values of the p struct, demonstrating successful unmarshaling

Unmarshaling into Maps and Slices

```
func main() {
    jsonData := []byte(`{"apple":1,"banana":2}`)
    var myMap map[string]int
    json.Unmarshal(jsonData, &myMap)
    fmt.Println(myMap) // Output: map[apple:1 banana:2]

    jsonData = []byte(`[1,2,3,4,5]`)
    var numbers []int
    json.Unmarshal(jsonData, &numbers)
    fmt.Println(numbers) // Output: [1 2 3 4 5]
}
```

Handling Errors

Unmarshaling can fail if the JSON data is invalid or if there's a type mismatch between the JSON data and the Go value you're trying to populate

- **Invalid JSON Syntax:** If the JSON data is not well-formed, `json.Unmarshal` will return a `*json.SyntaxError`
- **Type Mismatches:** If the JSON data types don't match the expected types in your Go value, `json.Unmarshal` will return an `*json.UnmarshalTypeError`

Always check the `err` value returned by `json.Unmarshal` and handle errors appropriately

Key Takeaways

- `json.Unmarshal` parses JSON-encoded byte slices and populates corresponding Go structs, maps, or slices
- Use struct tags to control the mapping between JSON field names and struct fields.
- Handle potential errors during unmarshaling, such as invalid JSON syntax or type mismatches
- Unmarshaling is essential for extracting structured data from JSON responses received from Web APIs or other sources

By mastering the art of unmarshaling, you can seamlessly convert JSON data into Go's native data structures, making it readily available for processing and manipulation within your programs. This capability opens the door to interacting with Web APIs, reading configuration files, and handling JSON data from various sources, further expanding the possibilities of your Go applications.

Making HTTP Requests to Web APIs

Go's `net/http` package not only empowers you to build web servers but also equips you with the tools to interact with external Web APIs. By making HTTP requests, you can fetch data, send information, and communicate with other services seamlessly, expanding the horizons of your Go applications.

Creating HTTP Clients: `http.Client`

The `http.Client` type is your gateway to making HTTP requests in Go. It provides a reusable and configurable client that handles the underlying network communication, connection pooling, and other complexities of HTTP interactions.

```go
client := &http.Client{}
```

Constructing HTTP Requests: `http.NewRequest`

The `http.NewRequest` function is used to create a new HTTP request.

Syntax

```go
req, err := http.NewRequest(method, url, body)
```

- `method`: The HTTP method for the request (e.g., `http.MethodGet`, `http.MethodPost`)
- `url`: The URL of the API endpoint you want to interact with
- `body`: An `io.Reader` representing the request body (optional, typically used for POST or PUT requests)

Setting Headers

You can set custom headers on the request using the `req.Header.Set` method.

```go
req.Header.Set("Content-Type", "application/json")
req.Header.Set("Authorization", "Bearer my-api-key")
```

Making Requests and Handling Responses

Once you've constructed the request, you can send it using the `client.Do` method, which returns an `*http.Response` representing the server's response.

Example: GET Request

```go
resp, err := client.Do(req)
if err != nil {
    // Handle the error
}
defer resp.Body.Close()

body, err := io.ReadAll(resp.Body)
if err != nil {
    // Handle the error
}

fmt.Println(string(body))
```

Example: POST Request

```go
data := map[string]string{"name": "Alice", "email": "alice@example.com"}
jsonData, _ := json.Marshal(data)

req, err := http.NewRequest(http.MethodPost, "https://api.example.com/users", bytes.NewBuffer(jsonData))
req.Header.Set("Content-Type", "application/json")

// ... send the request and handle the response
```

Key Points

- Use `http.Client` to create HTTP clients
- Construct HTTP requests using `http.NewRequest`
- Specify the request method, URL, headers, and body (if applicable)
- Send requests using `client.Do` and handle the responses

By mastering the art of making HTTP requests and handling responses, you can empower your Go programs to interact with the vast world of Web APIs, fetching data, sending information, and integrating with external services seamlessly.

Handling API Responses

Once you've sent an HTTP request to a Web API, the server will respond with an HTTP response containing valuable information, including the status code, headers, and, most importantly, the response body, which often holds the data you requested or feedback about the operation's outcome. Let's explore how to handle these API responses effectively in Go.

Reading the Response Body

The response body typically contains the data returned by the API, often encoded in JSON format. You can read the response body using the `io.ReadAll` function from the `io` package.

```go
body, err := io.ReadAll(resp.Body)
if err != nil {
    // Handle the error (e.g., log it or return an error to the caller)
}
```

- `resp.Body`: An `io.ReadCloser` representing the response body
- `body`: A byte slice containing the raw data from the response body
- `err`: An error value indicating any errors during reading

Checking the HTTP Status Code

The HTTP status code in the response provides crucial information about the outcome of the request

- **2xx Success:** Indicates that the request was successful
- **3xx Redirection:** Suggests that further action is needed to complete the request
- **4xx Client Error:** Indicates an error on the client side (e.g., bad request, unauthorized)
- **5xx Server Error:** Indicates an error on the server side (e.g., internal server error)

You can check the status code using the `resp.StatusCode` field

```go
if resp.StatusCode != http.StatusOK {
    // Handle the error (e.g., log it or return an error to the caller)
}
```

Unmarshaling JSON Responses

If the API returns data in JSON format, you'll need to unmarshal (decode) the JSON response body into Go data structures using the `json.Unmarshal` function

```go
type UserData struct {
    ID   int    `json:"id"`
    Name string `json:"name"`
}

var user UserData
```

```
err = json.Unmarshal(body, &user)
if err != nil {
    // Handle the error
}

fmt.Println(user.ID, user.Name)
```

Handling Successful and Error Responses

```
func fetchUserData(userID int) (*UserData, error) {
    // ... (construct the API request)

    resp, err := client.Do(req)
    if err != nil {
        return nil, fmt.Errorf("API request failed: %w", err)
    }
    defer resp.Body.Close()

    if resp.StatusCode != http.StatusOK {
        return nil, fmt.Errorf("API returned status code %d", resp.StatusCode)
    }

    var user UserData
    err = json.Unmarshal(body, &user)
    if err != nil {
        return nil, fmt.Errorf("failed to unmarshal JSON response: %w", err)
    }

    return &user, nil
}
```

In this example:

1. We make an HTTP request to fetch user data
2. We check for errors during the request
3. We check the status code to ensure a successful response
4. We unmarshal the JSON response into a `UserData` struct
5. We return the user data and a `nil` error (indicating success) or a `nil` user data and an error (indicating failure)

Key Takeaways

- Read the response body using `io.ReadAll`
- Check the HTTP status code using `resp.StatusCode`
- Unmarshal JSON responses into Go data structures using `json.Unmarshal`
- Handle both successful and error responses gracefully

By understanding how to handle API responses effectively, you can build Go programs that seamlessly interact with web services, fetch data, and integrate with external systems. Remember to always check for errors, handle different status codes appropriately, and unmarshal JSON data into suitable Go structures to make the most of the information returned by the API.

Error Handling and Robustness

When venturing into the realm of Web APIs, where your Go programs interact with external services over the vast expanse of the internet, the potential for errors looms large. Network hiccups, server glitches, invalid API keys, or unexpected data formats can all disrupt the smooth flow of communication. Robust error handling is paramount to ensure that your applications remain resilient, informative, and user-friendly even when faced with these challenges.

Potential Errors

1. **Network Errors**
   - **Connection Timeouts:** The network connection to the API server might time out due to network congestion, server overload, or other issues
   - **Server Unavailable:** The API server might be temporarily unavailable due to maintenance, outages, or other unforeseen circumstances.
   - **DNS Resolution Failures:** The domain name of the API server might not resolve to an IP address, preventing your program from establishing a connection
2. **API-Specific Errors**
   - **Invalid API Keys or Authentication:** The API might require authentication, and your requests might fail due to invalid API keys, expired tokens, or other authentication issues
   - **Rate Limits Exceeded:** Many APIs enforce rate limits to prevent abuse or overuse. If you exceed these limits, your requests might be throttled or rejected
   - **Invalid Input or Parameters:** The API might expect specific data formats or parameters in your requests. If your requests don't conform to these requirements, the server might return an error.
3. **JSON Parsing Errors**
   - **Invalid JSON Syntax:** The API response might contain malformed or invalid JSON data, causing the `json.Unmarshal` function to fail
   - **Type Mismatches:** The JSON data might not match the expected structure of your Go data types, leading to unmarshaling errors

Graceful Error Handling

When errors occur, it's essential to handle them gracefully, providing informative feedback to the user or taking appropriate corrective action

- **Informative Error Messages:** Use clear and descriptive error messages that explain the problem to the user, potentially suggesting solutions or workarounds
- **Logging:** Log errors to a file or a centralized logging system for later analysis and debugging. This helps you identify and track down the root causes of issues
- **Retries with Exponential Backoff:** For network errors or temporary server issues, implement retry mechanisms with exponential backoff. This involves retrying the request after a short delay, gradually increasing the delay between retries to avoid overwhelming the server
- **Fallback Mechanisms:** In some cases, you might be able to provide alternative functionality or gracefully degrade the user experience when an API is unavailable or encounters errors

Example

```go
resp, err := client.Do(req)
if err != nil {
    if errors.Is(err, net.ErrTimeout) {
        return nil, fmt.Errorf("API request timed out")
    } else if strings.Contains(err.Error(), "connection refused") {
        return nil, fmt.Errorf("API server is unavailable")
    } else {
        return nil, fmt.Errorf("API request failed: %w", err)
    }
}

if resp.StatusCode == http.StatusUnauthorized {
```

```go
        return nil, fmt.Errorf("invalid API key")
} else if resp.StatusCode == http.StatusTooManyRequests {
        return nil, fmt.Errorf("API rate limit exceeded")
} else if resp.StatusCode != http.StatusOK {
        return nil, fmt.Errorf("API returned an error status: %s", resp.Status)
}

// ... (unmarshal the JSON response)
```

In this example, we handle various potential errors:

- Network errors like timeouts or connection refused
- API-specific errors like unauthorized access or rate limit exceeded
- Unexpected status codes

Key Takeaways

- Error handling is crucial when working with Web APIs
- Anticipate potential errors like network issues, API-specific errors, and JSON parsing errors.
- Handle errors gracefully by providing informative messages, logging, retries, or fallback mechanisms

By incorporating robust error handling into your API interactions, you create Go programs that are resilient, user-friendly, and can navigate the unpredictable nature of the web with confidence.

Best Practices for Working with Web APIs

Interacting with Web APIs in Go involves more than just sending requests and receiving responses. To build robust and reliable applications that seamlessly integrate with external services, it's essential to follow best practices that ensure proper API usage, error handling, and security. Let's explore some key guidelines for working with Web APIs in Go.

1. API Documentation: Your North Star

- **Thorough Understanding:** Before you start making API requests, thoroughly read and understand the API documentation. This includes familiarizing yourself with the available endpoints, request and response formats, required headers, authentication mechanisms, and any rate limits or usage restrictions.
- **Stay Updated:** API documentation can change over time. Stay informed about any updates or deprecations to ensure your code remains compatible and functional.

2. Error Handling: The Safety Net

- **Anticipate Errors:** Assume that things can go wrong. Network issues, server outages, invalid API keys, or unexpected response formats are all possibilities. Implement robust error handling to gracefully handle these situations.
- **Informative Messages:** Provide clear and informative error messages to users or log them for debugging purposes. Include details about the specific error encountered and potential solutions or workarounds.
- **Retry Mechanisms:** For transient errors like network timeouts or temporary server issues, consider implementing retry mechanisms with exponential backoff. This involves retrying the request after a short delay, gradually increasing the delay between retries to avoid overwhelming the server.

3. Rate Limiting and Retries

- **Respect Rate Limits:** Many APIs enforce rate limits to prevent abuse or overuse. Be mindful of these limits and design your code to respect them. Exceeding rate limits can lead to your requests being throttled or even blocked.
- **Exponential Backoff:** If you encounter rate limit errors or other temporary server issues, implement retry mechanisms with exponential backoff. This strategy helps avoid overloading the server and ensures that your requests are eventually processed successfully.

4. Authentication: The Gatekeeper

- **Secure Access:** If the API requires authentication, use the appropriate authentication method, such as API keys, OAuth, or other mechanisms specified in the documentation.
- **Protect Credentials:** Store your API keys or other sensitive credentials securely, avoiding hardcoding them directly into your code. Consider using environment variables or configuration files to manage them.

5. Testing: The Assurance

- **Unit Tests:** Write unit tests to verify the correctness of your API interactions. Test different scenarios, including successful responses, error responses, and edge cases.
- **Mocking:** Consider using mocking frameworks to simulate API responses during testing, allowing you to test your code's behavior in isolation without relying on external services.

By following these best practices and approaching Web API interactions with a focus on documentation, error handling, rate limiting, authentication, and testing, you can build Go applications that are robust, reliable, and seamlessly integrated with external services. Remember that effective API usage is not just about functionality; it's about creating a positive and seamless experience for your users, even in the face of unexpected challenges.

Chapter Summary: Web APIs and JSON Handling in Go

In this chapter, we delved into the world of web APIs and JSON handling in Go, equipping you with the skills to build applications that interact seamlessly with external services and exchange data in a structured and efficient manner.

Key takeaways from this chapter:

- **Understanding Web APIs**: We explored the concept of Web APIs as a means for different software systems to communicate and exchange data over the web, highlighting their benefits in terms of modularity, reusability, integration, and data access.
- **JSON: The Data Interchange Format**: We introduced JSON as a lightweight and widely adopted data interchange format commonly used in Web APIs, emphasizing its human-readable and machine-readable nature, compactness, and language independence
- **The encoding/json Package**: We explored the encoding/json package as the primary tool for working with JSON data in Go, focusing on the Marshal and Unmarshal functions for converting between Go data structures and JSON representations
- **Marshaling and Unmarshaling**: You learned how to marshal Go data into JSON using json.Marshal and how to unmarshal JSON data into Go structures using json.Unmarshal, including handling struct tags, optional fields, and nested structs
- **Making HTTP Requests**: We demonstrated how to use the net/http package to make HTTP requests to Web APIs, create HTTP clients, construct requests, set headers, and handle responses
- **Handling API Responses**: You learned how to read response bodies, check HTTP status codes, and unmarshal JSON responses into Go data structures.
- **Error Handling and Robustness**: We emphasized the importance of error handling when working with Web APIs, discussing potential errors and demonstrating how to handle them gracefully

- **Best Practices**: We offered guidance on best practices for interacting with Web APIs, including consulting API documentation, implementing robust error handling, being mindful of rate limits and retries, using appropriate authentication methods, and writing unit tests

By mastering these concepts and techniques, you can now confidently build Go applications that interact with Web APIs, fetch data, send information, and integrate with external services. You have the tools to handle JSON data effectively, ensuring seamless communication and data exchange between your Go programs and the wider world of web services. Remember to prioritize error handling, security, and adherence to API documentation to create robust and reliable applications that provide a positive user experience.

As you progress further in your Go programming journey, you'll encounter numerous opportunities to apply these skills and build even more sophisticated and interconnected applications. The knowledge and experience gained in this chapter will serve as a solid foundation for your future endeavors in the world of web development with Go.

Section VI:
Advanced Go Techniques

Generics in Go: Writing Reusable Code

Outline

- The Need for Generics
- Understanding Generics
- Type Parameters
- Type Constraints
- Generic Functions
- Generic Types
- The `constraints` Package
- Common Use Cases for Generics
- Best Practices with Generics
- Chapter Summary

The Need for Generics

In the ever-evolving landscape of software development, the pursuit of code reusability stands as a guiding principle. Reusable code, akin to versatile building blocks, empowers developers to construct complex structures efficiently, avoiding the pitfalls of redundancy and promoting maintainability. It's the essence of "Don't Repeat Yourself" (DRY) principle, a cornerstone of software craftsmanship.

The Quest for Reusability

- **Efficiency & Productivity:** Reusable code saves time and effort by eliminating the need to write similar code multiple times for different data types. It accelerates development, allowing you to focus on the core logic of your application rather than getting bogged down in repetitive tasks.
- **Maintainability:** When you centralize functionality within reusable components, making updates or bug fixes becomes a breeze. A single change in the reusable code propagates to all its usages, ensuring consistency and reducing the risk of errors.
- **Readability & Clarity:** Reusable code promotes a cleaner and more organized codebase. By abstracting common patterns into reusable functions or types, you reduce code clutter and make your code more self-documenting.

Challenges without Generics

Before the introduction of generics in Go 1.18, achieving true code reusability was challenging.

- **Code Duplication:** Without generics, you often had to write separate functions or types for each data type you wanted to support. This led to code duplication, making your codebase larger and harder to maintain
- **Empty Interface Limitations:** The empty interface (`interface{}`) offered a workaround for handling values of different types, but it came with compromises. You had to rely on type assertions

or type switches to access the concrete values, sacrificing type safety and potentially introducing runtime errors.

Generics to the Rescue

Generics, introduced in Go 1.18, provide a powerful solution to these challenges. They allow you to write functions and types that can operate on values of various data types while maintaining type safety.

- **Type Parameters:** Generics introduce the concept of type parameters, which act as placeholders for concrete types. When you use a generic function or type, you provide specific type arguments, and the compiler generates specialized code for those types, ensuring type safety at compile time
- **Type Constraints:** You can define constraints on type parameters to restrict the types that can be used as arguments, further enhancing type safety and allowing you to perform specific operations within the generic code

Key Takeaways

- Code reusability is essential for efficient and maintainable software development
- Generics address the challenges of code duplication and the limitations of the empty interface.
- They allow you to write functions and types that work with various data types while maintaining type safety.

In the following sections, we'll explore the mechanics of generics in Go, including type parameters, type constraints, generic functions, and generic types. By mastering these concepts, you'll be equipped to write more reusable, flexible, and type-safe code, unlocking a new level of expressiveness and efficiency in your Go programs.

Understanding Generics

Generics in Go represent a significant leap forward in the quest for code reusability and type safety. They empower you to write functions and types that can operate on a variety of data types, all while ensuring that your code remains robust and free from type-related errors at compile time. At their core, generics introduce two fundamental concepts: type parameters and type constraints.

Type Parameters: The Versatile Placeholders

Imagine you're writing a function to find the maximum value in a slice. Without generics, you'd likely need to create separate functions for integers, floats, and other types. Generics liberate you from this repetition by introducing type parameters.

- **Placeholder Types:** Type parameters act as versatile placeholders within your function or type definitions. They are represented by names enclosed in square brackets [ ], such as [T].
- **Concrete Types at Instantiation:** When you use a generic function or type, you provide specific type arguments, replacing the type parameters with concrete types like `int`, `float64`, or even custom structs. The compiler then generates specialized code for each type argument, ensuring type safety.

Type Constraints: The Guardians of Safety

While type parameters offer flexibility, type constraints provide the necessary safeguards to prevent misuse and ensure that your generic code remains type-safe.

- **Restricting Type Arguments**: Type constraints impose restrictions on the types that can be used as arguments for your generic functions or types. This ensures that the operations within your generic code are valid for the provided types, preventing potential runtime errors.

- **The any Constraint:** The any constraint is the most permissive, allowing any type to be used as a type argument. However, it limits the operations you can perform within the generic code to those that are valid for all types.
- **Custom Constraints with Interfaces**: You can define custom constraints using interfaces. An interface constraint specifies that a type argument must implement a particular interface, granting you access to the methods defined in that interface within your generic code.

Example:

```go
func max[T constraints.Ordered](a, b T) T {
    if a > b {
        return a
    }
    return b
}
```

In this example:

- T is a type parameter representing any type that satisfies the `constraints.Ordered` constraint.
- The `constraints.Ordered` constraint ensures that the > operator is valid for the type T, guaranteeing type safety.

The Synergy of Type Parameters and Constraints

Type parameters offer flexibility, while type constraints enforce safety. Together, they empower you to write generic code that is both adaptable and robust. By carefully choosing appropriate type parameters and constraints, you can create reusable functions and types that work seamlessly with a variety of data types while maintaining the integrity and correctness of your Go programs.

Type Parameters

Type parameters, the cornerstone of generics in Go, act as versatile placeholders within your function or type definitions, waiting to be filled with concrete types when you actually use them. They unlock a new level of flexibility, enabling you to write code that can operate on a variety of data types without sacrificing type safety or resorting to cumbersome workarounds.

Syntax

You declare type parameters within square brackets [ ] immediately after the function or type name.

- **Function:**

    ```go
    func functionName[T1, T2, ...](parameters...) returnType {
        // ... function body
    }
    ```

- **Type:**

    ```go
    type typeName[T1, T2, ...] struct {
        // ... fields
    }
    ```

Type Parameters as Placeholders

- **Generic Blueprint**: Think of type parameters as creating a generic blueprint for your function or type. They represent abstract types that will be replaced with concrete types when the function or type is used.

- **Instantiation with Type Arguments:** When you call a generic function or create an instance of a generic type, you provide specific type arguments within angle brackets <>, replacing the type parameters with actual types.
- **Type Safety:** The Go compiler ensures that the provided type arguments satisfy any constraints defined for the type parameters. This guarantees type safety, preventing you from using the generic function or type with incompatible types.

Example

```
func printSlice[T any](s []T) {
    for _, v := range s {
        fmt.Println(v)
    }
}

func main() {
    intSlice := []int{1, 2, 3}
    stringSlice := []string{"apple", "banana", "orange"}

    printSlice(intSlice)      // Output: 1 2 3
    printSlice(stringSlice)   // Output: apple banana orange
}
```

In this example:

- The `printSlice` function is generic, with a type parameter T that can represent any type (any constraint).
- When we call `printSlice` with `intSlice`, the compiler generates a specialized version of the function where T is replaced with `int`.
- Similarly, when we call `printSlice` with `stringSlice`, T is replaced with `string`.
- This allows the same `printSlice` function to work with slices of different types while maintaining type safety.

Key Points

- Type parameters are declared within square brackets [ ] after the function or type name
- They act as placeholders for concrete types
- Type arguments are provided within angle brackets <> when using the generic function or type
- The compiler ensures type safety by checking that the type arguments satisfy any constraints

By understanding type parameters and how they work, you can start writing generic code in Go that is both flexible and type-safe.

Type Constraints

While type parameters in Go offer the flexibility to work with various data types, type constraints act as the guardians of type safety, ensuring that your generic code remains robust and free from potential runtime errors. They provide a way to specify restrictions on the types that can be used as arguments for your generic functions or types, allowing you to perform specific operations within the generic code while guaranteeing that those operations are valid for the provided types.

The any Constraint

The any constraint is the most permissive constraint in Go. It allows any type to be used as a type argument for a generic function or type.

- **Limited Operations:** However, the any constraint also limits the operations you can perform within the generic code. You can only use operations that are valid for all types, such as assignment or comparison using the == and != operators.

Example

```
func printValue[T any](value T) {
    fmt.Println(value)
}
```

In this example, the `printValue` function can accept a value of any type because of the any constraint on the type parameter T.

Custom Constraints with Interfaces

To enable more specific operations within your generic code, you can define custom constraints using interfaces. An interface constraint specifies that a type argument must implement a particular interface, granting you access to the methods defined in that interface.

- **Example:**

    ```
    type Number interface {
        int | int32 | int64 | float32 | float64
    }

    func sum[T Number](numbers []T) T {
        var total T
        for _, num := range numbers {
            total += num
        }
        return total
    }
    ```

    In this example:

    1. We define a custom constraint Number using a union of numeric types (`int`, `int32`, `int64`, `float32`, `float64`).
    2. The sum function has a type parameter T with the Number constraint, ensuring that it can only be used with slices of numeric types.
    3. Within the function, we can safely use the + operator on values of type T because the Number constraint guarantees that they support addition.

Key Points

- Type constraints restrict the types that can be used as type arguments for generic functions or types
- The any constraint allows any type but limits the operations you can perform
- Custom constraints can be defined using interfaces to enable specific operations
- Type constraints ensure type safety and prevent runtime errors

By understanding and utilizing type constraints effectively, you can create generic code in Go that is both flexible and robust. Type constraints empower you to write reusable functions and types that work with a variety of data types while maintaining the integrity and correctness of your programs.

Generic Functions

Generic functions in Go enable you to write reusable code that can operate on a variety of data types, enhancing the flexibility and efficiency of your programs. By using type parameters and constraints, you can create functions that adapt to different input types while maintaining type safety and ensuring correctness. Let's explore some illustrative examples of generic functions in Go.

Finding the Minimum or Maximum Value in a Slice

```
func min[T constraints.Ordered](slice []T) T {
    if len(slice) == 0 {
        var zero T // Return the zero value for the type if the slice is empty
        return zero
    }
    min := slice[0]
    for _, v := range slice {
        if v < min {
            min = v
        }
    }
    return min
}

func max[T constraints.Ordered](slice []T) T {
    // ... similar implementation for finding the maximum
}
```

In these examples:

- The min and max functions use a type parameter T with the constraints.Ordered constraint, ensuring that the < (or >) operator is valid for the type.
- This allows you to find the minimum or maximum value in a slice of any ordered type, such as int, float64, or even custom types that implement the constraints.Ordered interface.

Reversing a Slice

```
func reverse[T any](slice []T) {
    for i, j := 0, len(slice)-1; i < j; i, j = i+1, j-1 {
        slice[i], slice[j] = slice[j], slice[i]
    }
}
```

- The reverse function uses the any constraint, allowing it to work with slices of any type
- It reverses the elements of the slice in place

Filtering Elements

```
func filter[T any](slice []T, predicate func(T) bool) []T {
    var result []T
    for _, v := range slice {
        if predicate(v) {
            result = append(result, v)
        }
    }
    return result
}
```

- The `filter` function takes a slice of any type T and a `predicate` function that determines whether an element should be included in the filtered result
- It returns a new slice containing only the elements that satisfy the predicate

Key Points

- Generic functions use type parameters and constraints to operate on values of different types
- Type constraints ensure type safety and enable specific operations within the generic code
- Common use cases include operations on slices, data structures, and algorithms

By mastering the art of writing generic functions, you can create reusable and adaptable code that works seamlessly with various data types, promoting efficiency and maintainability in your Go projects.

Generic Types

Generic types in Go empower you to create reusable and adaptable data structures and interfaces that can work seamlessly with values of different types while preserving the crucial aspect of type safety. This ability to parameterize types with type parameters and constraints opens doors to building more flexible and expressive code, eliminating the need for repetitive type-specific implementations.

Defining Generic Types

You define generic types in Go, just like generic functions, by including type parameters within square brackets [ ] after the type name. You can also specify type constraints to restrict the types that can be used as arguments for these type parameters.

Syntax for Generic Structs:

```go
type MyGenericStruct[T any] struct {
    field1 T
    field2 []T
    // ... other fields
}
```

Syntax for Generic Interfaces:

```go
type MyGenericInterface[T any] interface {
    method1(param T)
    method2() T
    // ... other method signatures
}
```

Examples of Generic Types

Let's explore a few examples of how you can leverage generics to create reusable data structures in Go.

1. Stack

```go
type Stack[T any] struct {
    items []T
}

func (s *Stack[T]) Push(item T) {
    s.items = append(s.items, item)
}

func (s *Stack[T]) Pop() (T, bool) {
```

```
    if len(s.items) == 0 {
        var zero T
        return zero, false
    }
    top := s.items[len(s.items)-1]
    s.items = s.items[:len(s.items)-1]
    return top, true
}
```

In this example, we define a generic `Stack` struct that can hold elements of any type T. The `Push` and `Pop` methods provide the core stack operations, allowing you to push and pop elements of type T.

2. Queue

```
type Queue[T any] struct {
    items []T
}

func (q *Queue[T]) Enqueue(item T) {
    q.items = append(q.items, item)
}

func (q *Queue[T]) Dequeue() (T, bool) {
    if len(q.items) == 0 {
        var zero T
        return zero, false
    }
    front := q.items[0]
    q.items = q.items[1:]
    return front, true
}
```

Similarly, we define a generic `Queue` struct that can hold elements of any type T. The `Enqueue` and `Dequeue` methods implement the core queue operations.

3. Linked List

```
type Node[T any] struct {
    Value T
    Next  *Node[T]
}

type LinkedList[T any] struct {
    Head *Node[T]
}

// ... methods for inserting, deleting, and traversing the linked list
```

This example demonstrates a generic `LinkedList` implementation, where each node stores a value of type T and a pointer to the next node.

Key Points

- Generic types allow you to create reusable data structures and interfaces that work with different types.
- Use type parameters and constraints to define generic structs and interfaces.
- Generic types maintain type safety, preventing you from mixing incompatible types.
- Common use cases include stacks, queues, linked lists, and other data structures.

By mastering generic types, you can write more adaptable and reusable code in Go, reducing duplication and improving the overall maintainability of your projects. Remember to choose appropriate type constraints to ensure type safety and enable specific operations within your generic code.

The `constraints` Package

While you can define your own custom constraints using interfaces, Go's standard library offers a helping hand through the `constraints` package. This package provides a collection of predefined type constraints that you can readily use in your generic code, saving you the effort of defining your own interfaces for common scenarios.

Commonly Used Constraints

Let's explore some of the most frequently used constraints from the `constraints` package:

1. `Ordered`
   - **Purpose:** This constraint represents any ordered type, meaning types that can be compared using the <, >, <=, and >= operators.
   - **Applicable Types:** Numeric types (integers, floats), strings, and any custom types that implement the `comparable` interface with the < operator.
   - **Use Cases:** Sorting algorithms, finding minimum/maximum values, and other operations that rely on ordering.
2. `Comparable`
   - **Purpose:** This constraint represents any comparable type, meaning types that can be compared using the == and != operators.
   - **Applicable Types:** Basic types (integers, floats, strings, booleans), pointers, channels, interfaces, arrays of comparable types, structs with comparable fields, and any custom types that implement the `comparable` interface with the == operator
   - **Use Cases:** Searching for specific values, checking for duplicates, and other operations that involve equality comparisons
3. `Number`
   - **Purpose:** This constraint represents any numeric type, including integers, floats, and complex numbers
   - **Applicable Types:** All built-in numeric types (`int`, `int8`, `int16`, ..., `float32`, `float64`, `complex64`, `complex128`)
   - **Use Cases:** Mathematical operations, numerical algorithms, and any calculations involving numbers

Example Usage:

```
func findMax[T constraints.Ordered](slice []T) T {
    // ... (implementation to find the maximum value)
}

func contains[T comparable](slice []T, value T) bool {
    // ... (implementation to check if the slice contains the value)
}

func calculateAverage[T constraints.Number](numbers []T) T {
    // ... (implementation to calculate the average)
}
```

Benefits of the `constraints` Package:

- **Readability:** Predefined constraints enhance code readability by providing clear and concise ways to express type restrictions
- **Convenience:** You don't have to define custom interfaces for common constraints
- **Standardization:** Using predefined constraints promotes consistency and familiarity across different Go projects

Key Points

- The `constraints` package provides a collection of predefined type constraints
- Commonly used constraints include `Ordered`, `Comparable`, and `Number`
- Use constraints to restrict type arguments and enable specific operations within generic code

By leveraging the `constraints` package, you can write generic code in Go that is both expressive and type-safe. These predefined constraints simplify the process of defining type restrictions and enhance the clarity and maintainability of your generic functions and types.

Common Use Cases for Generics

Generics in Go shine brightly in scenarios where code reusability and type safety are paramount. Let's explore some common use cases where generics can significantly enhance your Go programs.

1. Data Structures: Building Blocks of Flexibility

- **Reusable Containers:** Generics empower you to create data structures like stacks, queues, linked lists, and trees that can seamlessly handle elements of various data types. This eliminates the need to write separate implementations for each type, leading to a more concise and maintainable codebase.
- **Type Safety:** With generics, you can enforce type safety at compile time, ensuring that your data structures only accept and operate on values of the specified types. This prevents runtime errors and enhances the robustness of your code.

2. Algorithms: The Power of Abstraction

- **Generic Algorithms:** Generics enable you to implement generic algorithms, such as sorting, searching, and filtering, that can operate on slices or other collections of different data types. This promotes code reusability and eliminates the need to write specialized algorithms for each type.
- **Type-Safe Operations:** By using type constraints, you can ensure that the operations performed within your generic algorithms are valid for the provided types, guaranteeing type safety and preventing unexpected behavior.

3. Utility Functions: Streamlining Common Tasks

- **Reusable Helpers:** Generics allow you to create utility functions that perform common operations on different data types. This reduces code duplication and makes your codebase more concise and maintainable.
- **Type-Agnostic Operations:** Generic utility functions can operate on values of any type that satisfies the specified constraints, providing a versatile toolset for handling various data manipulation tasks.

Illustrative Examples:

- **Generic Data Structure: Stack**

    ```go
    type Stack[T any] struct {
        items []T
    ```

```
}

func (s *Stack[T]) Push(item T) {
    s.items = append(s.items, item)
}

func (s *Stack[T]) Pop() (T, bool) {
    // ... (implementation)
}
```

- **Generic Algorithm: Find Maximum**

```
func findMax[T constraints.Ordered](slice []T) T {
    // ... (implementation)
}
```

- **Generic Utility Function: Reverse**

```
func reverse[T any](s []T) {
    // ... (implementation)
}
```

Key Takeaways:

- Generics excel in scenarios where code reusability and type safety are important.
- They allow you to create reusable data structures, algorithms, and utility functions that work with various data types.
- Type constraints ensure type safety and enable specific operations within generic code.

By embracing generics in your Go projects, you can write more adaptable, efficient, and maintainable code. They empower you to create reusable components that work seamlessly with different data types, promoting code clarity and reducing the need for repetitive implementations. As you continue to explore Go's capabilities, consider leveraging generics whenever you encounter opportunities for code reusability and type safety.

Best Practices with Generics

While generics offer a powerful tool for code reusability and type safety in Go, their effective usage requires careful consideration and adherence to best practices. Let's explore some guidelines to help you harness the full potential of generics while maintaining code clarity, efficiency, and robustness.

1. Clarity and Readability

- **Descriptive Names:** Choose meaningful and descriptive names for your type parameters and constraints. Avoid single-letter names or cryptic abbreviations that might obscure the purpose or intent of the generic code.
- **Comments and Documentation:** Use comments and Godoc-style documentation to explain the purpose of your generic functions or types, the role of type parameters, and any specific constraints or assumptions.
- **Clear Error Messages:** When type constraints are not satisfied, provide clear and informative error messages that guide users on how to use your generic code correctly.

2. Minimal Constraints

- **Balance Flexibility and Safety:** Strive to use the least restrictive constraints necessary to achieve the desired functionality while maintaining type safety. Overly restrictive constraints can limit the reusability of your generic code.

- **Interface Constraints:** When possible, prefer interface constraints over concrete type constraints. This allows for greater flexibility, as any type that implements the interface can be used as a type argument.
- **Avoid any When Possible:** While the any constraint offers maximum flexibility, it also limits the operations you can perform within the generic code. Use more specific constraints whenever possible to enable type-specific operations and improve code clarity.

3. Testing: The Cornerstone of Confidence

- **Thorough Testing:** Generic code, by its nature, is designed to work with multiple types. Therefore, it's crucial to test your generic functions and types with a variety of type arguments to ensure their correctness and robustness.
- **Edge Cases:** Pay special attention to edge cases, such as empty slices, zero values, or boundary conditions, to ensure that your generic code handles them gracefully.
- **Table-Driven Tests:** Consider using table-driven tests to systematically test your generic code with different type combinations and input values.

Key Takeaways

- Choose descriptive names for type parameters and constraints.
- Use the least restrictive constraints necessary while maintaining type safety
- Thoroughly test your generic code with different type arguments

By adhering to these best practices, you can write generic code in Go that is not only reusable and type-safe but also clear, maintainable, and reliable. Remember, generics are a powerful tool, but their effective usage requires thoughtful design and thorough testing. With practice and experience, you'll develop the intuition and skills to leverage generics to their full potential and create elegant and efficient Go programs.

Chapter Summary

In this chapter, we embarked on a journey to explore the world of generics in Go, a powerful feature that empowers you to write reusable and type-safe code. We covered the following key concepts:

- **The Need for Generics:** We discussed the importance of code reusability and the challenges of achieving it in Go without generics, highlighting the issues of code duplication and the limitations of the empty interface.
- **Understanding Generics:** We introduced generics as a way to write functions and types that operate on values of different types in a type-safe manner, explaining the core concepts of type parameters and type constraints.
- **Type Parameters:** We described the syntax for declaring type parameters and how they act as placeholders for concrete types when the generic function or type is instantiated.
- **Type Constraints:** We explored how type constraints restrict the types that can be used as type arguments, ensuring type safety and enabling specific operations within generic code. We discussed the any constraint and how to define custom constraints using interfaces.
- **Generic Functions:** We demonstrated how to define generic functions with type parameters and constraints, providing examples of generic functions for common operations like finding the minimum or maximum value in a slice, reversing a slice, or filtering elements.
- **Generic Types:** We explained how to define generic types (structs, interfaces) with type parameters and constraints, showcasing examples of generic data structures like stacks, queues, and linked lists.
- **The constraints Package**: We introduced the constraints package, which provides predefined type constraints for common scenarios, enhancing code readability and convenience.

- **Common Use Cases:** We discussed typical scenarios where generics are beneficial, including building reusable data structures, implementing generic algorithms, and writing generic utility functions
- **Best Practices:** We offered guidance on best practices for using generics effectively, emphasizing clarity, minimal constraints, and thorough testing

By mastering generics in Go, you've added a valuable tool to your programming arsenal. Generics enable you to write more reusable, adaptable, and type-safe code, leading to cleaner, more maintainable, and more efficient Go programs. As you continue to explore Go's capabilities, embrace the power of generics to create elegant and versatile solutions for a wide range of programming challenges.

In the next chapter, we will shift our focus to testing and benchmarking in Go. You will learn how to write unit tests, table-driven tests, and benchmarks to ensure the correctness, reliability, and performance of your Go code. Get ready to elevate the quality and robustness of your Go projects through effective testing and benchmarking practices.

Testing and Benchmarking in Go

Outline

- The Importance of Testing
- The `testing` Package
- Writing and Running Tests
- Table-Driven Tests
- Testing with Test Doubles (Mocks and Stubs)
- Benchmarking with the `testing` Package
- Profiling and Optimization
- Test Coverage
- Chapter Summary

The Importance of Testing

In the intricate world of software development, where even the most meticulous code can harbor hidden flaws, testing emerges as the vigilant sentinel that guards against bugs, regressions, and unexpected behavior. It's not merely a formality or an optional step; it's a cornerstone of building robust and reliable software that instills confidence in its correctness and functionality.

The Guardian Against Bugs

- **Early Detection:** Tests act as an early warning system, catching bugs and errors during development, when they are easier and less expensive to fix. By systematically exercising your code with various inputs and scenarios, tests expose hidden flaws and inconsistencies, allowing you to address them before they impact users or cause system failures.
- **Regression Prevention:** As your codebase evolves and new features are added, tests act as a safety net, preventing regressions – the unintentional reintroduction of previously fixed bugs. By running your tests after every change, you can quickly identify if any modifications have inadvertently broken existing functionality.
- **Confidence and Peace of Mind:** A comprehensive suite of tests provides a sense of confidence in the correctness of your code. Knowing that your code has been thoroughly exercised and validated through tests gives you the peace of mind to deploy it to production or share it with others.

Go's Built-in Testing Support

Go's creators recognized the importance of testing from the outset, and the language comes with built-in support for testing and benchmarking. The `testing` package in the standard library provides the essential tools and conventions for writing and running tests in a structured and efficient manner.

Key Benefits

- **Simplicity:** Go's testing framework is designed for simplicity and ease of use. You can write tests using plain Go code, leveraging the familiar syntax and constructs of the language.
- **Integration:** The `testing` package seamlessly integrates with the Go toolchain, making it easy to run tests from the command line using the `go test` command
- **Flexibility:** Go's testing framework supports various types of tests, including unit tests, table-driven tests, and benchmarks, allowing you to tailor your testing approach to the specific needs of your project.

In Essence

Testing is not just about finding bugs; it's about building confidence in your code, ensuring its correctness, preventing regressions, and facilitating collaboration and maintainability. Go's built-in testing support and the `testing` package make it easy to incorporate testing into your development workflow, leading to more robust, reliable, and ultimately successful software projects.

In the following sections, we'll delve deeper into the specifics of writing and running tests in Go, exploring the `testing` package's functionalities, best practices, and advanced testing techniques. Get ready to embrace the power of testing and elevate the quality of your Go code!

The `testing` Package

At the heart of Go's testing ecosystem resides the `testing` package, a cornerstone that provides the essential tools and conventions for writing and running tests in a structured and effective manner. This package empowers you to systematically verify the correctness of your code, catch bugs early, and ensure that your programs behave as expected.

Core Components

1. **The `testing.T` Type:**
   - **Test Instance**: The `testing.T` type represents a single test instance. It acts as a central hub for managing the execution of your test code and provides methods for reporting test failures, logging messages, and controlling the test's behavior
   - **Key Methods:**
     - `t.Error(args ...any)`: Reports a test failure with the provided arguments.
     - `t.Errorf(format string, args ...any)`: Reports a formatted test failure.
     - `t.Fail()`: Marks the test as failed but continues execution
     - `t.Fatal(args ...any)`: Reports a test failure and immediately stops the test's execution.
     - `t.Log(args ...any)`: Logs messages during the test execution.
     - `t.Skip(args ...any)`: Skips the current test, providing a reason for skipping
2. **Test Functions:**
   - **Naming Convention:** Test functions are regular Go functions that adhere to a specific naming convention. They must start with the prefix `Test` followed by a descriptive name that starts with a capital letter (e.g., `TestAdd`, `TestIsValid`).
   - **Parameter:** Each test function takes a single parameter of type `*testing.T`, which provides access to the test instance and its methods for reporting failures and logging.
   - **Test Logic:** The body of a test function contains the actual test logic. This typically involves setting up test data, calling the function or method under test, and using assertions to verify that the output or behavior matches the expected results.
3. **The `go test` Command**
   - **Command-Line Execution:** The `go test` command is the command-line tool you use to run your tests. It automatically discovers and executes all test functions within a package or a set of packages
   - **Common Usage:**
     - `go test`: Runs tests for the current package
     - `go test ./mypackage`: Runs tests for the specified package
     - `go test ./...`: Runs tests for all packages in the current directory and its subdirectories
   - **Useful Flags:**

- `-v`: Enables verbose output, showing details about each test case.
- `-run <pattern>`: Runs only tests whose names match the specified pattern
- `-cover`: Generates a test coverage report, showing which parts of your code are exercised by the tests.

Key Takeaways

- The `testing` package provides the core framework for testing in Go
- The `testing.T` type represents a test instance and offers methods for reporting failures and logging
- Test functions are named with the prefix `Test` and contain the test logic
- The `go test` command is used to run tests from the command line

By understanding these core components, you're ready to start writing and running tests in Go.

Writing and Running Tests

Writing Test Functions

In Go, test functions are the heart of your test suite, encapsulating the logic to verify the behavior of your code. They follow a specific naming convention and structure, allowing the `go test` command to automatically discover and execute them.

Conventions for Test Functions

1. **Name:** Test functions must start with the prefix `Test` followed by a descriptive name that starts with a capital letter. This naming convention is crucial for the `go test` command to recognize them as test functions.
   - Examples: `TestAdd`, `TestIsValid`, `TestCalculateAverage`
2. **Parameter:** Each test function takes a single parameter of type `*testing.T`. This parameter provides access to the test instance and its methods for reporting test failures, logging messages, and controlling the test's behavior.
3. **Body:** The function body contains the actual test logic. This typically involves:
   - **Setting Up Test Data:** Preparing the necessary input data or test fixtures for the function or method you're testing.
   - **Calling the Code Under Test:** Invoking the function or method you want to test, passing the prepared test data.
   - **Assertions:** Using assertions to verify that the output or behavior of the code under test matches the expected results. Go's `testing` package provides methods like `t.Error` and `t.Errorf` for reporting test failures.

Examples of Simple Test Functions

```
func TestAdd(t *testing.T) {
    result := add(2, 3)
    expected := 5
    if result != expected {
        t.Errorf("Expected %d, but got %d", expected, result)
    }
}

func TestIsValidEmail(t *testing.T) {
    email := "test@example.com"
    if !isValidEmail(email) {
```

```
        t.Error("Expected email to be valid, but it was not")
    }

    invalidEmail := "invalid-email"
    if isValidEmail(invalidEmail) {
        t.Error("Expected email to be invalid, but it was valid")
    }
}
```

In these examples:

- The `TestAdd` function tests the `add` function, comparing its output to the expected result and reporting an error if they don't match
- The `TestIsValidEmail` function tests the `isValidEmail` function with both valid and invalid email addresses, using `t.Error` to report failures.

Key Points

- Test functions must start with the prefix `Test` and a descriptive name
- They take a `*testing.T` parameter for reporting failures and logging
- The function body contains the test logic, including assertions to verify expected behavior
- Use `t.Error` or `t.Errorf` to report test failures

By adhering to these conventions and incorporating assertions into your test functions, you can create a robust test suite that helps ensure the correctness and reliability of your Go code.

Running Tests

Once you've crafted your test functions, it's time to unleash the power of the `go test` command to execute your test suite and verify the correctness of your code. This command, seamlessly integrated into the Go toolchain, automates the process of discovering and running test functions, providing valuable feedback about the behavior of your program.

Executing Tests

1. **Navigate to the Package Directory:** Open your terminal and use the `cd` command to navigate to the directory containing the package you want to test.
2. **Run go test:** Execute the `go test` command without any arguments to run all test functions within the current package.

    ```
    go test
    ```

    - Go will automatically scan the package for functions that start with the `Test` prefix and execute them as test cases.
    - The output will indicate whether each test passed or failed, along with any error messages or log output generated by the tests.
3. **Testing Specific Packages:** You can specify the package path to run tests for a particular package within your project.

    ```
    go test ./mypackage
    ```

4. **Testing All Packages:** To run tests for all packages in the current directory and its subdirectories, use the ./... pattern.

    ```
    go test ./...
    ```

This is useful for running tests across your entire project.

Useful Flags

The go test command offers several flags to customize test execution

- **-v (Verbose Output):** This flag provides more detailed output, including information about each test case and any log messages generated during the test run.

    ```
    go test -v
    ```

- **-run <pattern> (Run Specific Tests):** This flag allows you to run only the tests whose names match the specified pattern.

    ```
    go test -run TestAdd
    ```

- **-cover (Test Coverage):** This flag generates a test coverage report, indicating which parts of your code are exercised by the tests. It's a valuable tool for assessing the thoroughness of your test suite.

    ```
    go test -cover
    ```

- **Other Flags:** The go test command has many other flags for customizing test execution. You can explore them using go help test.

Key Takeaways

- Use the go test command to run tests within a package
- Specify package paths to run tests for specific packages or use ./... to test all packages
- The -v flag provides verbose output
- The -run flag allows you to run specific tests
- The -cover flag generates a test coverage report

By mastering the go test command and its flags, you can efficiently execute your test suite, gain valuable insights into the behavior of your code, and ensure the correctness and reliability of your Go programs.

Table-Driven Tests

When you need to test a function or method with multiple input values and their corresponding expected outputs, table-driven tests in Go offer a structured and maintainable approach. They involve defining a table (often a slice of structs) that holds test cases, each containing input data and the expected result. You then iterate over this table, executing each test case and verifying that the actual output matches the expected output.

Benefits of Table-Driven Tests

- **Organization and Clarity**: Table-driven tests organize your test cases in a clear and concise table format, making it easier to understand the different scenarios being tested and their expected outcomes
- **Maintainability**: Adding or modifying test cases is straightforward, as you simply add or update rows in the table
- **Readability**: The table structure enhances the readability of your tests, making it easier to grasp the test inputs and expected outputs at a glance

- **Reusability**: You can reuse the same table-driven test structure for different functions or methods, promoting code reusability

Structure of a Table-Driven Test

1. **Test Table**: Define a slice of structs (or other suitable data structure) to represent your test table. Each struct typically contains fields for the input data and the expected output
2. `for-range` **Loop**: Use a `for-range` loop to iterate over the test table
3. **Execute Test Case**: Within the loop, extract the input data and expected output from the current test case
4. **Call the Function Under Test**: Call the function or method you're testing, passing the input data.
5. **Assertion**: Compare the actual output from the function with the expected output using an assertion. If they don't match, report a test failure using `t.Errorf`.

Example: Testing a `fibonacci` Function

```
func TestFibonacci(t *testing.T) {
    testCases := []struct {
        input    int
        expected int
    }{
        {0, 0},
        {1, 1},
        {2, 1},
        {3, 2},
        {4, 3},
        {5, 5},
        {10, 55},
    }

    for _, tc := range testCases {
        actual := fibonacci(tc.input)
        if actual != tc.expected {
            t.Errorf("For input %d, expected %d but got %d", tc.input, tc.expected, actual)
        }
    }
}
```

In this example:

- We define a `testCases` slice of structs, each containing an `input` value and the `expected` Fibonacci number
- We iterate over the `testCases` using a `for-range` loop
- For each test case, we call the `fibonacci` function, compare the `actual` result with the `expected` value, and report an error if they don't match

Key Takeaways

- Table-driven tests provide a structured and maintainable way to organize and execute multiple test cases
- They involve defining a table of test cases and iterating over it to execute each case
- They improve code clarity, readability, and reusability

By adopting table-driven tests in your Go testing practices, you can create more organized, maintainable, and expressive test suites that thoroughly exercise your code and contribute to the overall robustness and reliability of your applications

Testing with Test Doubles (Mocks and Stubs)

In the pursuit of effective testing, the concept of test doubles emerges as a valuable ally. Test doubles, which include mocks and stubs, are objects or functions that simulate the behavior of real dependencies within your code. They allow you to isolate the code under test from its external interactions, enabling focused and controlled testing.

Isolation and Control

Imagine you're testing a function that interacts with a database. Relying on the actual database during testing can introduce complexities and dependencies, such as the need for a live database connection, potential data modifications, and the impact of network latency. Test doubles provide a way to bypass these dependencies by simulating the database's behavior, giving you precise control over the interactions and responses during your tests.

Mocks and Stubs

- **Mocks:** Mocks are objects that mimic the behavior of real objects, allowing you to set expectations about how they should be called and what responses they should provide. They are useful for verifying that your code interacts with its dependencies correctly.
- **Stubs:** Stubs are simpler versions of real objects that provide canned responses or perform minimal actions. They are helpful when you need to provide a basic implementation of a dependency without its full complexity.

Benefits of Test Doubles

- **Isolation:** Test doubles isolate the code under test from its external dependencies, allowing you to focus on testing its internal logic and behavior.
- **Control:** You have complete control over the behavior of test doubles, allowing you to simulate various scenarios, including error conditions, edge cases, and success paths.
- **Speed:** Test doubles often execute faster than real dependencies, leading to faster test execution times.
- **Determinism:** Test doubles provide consistent and predictable behavior, making your tests more reliable and repeatable.

Encouragement to Explore Mocking Frameworks

While Go's standard library doesn't include built-in mocking capabilities, there are numerous third-party mocking frameworks available that can simplify the creation and management of mocks and stubs. These frameworks offer features like automatic mock generation, expectation setting, and verification, making your tests even more powerful and expressive.

Key Points

- Test doubles (mocks and stubs) simulate the behavior of real dependencies during testing
- They isolate the code under test, provide control over interactions, and improve test speed and determinism
- Explore third-party mocking frameworks for advanced mocking capabilities

By incorporating test doubles into your testing strategy, you can create more focused, reliable, and maintainable tests that thoroughly exercise your Go code and ensure its correctness.

Benchmarking with the `testing` Package

In the realm of performance optimization, where speed and efficiency reign supreme, benchmarking emerges as a crucial tool for measuring and analyzing the performance of your Go code. It empowers you to identify bottlenecks, compare different implementations, and make informed decisions about optimizations. Go's `testing` package provides built-in support for benchmarking, making it easy to measure the execution time and other performance metrics of your functions and algorithms.

The Power of Benchmarking

- **Performance Measurement:** Benchmarking allows you to quantitatively measure how long it takes for your code to execute under various conditions. This data can help you identify areas where your code might be slow or inefficient.
- **Comparison and Optimization:** By comparing the benchmarks of different implementations or algorithms, you can identify which one performs better and make informed decisions about optimizations.
- **Regression Testing:** Benchmarking can be incorporated into your test suite to ensure that performance doesn't regress as your codebase evolves.

Benchmark Functions

Benchmark functions in Go are special functions that adhere to a specific naming convention and structure, allowing the `go test` command to recognize and execute them as benchmarks.

- **Naming Convention:** Benchmark functions must start with the prefix Benchmark followed by a descriptive name that starts with a capital letter (e.g., BenchmarkSort, BenchmarkFibonacci).
- **Parameter:** Each benchmark function takes a single parameter of type *testing.B. This parameter provides control over the benchmarking process and access to methods for measuring performance.
- **The b.N Field:** The b.N field within the *testing.B parameter represents the number of iterations the benchmark should run. The testing package automatically adjusts this value to achieve a statistically significant measurement.
- **Benchmark Logic:** The body of a benchmark function contains the code you want to benchmark. This typically involves setting up any necessary data or context and then repeatedly executing the code under test within a loop that runs b.N times.

Example: Benchmarking String Concatenation

```go
func BenchmarkStringConcat(b *testing.B) {
    var s string
    for i := 0; i < b.N; i++ {
        s += "hello"
    }
}
```

In this example:

- The BenchmarkStringConcat function benchmarks the performance of string concatenation using the + operator
- It repeatedly appends the string "hello" to the s variable within a loop that runs b.N times.
- The testing package measures the total time taken to execute the loop and reports the average time per operation.

Running Benchmarks

To run benchmarks within a package, use the `go test` command with the -bench flag

```
go test -bench=.
```

- The `.` in the `-bench` flag indicates that you want to run all benchmark functions in the current package.
- You can also specify a pattern to run specific benchmarks (e.g., `-bench=BenchmarkStringConcat`).

Key Takeaways

- Benchmarking helps measure the performance of your code
- Benchmark functions are named with the prefix Benchmark and take a `*testing.B` parameter.
- Use the `b.N` field to control the number of iterations.
- Run benchmarks using the `go test -bench` command

By incorporating benchmarking into your development process, you can gain valuable insights into the performance characteristics of your Go code. This enables you to identify bottlenecks, compare different implementations, and make informed decisions about optimizations, leading to faster and more efficient Go programs.

Profiling and Optimization

While benchmarking provides a quantitative measure of your code's performance, profiling delves deeper, offering insights into the specific parts of your code that consume the most time or resources. It helps you pinpoint performance bottlenecks, allowing you to focus your optimization efforts on the areas that matter most.

Profiling: Unveiling the Performance Landscape

- **Identifying Bottlenecks:** Profiling tools like the Go profiler (`go tool pprof`) collect data about your program's execution, including CPU usage, memory allocation, and goroutine behavior. This data can be visualized and analyzed to identify functions or code sections that are consuming a disproportionate amount of resources, revealing potential areas for optimization
- **Targeted Optimization:** By understanding where your program spends most of its time, you can focus your optimization efforts on those specific areas, leading to more efficient and performant code.

The Go Profiler: Your Performance Detective

- `go tool pprof`: The Go profiler is a powerful tool that can be used to collect and analyze profiling data from your running Go programs. It provides various visualization options, such as flame graphs and call graphs, to help you understand the performance characteristics of your code.
- **Profiling Modes**: The Go profiler supports different profiling modes, including CPU profiling (measures CPU time spent in different functions), memory profiling (tracks memory allocations), and block profiling (identifies goroutines that are blocked waiting for synchronization).

Beyond Profiling: Optimization Techniques

While profiling helps you identify performance bottlenecks, optimization techniques are the tools you use to address those bottlenecks and improve the efficiency of your code. Some common optimization techniques in Go include:

- **Algorithm Optimization:** Choose more efficient algorithms or data structures to reduce computational complexity
- **Code Refactoring:** Restructure your code to eliminate unnecessary operations, reduce memory allocations, or improve cache locality

- **Concurrency Optimization:** Fine-tune your goroutine and channel usage to avoid contention and maximize parallelism
- **Low-Level Optimizations:** In performance-critical scenarios, you might consider using low-level techniques like inline assembly or optimizing memory layouts

Key Takeaways

- Profiling is essential for identifying performance bottlenecks in your Go code
- The Go profiler (`go tool pprof`) provides powerful tools for collecting and analyzing profiling data
- Optimization techniques, such as algorithm optimization, code refactoring, and concurrency optimization, can be used to improve performance based on profiling insights.

By incorporating profiling and optimization into your development process, you can create Go programs that are not only functionally correct but also performant and efficient. Remember, optimization should be a data-driven process, guided by profiling insights and careful analysis. As you gain more experience with Go, continue to explore profiling and optimization techniques to push the boundaries of performance and create software that runs smoothly and efficiently.

Test Coverage

In the pursuit of comprehensive testing, where the goal is to ensure that every nook and cranny of your code is thoroughly exercised, **test coverage** emerges as a valuable metric. It quantifies the extent to which your test suite actually executes your code, providing insights into areas that might be lacking sufficient testing. Think of test coverage as a spotlight that illuminates the parts of your code that your tests have touched, revealing any shadowy corners that might harbor lurking bugs.

Measuring Code Execution

Test coverage tools, seamlessly integrated into Go's testing framework, analyze your code and track which statements, branches, and functions are executed during your test runs. This information is then presented in the form of a coverage report, which highlights the percentage of your code that has been covered by your tests.

Using `go test -cover`

Go's `testing` package provides a built-in mechanism for generating test coverage reports. By adding the `-cover` flag to the `go test` command, you instruct Go to instrument your code and collect coverage data during test execution.

```
go test -cover
```

- **Coverage Report**: After running your tests with the `-cover` flag, Go will print a summary of the coverage results to the console, indicating the overall percentage of statements covered by your tests.
- **Detailed Report (Optional):** You can generate a more detailed HTML report using the `-coverprofile` flag, which saves the coverage data to a file that can be visualized in a web browser.

Interpreting Coverage Information

- **Percentage:** The coverage percentage indicates the proportion of your code's statements that were executed during the tests

- **Statements, Branches, Functions**: Coverage reports often break down the coverage information by statements, branches (decision points in your code), and functions, giving you a more granular view of which parts of your code are well-tested and which might need more attention.
- **Visualizations:** The HTML coverage report provides a visual representation of your code, highlighting the lines that were covered (green) and those that were not (red), making it easier to identify areas that need additional testing

Striving for High Test Coverage

While 100% test coverage is not always feasible or necessary, aiming for high coverage is a good practice. High test coverage indicates that a significant portion of your code has been exercised by your tests, increasing your confidence in its correctness and reducing the likelihood of undiscovered bugs.

Key Takeaways

- Test coverage measures how much of your code is executed by your tests
- Use the `go test -cover` flag to generate test coverage reports
- Interpret coverage information to identify areas of your code that need more testing
- Strive for high test coverage to ensure the thoroughness of your test suite

By incorporating test coverage analysis into your Go development workflow, you can gain valuable insights into the effectiveness of your tests and identify areas where additional testing is needed. This proactive approach to testing helps you build more robust and reliable software, minimizing the risk of unexpected bugs and ensuring a smoother user experience. Remember, testing is an investment in the quality and maintainability of your code, and high test coverage is a key indicator of a well-tested and trustworthy codebase.

Chapter Summary

In this chapter, we delved into the crucial practices of testing and benchmarking in Go, equipping you with the tools and techniques to ensure the correctness, reliability, and performance of your code. We covered the following key aspects:

- **The Importance of Testing:** We discussed why testing is fundamental for building robust software, highlighting how tests help catch bugs early, prevent regressions, and instill confidence in your code's behavior.
- **The `testing` Package:** You were introduced to the `testing` package as the core of Go's testing framework, exploring its main components: the `testing.T` type, test functions, and the `go test` command
- **Writing and Running Tests:** We explained the conventions for writing test functions, including their naming, parameters, and structure. You learned how to use assertions to verify expected behavior and how to run tests using the `go test` command with various flags for customization
- **Table-Driven Tests:** You discovered how to organize and execute multiple test cases efficiently using table-driven tests, improving code clarity and maintainability
- **Testing with Test Doubles:** We briefly introduced the concept of test doubles (mocks and stubs) for isolating code under test and simulating dependencies, encouraging you to explore third-party mocking frameworks
- **Benchmarking:** You learned how to measure the performance of your code using benchmark functions and the `testing` package's benchmarking capabilities
- **Profiling and Optimization:** We touched upon the importance of profiling to identify performance bottlenecks and encouraged you to explore profiling tools and optimization techniques to enhance the efficiency of your Go programs
- **Test Coverage:** We discussed test coverage as a metric for measuring how much of your code is exercised by your tests and how to generate coverage reports using the `go test -cover` flag

By embracing testing and benchmarking as integral parts of your Go development workflow, you can significantly elevate the quality and reliability of your software. Tests act as a safety net, catching bugs early, preventing regressions, and providing confidence in your code's behavior. Benchmarking helps you identify performance bottlenecks and make informed decisions about optimizations. Strive for high test coverage to ensure that your test suite thoroughly exercises your code and leaves no room for hidden surprises

In the next chapter, we will explore best practices and optimization tips for Go code, providing guidance on writing clean, efficient, and idiomatic Go programs that are both performant and maintainable.

Best Practices and Optimization Tips for Go Code

Outline

- Writing Clean and Idiomatic Go Code
- Performance Optimization
- Concurrency Optimization
- Tooling and Profiling
- Common Pitfalls and How to Avoid Them
- Chapter Summary

Writing Clean and Idiomatic Go Code

In the world of Go programming, where simplicity and clarity are paramount, writing clean and idiomatic code is not just a matter of aesthetics; it's a fundamental principle that fosters maintainability, collaboration, and long-term project health. By adhering to established conventions and best practices, you can create Go code that is not only functional but also elegant, readable, and a pleasure to work with.

Code Formatting: The `gofmt` Enforcer

Go takes a strong stance on code formatting, enforcing a consistent style across all Go projects through the `gofmt` tool. This tool automatically formats your code according to Go's official style guidelines, eliminating debates about code style and ensuring that all Go code looks uniform and familiar.

- **Benefits of gofmt:**
  - **Consistency**: Enforces a standardized code style, making your code easier to read and navigate, regardless of who wrote it
  - **Readability:** Improves code readability by automatically handling indentation, spacing, and other formatting details
  - **Collaboration:** Eliminates conflicts and debates about code style, allowing developers to focus on the logic and functionality of the code
  - **Automation**: Can be integrated into your editor or IDE to automatically format your code as you type or save

Naming Conventions: The Art of Clarity

Choosing clear and descriptive names for your variables, functions, types, and packages is crucial for code readability and maintainability.

- **Variables and Functions:** Use camelCase for variable and function names (e.g., `myVariable`, `calculateSum`).
- **Types and Packages:** Use PascalCase for type and package names (e.g., `Person`, `MyPackage`).
- **Meaningful Names:** Choose names that accurately reflect the purpose or content of the identifier. Avoid single-letter names or cryptic abbreviations that might obscure the meaning
- **Short but Descriptive:** Strive for concise names that are easy to read and understand, but avoid sacrificing clarity for brevity.

Error Handling: The Graceful Responder

Go's explicit error-handling mechanism encourages you to handle errors proactively and gracefully.

- **Check for Errors:** Always check for errors returned from functions that might fail. Don't assume that everything will always work as expected
- **Informative Error Messages:** Provide clear and descriptive error messages that help users or developers understand the cause of the error and potential solutions
- **Error Wrapping:** Use `fmt.Errorf` to wrap errors with additional context, such as the location in your code where the error occurred or the specific operation that failed.

Comments and Documentation: The Guiding Narrator

Well-written comments and documentation are invaluable for making your code understandable and maintainable.

- **Explain the "Why":** Use comments to explain the reasoning behind your code choices, especially for non-obvious or complex logic
- **Document APIs**: Write clear and concise Godoc comments for your exported functions, types, and packages to provide guidance to other developers who might use your code
- **Keep it Up-to-Date:** Ensure that your comments and documentation remain accurate and reflect any changes in your code

Simplicity and Clarity: The Go Way

Go's philosophy embraces simplicity and clarity. Strive to write code that is:

- **Easy to Read**: Use clear and concise syntax, meaningful names, and proper formatting to make your code easy to read and understand.
- **Straightforward**: Avoid unnecessary complexity or clever tricks that might obfuscate the code's intent
- **Idiomatic**: Follow Go's established conventions and idioms to write code that feels natural and familiar to other Go developers

By adhering to these best practices and embracing Go's philosophy of simplicity, you can create clean, idiomatic code that is not only functional but also a pleasure to work with. Remember, writing good Go code is not just about getting the job done; it's about crafting code that is maintainable, collaborative, and a testament to the elegance and power of the Go language.

Performance Optimization

In the realm of Go programming, where efficiency and speed are often paramount, performance optimization is the art of fine-tuning your code to extract the maximum potential from your hardware. While Go's inherent performance characteristics provide a solid foundation, there's always room for improvement. Let's delve into some techniques and best practices for optimizing the performance of your Go code.

Profiling: Illuminating the Bottlenecks

Before embarking on any optimization journey, it's crucial to identify the areas of your code that are causing performance bottlenecks. Profiling tools, such as the Go profiler (`go tool pprof`), come to the rescue by providing detailed insights into your program's execution, including CPU usage, memory allocations, and goroutine behavior. By analyzing profiling data, you can pinpoint the functions or code sections that consume the most resources, allowing you to focus your optimization efforts on the areas that matter most.

Efficient Algorithms and Data Structures

The choice of algorithms and data structures can significantly impact the performance of your Go programs.

- **Algorithmic Complexity:** Analyze the time and space complexity of your algorithms. Consider alternative algorithms or optimizations that can reduce the computational complexity and improve performance.
- **Suitable Data Structures:** Choose data structures that align with your access patterns and operations. For example, if you need frequent insertions and deletions, a linked list might be more efficient than an array.
- **Standard Library:** Leverage the efficient implementations of data structures and algorithms provided by Go's standard library whenever possible.

Minimizing Allocations

Memory allocations and garbage collection can introduce overhead in Go programs. Minimizing unnecessary allocations can lead to performance gains.

- **Object Pooling:** Reuse objects instead of creating new ones for every operation, especially for frequently used objects.
- **Buffer Reuse:** Reuse buffers for I/O operations or string manipulation to avoid repeated memory allocations.
- **sync.Pool:** Utilize the `sync.Pool` from the `sync` package to manage a pool of reusable temporary objects, reducing allocation overhead.

Avoiding Unnecessary Work

Eliminating redundant computations or unnecessary operations can significantly improve performance.

- **Lazy Evaluation:** Defer computations until their results are actually needed.
- **Caching:** Store the results of expensive computations to avoid recalculating them repeatedly.
- **Loop Optimizations:** Minimize the number of iterations in loops and avoid unnecessary calculations within loops.

Key Takeaways

- Profiling tools like `go tool pprof` help identify performance bottlenecks
- Choose efficient algorithms and data structures
- Minimize memory allocations and garbage collection overhead
- Eliminate redundant computations and unnecessary work

By applying these performance optimization techniques and using profiling tools to guide your efforts, you can create Go programs that are not only functionally correct but also lightning-fast and resource-efficient. Remember, optimization is an iterative process. Continuously measure, analyze, and refine your code to achieve the best possible performance for your Go applications.

Concurrency Optimization

Concurrency, while a powerful tool in Go, can also introduce complexities and potential performance bottlenecks if not managed carefully. Optimizing concurrent programs requires a nuanced understanding of goroutine lifecycles, channel usage, and strategies for minimizing contention on shared resources. Let's explore some key tips for maximizing the efficiency and performance of your concurrent Go code.

Goroutine Management

- **Lifecycle Control with `context.Context`**: Goroutines can run indefinitely, potentially leading to resource leaks if not managed properly. The `context.Context` type provides a mechanism for signaling cancellation or deadlines to goroutines, allowing you to gracefully terminate them when they are no longer needed.
- **Avoid Goroutine Leaks:** Be mindful of goroutines that might get stuck waiting on channels or other synchronization primitives. Ensure that all goroutines have a clear exit path, either by completing their tasks successfully or by responding to cancellation signals.
- **Limit Goroutine Creation**: While goroutines are lightweight, creating an excessive number of them can still lead to overhead. Consider using worker pools or other techniques to manage the number of active goroutines and avoid overloading the system.

Channel Usage

- **Choosing Buffer Sizes:** The choice between unbuffered and buffered channels, and the size of the buffer for buffered channels, can impact performance.
    - **Unbuffered Channels:** Provide strict synchronization but can lead to contention if goroutines are frequently blocked waiting on each other
    - **Buffered Channels:** Offer some decoupling between sender and receiver goroutines, potentially improving throughput but also consuming more memory.
    - **Optimal Buffer Size:** Experiment with different buffer sizes to find the right balance between synchronization and throughput for your specific use case
- **Channel Patterns:** Utilize appropriate channel patterns, such as worker pools, pipelines, or fan-in/fan-out, to structure your concurrent communication and data flow effectively

Avoiding Contention

- **Shared Data Access:** When multiple goroutines access or modify the same shared data, contention can occur, leading to performance degradation.
- **Fine-Grained Locking:** Use mutexes (`sync.Mutex`) strategically to protect critical sections of your code where shared data is accessed or modified. Strive for fine-grained locking, where you lock only the specific data that needs protection, rather than locking large sections of code unnecessarily
- **Lock-Free Data Structures:** In some cases, you might be able to use lock-free data structures or algorithms that avoid the need for explicit locking, potentially improving performance in highly concurrent scenarios
- **Atomic Operations:** For simple operations on shared variables, consider using atomic operations from the `sync/atomic` package. These operations provide low-level synchronization without the need for explicit locks

Key Takeaways

- Manage goroutine lifecycles effectively using `context.Context` and avoid goroutine leaks
- Choose appropriate channel buffer sizes and patterns to optimize communication and synchronization
- Minimize contention on shared resources using techniques like fine-grained locking, lock-free data structures, or atomic operations

By applying these concurrency optimization tips and understanding the trade-offs involved in different approaches, you can fine-tune your Go programs to achieve optimal performance, scalability, and reliability in concurrent environments. Remember that concurrency optimization is an iterative process. Continuously measure, analyze, and refine your code to ensure that your goroutines work together harmoniously and efficiently.

Tooling and Profiling

The Go ecosystem boasts a rich collection of tools that streamline development, testing, and performance analysis. These tools, both built-in and from the community, empower you to write better code, catch errors early, and optimize your programs for peak performance. Let's explore some essential tools that every Go developer should have in their arsenal.

Go Tools: Your Everyday Companions

Go comes with a powerful set of command-line tools that are indispensable for building, testing, and documenting your projects.

- `go build`: Compiles your Go source code into executable binaries.
- `go run`: Compiles and runs your Go program directly, without creating a separate executable.
- `go test`: Automates the execution of your test functions, ensuring the correctness of your code
- `go get`: Downloads and installs Go packages from remote repositories, handling dependencies seamlessly.
- `go doc`: Provides access to Go's extensive documentation from the command line, allowing you to explore packages, types, and functions.

Linters: Your Code Style Guardians

Linters, like `golangci-lint`, are static analysis tools that scan your code for potential issues, style inconsistencies, and adherence to best practices. They act as vigilant guardians, helping you catch errors early, enforce a consistent code style, and promote code quality.

- **Benefits of Linters:**
    - **Error Detection**: Linters can identify potential bugs, unused variables, inefficient code patterns, and other issues that might slip through the cracks during development.
    - **Code Style Enforcement**: They help maintain a consistent code style across your project, making your code more readable and easier to collaborate on
    - **Best Practices**: Linters can guide you towards adopting Go's recommended best practices, leading to cleaner and more idiomatic code.

Profilers: Performance Detectives

Profilers, such as the Go profiler (`go tool pprof`), provide deep insights into the performance characteristics of your running Go programs. They collect data about CPU usage, memory allocation, blocking operations, and other metrics, allowing you to visualize and analyze performance bottlenecks and identify areas for optimization

- **Benefits of Profilers**
    - **Performance Bottleneck Identification**: Profilers pinpoint the functions or code sections that consume the most time or resources, guiding your optimization efforts
    - **Performance Visualization:** They provide visual representations like flame graphs and call graphs, making it easier to understand the performance landscape of your code
- **Other Profilers:** In addition to the built-in Go profiler, various third-party profiling tools and visualization libraries are available to further enhance your performance analysis capabilities

Key Takeaways

- Go's built-in tools streamline development, testing, and documentation.
- Linters like `golangci-lint` enforce code style and catch potential issues

- Profilers like go `tool pprof` help you analyze performance and identify optimization opportunities

By incorporating these tools into your Go development workflow, you can write cleaner, more efficient, and more reliable code. Linters help you maintain code quality and consistency, while profilers guide your optimization efforts, ensuring that your Go programs perform at their best. Remember, these tools are your allies in the pursuit of Go programming mastery. Leverage them effectively to enhance your productivity, improve the quality of your code, and build high-performance applications that meet the demands of the modern software landscape.

Common Pitfalls and How to Avoid Them

As you embark on your Go programming journey, it's essential to be aware of common pitfalls that can trip up even experienced developers. By recognizing these potential stumbling blocks and adopting preventive measures, you can write cleaner, safer, and more efficient Go code.

1. Nil Pointer Dereferences: The Silent Crash

- **The Pitfall**: Attempting to dereference a `nil` pointer (i.e., access the value it points to) will trigger a runtime panic, causing your program to crash abruptly.
- **The Solution:** Always check if a pointer is `nil` before dereferencing it using an `if` statement.

    ```go
    if ptr != nil {
        // Safe to dereference the pointer
        fmt.Println(*ptr)
    }
    ```

2. Unclosed Resources: The Leaky Faucet

- **The Pitfall:** Forgetting to close resources like files, network connections, or database handles can lead to resource leaks, where your program consumes system resources unnecessarily, potentially impacting performance and stability.
- **The Solution**: Use the `defer` statement to schedule resource cleanup at the end of a function, ensuring that resources are always closed, even if an error occurs or the function panics.

    ```go
    file, err := os.Open("data.txt")
    if err != nil {
        // Handle the error
    }
    defer file.Close() // Ensures the file is closed when the function exits
    ```

3. Race Conditions: The Concurrency Conundrum

- **The Pitfall:** In concurrent programs, multiple goroutines might attempt to access or modify the same shared data simultaneously, leading to race conditions and unpredictable behavior.
- **The Solution**: Use synchronization mechanisms like channels, mutexes, or atomic operations to protect shared data and ensure that only one goroutine can access it at a time.

    ```go
    var mutex sync.Mutex
    var data int

    func increment() {
        mutex.Lock()
        data++
        mutex.Unlock()
    }
    ```

4. Inefficient String Concatenation: The Performance Bottleneck

- **The Pitfall:** Repeatedly concatenating strings using the + operator can lead to performance issues, as it creates new string objects with each concatenation
- **The Solution:** Use the `strings.Builder` type for efficient string concatenation. It provides a mutable buffer that allows you to append strings without creating new objects on each operation.

```
var sb strings.Builder
for i := 0; i < 1000; i++ {
    sb.WriteString("hello")
}
result := sb.String()
```

5. Ignoring Errors: The Silent Troublemaker

- **The Pitfall**: Ignoring errors returned from functions can lead to unexpected behavior, data corruption, or even security vulnerabilities
- **The Solution**: Always check for errors after calling functions that might return them. Handle errors appropriately by logging them, returning them to the caller, or taking corrective actions based on the specific error.

By being mindful of these common pitfalls and adopting the suggested solutions, you can write Go code that is not only functional but also robust, efficient, and maintainable. Remember, writing good Go code involves not just getting the job done but also anticipating potential issues and handling them gracefully, ensuring a smooth and reliable experience for your users and fellow developers.

Chapter Summary

In this chapter, we delved into the realm of best practices and optimization techniques, empowering you to write Go code that is not only functional but also clean, efficient, and idiomatic. We covered a range of topics aimed at elevating the quality and performance of your Go programs:

- **Writing Clean and Idiomatic Go Code:** We emphasized the importance of code formatting, naming conventions, error handling, comments, and documentation, and encouraged you to embrace simplicity and clarity in your Go code.
- **Performance Optimization:** We explored techniques for optimizing performance, such as profiling to identify bottlenecks, choosing efficient algorithms and data structures, minimizing memory allocations, and avoiding unnecessary work.
- **Concurrency Optimization:** We provided tips for optimizing concurrent Go programs, including managing goroutine lifecycles, choosing appropriate channel patterns, and minimizing contention on shared resources.
- **Tooling and Profiling:** We highlighted the value of using Go's built-in tools and external tools for development, testing, and profiling, empowering you to streamline your workflow, catch errors early, and analyze performance.
- **Common Pitfalls and How to Avoid Them**: We discussed common mistakes and pitfalls in Go programming, such as nil pointer dereferences, unclosed resources, race conditions, inefficient string concatenation, and ignoring errors. We offered guidance on how to avoid these pitfalls and write more robust and reliable code.

By internalizing these best practices and optimization tips, you're well on your way to becoming a Go programming maestro. Remember, writing good Go code is an ongoing journey of learning and improvement. Continuously strive for clarity, efficiency, and maintainability, and leverage the tools and techniques at your disposal to create Go programs that are not only functional but also elegant, performant, and a joy to work with.

In the next section of the book, we will embark on exciting real-world projects, applying the knowledge and skills you've acquired to build practical applications. From command-line tools to web servers and chat applications, you'll witness the power and versatility of Go in action. Get ready to transform your ideas into reality and build impressive projects that showcase your Go programming mastery!

Section VII:
Building Real-World Applications

Building a CLI Tool with Go

Outline

- Introduction to CLI Tools
- The `flag` Package
- Parsing Command-Line Arguments
- Handling Flags and Options
- Structuring CLI Applications
- Handling User Input and Output
- Error Handling and User Feedback
- Testing CLI Applications
- Advanced CLI Techniques
- Chapter Summary

Introduction to CLI Tools

In the digital age, where automation and efficiency are paramount, Command-Line Interface (CLI) tools stand as indispensable companions for developers and power users alike. They offer a text-based interface for interacting with computer systems, executing commands, and managing tasks, all through the power of the terminal or command prompt. CLI tools have been instrumental in shaping the computing landscape, from the early days of Unix to the modern world of DevOps and cloud infrastructure management.

The Importance of CLI Tools

1. **Automation:** CLI tools excel at automating repetitive tasks, freeing you from the tedium of manual execution. Whether it's compiling code, running tests, deploying applications, or managing system configurations, CLI tools empower you to streamline your workflow and boost productivity.
2. **System Interaction:** CLI tools provide a direct and powerful way to interact with your operating system, file system, network, and other system-level components. They allow you to perform a wide range of operations, from creating and managing files and directories to executing system commands and configuring network settings.
3. **Command-Line Interfaces for Applications:** Many applications, especially developer tools, server applications, and system utilities, offer CLI interfaces to provide fine-grained control and access to advanced features. CLI tools can be used to manage databases, interact with cloud services, control version control systems, and much more.

Why Build CLI Tools with Go?

Go's unique blend of features makes it a compelling choice for building CLI tools.

1. **Cross-Platform Compatibility:** Go's compilation process produces statically linked binaries that can run on various operating systems and architectures without external dependencies. This makes

it easy to distribute and install your CLI tools, ensuring they work seamlessly across different environments.
2. **Performance and Efficiency:** Go's compiled nature and efficient memory management result in fast and lightweight executables. This is crucial for CLI tools, which are often expected to perform tasks quickly and with minimal resource overhead.
3. **Rich Standard Library:** Go's standard library offers a wealth of packages for handling I/O, file system operations, network communication, and other tasks commonly required in CLI tools. This reduces the need for external dependencies and simplifies development.
4. **Easy Distribution and Installation:** Go's compiled binaries are self-contained and easy to distribute. You can simply share the binary with users, and they can run it without needing to install Go or any additional libraries.

Key Points

- CLI tools are text-based interfaces for interacting with systems and automating tasks
- They are essential for automation, system interaction, and providing command-line interfaces for applications.
- Go is well-suited for building CLI tools due to its cross-platform compatibility, performance, rich standard library, and easy distribution.

In the following sections, we'll explore the `flag` package, Go's built-in library for parsing command-line arguments, and dive into the practical aspects of building CLI tools with Go. Get ready to unleash the power of the command line and create efficient and versatile tools that streamline your workflow and enhance your productivity!

The `flag` Package

In the realm of command-line interfaces, where users interact with your programs through text-based commands and options, the `flag` package emerges as your trusty assistant. It is Go's built-in library for parsing command-line flags and options, providing a structured and convenient way to handle user-provided input directly from the terminal.

Think of flags as switches or settings that modify the behavior of your CLI tool. They allow users to customize the execution of your program, providing input values, enabling or disabling features, or specifying alternative actions. The `flag` package takes the raw command-line arguments provided by the user and transforms them into meaningful values that your Go code can understand and act upon.

The Role of the `flag` Package

- **Flag Definition**: It allows you to define various types of flags, such as strings, integers, booleans, and more, each associated with a name and a default value.
- **Argument Parsing**: It parses the command-line arguments provided by the user, extracting the values for the defined flags and storing them in corresponding variables.
- **Usage Information**: It can automatically generate and display helpful usage messages that guide users on how to use your CLI tool correctly, including the available flags and their descriptions.
- **Flexibility**: It offers flexibility in defining flag names (short and long forms), setting default values, marking flags as required, and handling custom flag parsing logic for more complex scenarios

In essence

The `flag` package acts as the interpreter between the user's command-line input and your Go program's logic. It simplifies the process of handling user-provided options, making it easier to create user-friendly and configurable CLI tools.

Parsing Command-Line Arguments

Let's delve into the practical aspects of using the `flag` package to define, parse, and handle command-line arguments in your Go CLI tools. We'll explore how to define flags of various types, parse the user's input, and provide helpful usage messages.

Defining Flags

The `flag` package provides a set of functions for defining flags of different data types.

- **`flag.String(name, value, usage string) *string`**: Defines a string flag with the specified name, default value, and usage description. It returns a pointer to a string variable that will hold the parsed flag value.
- **`flag.Int(name, value, usage string) *int`**: Defines an integer flag.
- **`flag.Bool(name, value, usage string) *bool`**: Defines a boolean flag

Example:

```go
var name string
var age int
var verbose bool

func init() {
    flag.StringVar(&name, "name", "Guest", "Name of the user")
    flag.IntVar(&age, "age", 0, "Age of the user")
    flag.BoolVar(&verbose, "verbose", false, "Enable verbose output")
}
```

In this example, we define three flags:

- `-name`: A string flag with the default value "Guest"
- `-age`: An integer flag with the default value 0
- `-verbose`: A boolean flag with the default value `false`

Parsing Arguments: `flag.Parse()`

After defining your flags, you need to call `flag.Parse()` to parse the command-line arguments and populate the flag variables with the values provided by the user.

```go
func main() {
    // ... define flags ...

    flag.Parse() // Parse the command-line arguments

    fmt.Println("Name:", name)
    fmt.Println("Age:", age)
    fmt.Println("Verbose:", verbose)
}
```

Providing Usage Information: `flag.Usage()`

The `flag.Usage()` function prints a helpful usage message to the console, guiding users on how to use your CLI tool correctly. It automatically includes the defined flags, their default values, and their usage descriptions

- **Automatic Trigger**: `flag.Usage()` is automatically called when the user provides invalid or unrecognized flags
- **Custom Trigger**: You can also call `flag.Usage()` explicitly within your code to display the usage message whenever you deem it necessary

Example:

If the user runs your program with an invalid flag (e.g., `./myprogram -invalid`), the following usage message will be printed:

```
Usage of ./myprogram:
  -age int
        Age of the user (default 0)
  -name string
        Name of the user (default "Guest")
  -verbose
        Enable verbose output
exit status 2
```

Key Takeaways

- Use `flag.String`, `flag.Int`, `flag.Bool`, and other functions to define flags
- Call `flag.Parse()` to parse command-line arguments
- `flag.Usage()` provides a helpful usage message

By leveraging the `flag` package, you can create CLI tools that are user-friendly, configurable and provide clear guidance to users.

Handling Flags and Options

Once you've parsed the command-line arguments using the `flag` package, you need to process the flag values within your CLI tool to customize its behavior and provide the desired functionality to the user. Let's explore some strategies for effectively handling flags and options in your Go code.

1. Conditional Logic Based on Flag Values

Flags often act as switches that control the execution flow of your program. You can use `if` statements or other conditional constructs to make decisions based on the values of the parsed flags

Example:

```go
if verbose {
    fmt.Println("Verbose mode enabled")
    // ... perform additional logging or output
}

if outputFile != "" {
    // Write output to the specified file
} else {
    // Print output to the console
}
```

2. Setting Default Values for Flags

When defining flags using the `flag` package functions, you can provide default values. These default values will be used if the user doesn't explicitly provide a value for the flag on the command line

Example:

```
flag.StringVar(&name, "name", "Guest", "Name of the user")
flag.IntVar(&port, "port", 8080, "Port number to listen on")
```

In this example, the name flag has a default value of "Guest", and the `port` flag has a default value of 8080

3. Handling Required vs. Optional Flags

- **Required Flags:** If a flag is essential for your CLI tool to function correctly, you can mark it as required using the `flag.Required` function after defining the flag.

    ```
    flag.StringVar(&filename, "file", "", "Input file to process")
    flag.Parse()

    if filename == "" {
        flag.Usage() // Print the usage message and exit
        os.Exit(1)
    }
    ```

- **Optional Flags:** Flags that provide additional functionality or customization but are not strictly required can be left as optional with default values.

4. Providing Informative Error Messages

When users provide invalid or missing flags, it's crucial to provide clear and informative error messages that guide them on how to use your CLI tool correctly

- **`flag.Usage()`**: The `flag.Usage()` function automatically prints a usage message that includes the defined flags, their default values, and their usage descriptions. It's automatically triggered when the user provides invalid flags.
- **Custom Error Messages**: You can also create custom error messages using `fmt.Errorf` or other error handling techniques to provide more specific feedback to the user.

    ```
    if port < 1 || port > 65535 {
        fmt.Println("Invalid port number. Please specify a port between 1 and 65535")
        os.Exit(1)
    }
    ```

Key Takeaways

- Use conditional logic to customize your CLI tool's behavior based on flag values
- Set default values for flags to provide sensible defaults when users don't specify values.
- Mark essential flags as required and handle missing or invalid flags with informative error messages.

By implementing these strategies, you can create CLI tools that are user-friendly, flexible, and robust, providing a seamless command-line experience for your users.

Structuring CLI Applications

As your CLI tool grows in complexity, maintaining a well-structured and organized codebase becomes increasingly important. A clear structure not only enhances code readability and maintainability but also makes it easier to add new features, fix bugs, and collaborate with other developers. Let's explore some effective strategies for structuring your CLI applications in Go.

The `main` Function: The Conductor

The `main` function, residing within the `main` package, serves as the entry point for your CLI tool. It acts as the conductor, orchestrating the overall flow of the application.

- Responsibilities:
    - **Flag Parsing**: Typically, the `main` function starts by defining and parsing command-line flags using the `flag` package.
    - **Subcommand Handling**: If your CLI tool has subcommands, the `main` function delegates the execution to the appropriate subcommand handler based on the user's input.
    - **Core Logic Execution**: For simple CLI tools without subcommands, the `main` function might contain the core logic of the application itself.
    - **Error Handling**: The `main` function should also include error handling mechanisms to gracefully handle any errors that might occur during the execution of the tool.

Subcommands: Divide and Conquer

For complex CLI tools with multiple functionalities, subcommands provide a way to break down the tool into smaller, more manageable units. Each subcommand represents a distinct action or operation that the tool can perform, and it can have its own set of flags and options.

- **Benefits:**
    - **Organization:** Subcommands help organize your CLI tool's functionality into logical groups, making it easier for users to understand and navigate.
    - **Modularity:** Each subcommand can be implemented as a separate function or even a separate package, promoting modularity and code reusability
    - **Flexibility:** Subcommands can have their own flags and options, allowing you to tailor the user experience for each specific command
- **Implementation:**
    - You can use third-party libraries like `spf13/cobra` or `urfave/cli` to simplify the implementation of subcommands in your Go CLI tools. These libraries provide a structured way to define subcommands, handle their flags, and generate usage messages.

Helper Functions: Encapsulation and Reusability

As your CLI tool's logic grows, it's essential to break down complex tasks into smaller, reusable functions. Helper functions encapsulate specific pieces of functionality, improving code readability, maintainability, and testability.

- **Benefits**
    - **Readability:** Helper functions make your code more readable by abstracting away implementation details and focusing on the core logic.
    - **Reusability:** You can reuse helper functions in different parts of your CLI tool or even across multiple projects, saving development time and effort.
    - **Testability:** Helper functions are easier to test in isolation, allowing you to verify their correctness independently.

Key Takeaways

- The `main` function acts as the entry point and orchestrates the overall flow of your CLI tool
- Subcommands help organize complex CLI tools into smaller, more manageable commands

- Helper functions encapsulate reusable logic and improve code readability

By adopting these structuring strategies, you can create CLI tools that are not only functional but also well-organized, maintainable, and scalable. A clear and logical structure empowers you to add new features, fix bugs, and collaborate with other developers effectively, ensuring the long-term success of your Go CLI projects.

Handling User Input and Output

CLI tools are not just about processing command-line arguments; they also need to interact with users, gather input, and provide meaningful feedback. Go's standard library offers various tools and techniques for handling user input and output effectively, enabling you to create interactive and user-friendly command-line experiences.

Reading Input from the User

The `bufio` package provides a convenient way to read input from the user through the standard input (stdin).

- **`bufio.NewReader`**: Create a buffered reader that wraps `os.Stdin` to read input efficiently.
- **`reader.ReadString('\n')`**: Read a line of text from the user, including the newline character.

```go
package main

import (
    "bufio"
    "fmt"
    "os"
    "strings"
)

func main() {
    reader := bufio.NewReader(os.Stdin)
    fmt.Print("Enter your name: ")
    name, _ := reader.ReadString('\n')
    name = strings.TrimSpace(name) // Remove leading/trailing whitespace
    fmt.Println("Hello,", name+"!")
}
```

In this example, we prompt the user to enter their name, read the input using `reader.ReadString('\n')`, and then print a personalized greeting.

Providing Output to the User

The `fmt` package is your go-to tool for displaying output to the user on the command line

- **`fmt.Println`, `fmt.Printf`, `fmt.Fprintf`**: Print formatted output to the console, allowing you to include variables, format specifiers, and other elements to create structured and informative messages.
- **Progress Bars**: You can use third-party libraries like `cheggaaa/pb` or `schollz/progressbar` to create progress bars that visually indicate the progress of long-running operations, enhancing the user experience.
- **Tables**: For tabular data, consider using third-party libraries like `olekukonko/tablewriter` to generate well-formatted tables that present information in a clear and organized way

Example: Progress Bar

```
import "github.com/cheggaaa/pb/v3"

func main() {
    count := 100
    bar := pb.StartNew(count)
    for i := 0; i < count; i++ {
        bar.Increment()
        time.Sleep(time.Millisecond * 50) // Simulate some work
    }
    bar.Finish()
}
```

This example demonstrates how to create a simple progress bar using the `cheggaaa/pb` library

Key Takeaways:

- Use the `bufio` package to read input from the user
- Use the `fmt` package to print formatted output to the console
- Consider using third-party libraries for progress bars and tables

By mastering these techniques for handling user input and output, you can create CLI tools that are not only functional but also interactive and user-friendly. Clear prompts, informative output, and visual feedback like progress bars can significantly enhance the user experience and make your CLI tools a pleasure to use.

Error Handling and User Feedback

In the realm of CLI tools, where users interact directly with your program through the command line, robust error handling and informative user feedback are essential for creating a positive and seamless experience. Unexpected errors, invalid input, or unforeseen circumstances can disrupt the user's workflow and lead to frustration. By anticipating potential issues and handling them gracefully, you can build CLI tools that are not only functional but also user-friendly and resilient.

Handling Errors Gracefully

- **Anticipate and Catch Errors**: Throughout your CLI tool's code, proactively anticipate potential error scenarios. Use `if err != nil` checks after operations that might fail, such as file I/O, network requests, or user input parsing
- **Error Types:** Leverage Go's error handling mechanism to categorize errors based on their underlying cause. This allows you to provide more specific and helpful feedback to the user
- **Graceful Recovery or Exit:** When an error occurs, decide whether to attempt recovery (e.g., retrying an operation, prompting the user for alternative input) or gracefully terminate the program with a clear error message

Example: Handling File Errors

```
func processFile(filename string) {
    data, err := os.ReadFile(filename)
    if err != nil {
        if errors.Is(err, os.ErrNotExist) {
            fmt.Println("Error: File not found:", filename)
        } else if errors.Is(err, os.ErrPermission) {
            fmt.Println("Error: Permission denied to read file:", filename)
        } else {
            fmt.Println("Error reading file:", err)
        }
```

```
        os.Exit(1) // Exit with a non-zero status code to indicate failure
    }

    // ... process the file data
}
```

In this example, we handle different types of file errors, providing specific messages to the user and exiting the program gracefully

Providing Informative Error Messages

- **Clarity:** Craft error messages that are clear, concise, and easy for users to understand
- **Context:** Include relevant context in the error message, such as the specific file or operation that caused the error
- **Suggestions:** Whenever possible, offer suggestions on how the user can resolve the issue or provide alternative actions

Example: Invalid Input

```
age, err := strconv.Atoi(input)
if err != nil {
    fmt.Println("Invalid age input. Please enter a valid number")
} else if age < 0 {
    fmt.Println("Age cannot be negative. Please enter a positive number")
}
```

In this example, we provide clear error messages for invalid age input, guiding the user on how to correct the issue

Key Takeaways

- Anticipate and handle errors gracefully in your CLI tools
- Use `if err != nil` checks and error types for targeted error handling
- Provide clear, contextual, and informative error messages to the user
- Consider offering suggestions or alternative actions to help the user resolve the issue

By prioritizing error handling and user feedback, you can create CLI tools that are not only functional but also robust, user-friendly, and capable of handling unexpected situations gracefully. This contributes to a positive user experience and enhances the overall reliability and professionalism of your Go applications

Testing CLI Applications

Testing is as crucial for CLI tools as it is for any other type of software. It ensures that your tool functions correctly, handles various inputs gracefully, and produces the expected output. In the context of CLI applications, testing typically involves two main approaches: unit tests and integration tests.

Unit Tests for Individual Functions and Components

Unit tests focus on testing the smallest testable units of your code, such as individual functions or methods. They aim to verify that each unit behaves correctly in isolation, given specific inputs and expected outputs.

- **Isolation:** Unit tests should ideally isolate the unit under test from its dependencies, using techniques like mocking or stubbing to simulate the behavior of external components.
- **Focus on Logic:** They primarily focus on testing the internal logic and algorithms within the unit, ensuring that they produce the correct results.
- **Example:**

```go
func TestCalculateAverage(t *testing.T) {
    numbers := []float64{1, 2, 3, 4, 5}
    expected := 3.0
    actual := calculateAverage(numbers)
    if actual != expected {
        t.Errorf("Expected %f, but got %f", expected, actual)
    }
}
```

In this example, the TestCalculateAverage function tests the calculateAverage function in isolation, verifying that it correctly calculates the average of a slice of numbers.

Integration Tests for End-to-End Functionality

Integration tests, on the other hand, take a broader perspective, testing the interaction between multiple components or modules of your CLI tool. They aim to verify that the entire system works as expected when different parts are combined.

- **Simulating User Interactions:** Integration tests often involve simulating user interactions with the command line, passing arguments and flags, and capturing the output to verify its correctness.
- **End-to-End Testing:** They focus on testing the complete flow of the CLI tool, from parsing command-line arguments to performing actions and producing output.
- **Example:**

```go
func TestMyCLI_EndToEnd(t *testing.T) {
    // ... set up test environment ...

    // Execute the CLI tool with specific arguments
    output, err := exec.Command("./mycli", "-flag1", "value1", "arg1", "arg2").Output()
    if err != nil {
        t.Fatal(err)
    }

    // Verify the output
    expectedOutput := "Expected output based on the arguments"
    if string(output) != expectedOutput {
        t.Errorf("Expected '%s', but got '%s'", expectedOutput, string(output))
    }
}
```

In this example, the TestMyCLI_EndToEnd function simulates executing the mycli tool with specific arguments and verifies that the output matches the expected result.

Key Takeaways

- Unit tests focus on testing individual functions or components in isolation
- Integration tests verify the end-to-end functionality of the CLI tool
- Use mocking or stubbing to isolate units under test in unit tests
- Simulate user interactions and verify output in integration tests

By combining unit tests and integration tests, you can create a comprehensive test suite that covers both the internal logic of your CLI tool and its overall behavior when interacting with the command line. This approach helps ensure the correctness, reliability, and maintainability of your Go CLI applications.

Advanced CLI Techniques

While the core concepts and tools we've explored provide a solid foundation for building CLI tools in Go, there are several advanced techniques you can employ to enhance the user experience, handle complex scenarios, and create more sophisticated command-line interfaces. Let's briefly touch upon some of these techniques:

Custom Flag Parsing

- **Beyond the Basics:** Go's built-in `flag` package handles most common flag parsing needs. However, for more intricate scenarios, you might require custom flag parsing logic.
- **Flexibility and Control:** You can implement custom flag parsing by directly working with the `os.Args` slice, which contains the raw command-line arguments. This allows you to handle complex flag combinations, nested flags, or flags with specific validation requirements.

Interactive Prompts

- **Guiding User Input:** For complex tasks that require multiple inputs or user choices, interactive prompts can guide the user through the process, making the CLI tool more user-friendly and intuitive
- **Libraries:** Several third-party libraries, such as `AlecAivazis/survey` or `manifoldco/promptui`, provide convenient functions and structures for creating interactive prompts, handling user input validation, and presenting choices in a visually appealing manner.

Progress Bars and Visual Feedback

- **User Engagement:** For long-running operations, providing visual feedback like progress bars or spinners keeps the user informed and engaged, preventing them from assuming that the program has stalled or crashed
- **Libraries:** Go offers various libraries for creating progress bars and other visual feedback elements, such as `cheggaaa/pb`, `schollz/progressbar`, or `gosuri/uiprogress`.

The Journey Continues

We encourage you to delve deeper into these advanced CLI techniques as you gain more experience with Go and embark on more ambitious projects. They offer a pathway to create CLI tools that are not only functional but also user-friendly, interactive, and capable of handling complex scenarios.

Remember, the command line is a powerful tool, and Go provides the capabilities to build CLI applications that are both efficient and enjoyable to use. By applying your knowledge and exploring these advanced techniques, you can create CLI tools that streamline your workflow, automate tasks, and empower you to interact with systems and applications in a powerful and intuitive way.

Chapter Summary

In this chapter, we embarked on a journey to explore the world of building command-line interface (CLI) tools with Go. You learned how to harness the power of the command line to create efficient and versatile tools that automate tasks, interact with systems, and provide command-line interfaces for your applications.

Here are the key takeaways from this chapter:

- **Introduction to CLI Tools:** We discussed the importance of CLI tools in automation, system interaction, and application interfaces, highlighting Go's suitability for building such tools due to its cross-platform compatibility, performance, rich standard library, and ease of distribution.

- **The `flag` Package:** We introduced the `flag` package as Go's built-in library for parsing command-line flags and options, enabling you to handle user-provided input in a structured and convenient way
- **Parsing Command-Line Arguments:** You learned how to define and parse flags of different types using functions like `flag.String`, `flag.Int`, and `flag.Bool`, and how to use `flag.Parse()` to process the command-line arguments
- **Handling Flags and Options:** We explored strategies for handling parsed flags, including conditional logic, default values, required vs. optional flags, and informative error messages.
- **Structuring CLI Applications:** We discussed effective ways to structure CLI applications, emphasizing the role of the `main` function, the use of subcommands for organizing complex tools, and the benefits of helper functions for encapsulation and reusability.
- **Handling User Input and Output:** You learned how to interact with users through the command line, reading input using the `bufio` package and providing formatted output using the `fmt` package or third-party libraries for progress bars and tables
- **Error Handling and User Feedback:** We stressed the importance of error handling and providing clear feedback to the user, demonstrating how to catch and handle errors gracefully and create informative error messages.
- **Testing CLI Applications**: We discussed strategies for testing CLI tools, including unit tests for individual functions and integration tests for end-to-end functionality
- **Advanced CLI Techniques**: We briefly touched upon advanced techniques like custom flag parsing, interactive prompts, and progress bars, encouraging you to explore them further as you gain more experience.

By mastering these concepts and techniques, you're now equipped to build your own powerful CLI tools with Go. You can automate tasks, interact with systems, and create command-line interfaces for your applications, all while leveraging Go's strengths in performance, cross-platform compatibility, and ease of distribution. Remember to prioritize code organization, error handling, user feedback, and testing to create CLI tools that are not only functional but also user-friendly, reliable, and maintainable.

In the next chapter, we will continue our exploration of real-world applications by learning how to create a simple web server in Go. You will discover how to handle HTTP requests, serve dynamic content, and build the foundation for more complex web applications using Go's `net/http` package.

Creating a Simple Web Server in Go

Outline

- Setting the Stage: Web Servers and Go
- Laying the Foundation: The net/http Package
- The "Hello, World!" Web Server
- Handling HTTP Requests and Responses
- Serving Static Files
- Basic Routing
- Going Beyond: Expanding Your Web Server
- Chapter Summary

Setting the Stage: Web Servers and Go

In the vast interconnected landscape of the internet, web servers play a pivotal role as the tireless workhorses that deliver web pages and handle client requests. They stand as the intermediaries between users browsing the web and the vast repositories of information and services residing on remote servers. When you type a URL into your browser, it's the web server that receives your request, processes it, and sends back the corresponding web page or data, rendering it seamlessly in your browser window.

Go, with its blend of performance, concurrency support, and a robust standard library, has emerged as a formidable contender in the realm of web development. Its compiled nature and efficient memory management lead to high-performance web servers capable of handling a multitude of concurrent requests. The built-in net/http package, a cornerstone of Go's web development capabilities, provides the essential tools and abstractions for building web servers, handling HTTP requests and responses, and creating dynamic web applications.

Go's Strengths in Web Development

- **Performance:** Go's compiled nature and efficient garbage collection mechanism result in web servers that are blazingly fast and capable of handling heavy loads.
- **Concurrency:** Go's built-in concurrency model, based on goroutines and channels, makes it exceptionally well-suited for handling concurrent requests from multiple clients, ensuring a responsive and scalable web server.
- **net/http Package:** The net/http package offers a comprehensive and easy-to-use API for building web servers, handling requests, routing, serving static files, and more.
- **Simplicity:** Go's clean and concise syntax leads to web server code that is easy to read, understand, and maintain, promoting developer productivity.
- **Standard Library:** Go's standard library provides a rich collection of packages for various web development tasks, such as handling JSON data, working with templates, and implementing secure communication protocols.

By leveraging Go's strengths and the capabilities of the net/http package, you can create web servers that are not only performant and scalable but also maintainable and easy to develop. In the next section, we'll dive into the net/http package and explore its key components, laying the foundation for building your own web server in Go.

Laying the Foundation: The net/http Package

The net/http package in Go's standard library is the bedrock upon which you'll construct your web applications. It provides a comprehensive suite of tools and abstractions that simplify the process of building web servers, handling requests, and generating responses. Let's delve into some of its key components:

1. **http.Server**
   - The Centerpiece: This struct represents an HTTP server instance. It holds the server's configuration, including the address and port to listen on, timeouts, and other settings.
   - Customization: You can create an http.Server instance and customize its behavior by setting various fields, such as Addr (the network address to listen on), ReadTimeout, WriteTimeout, and more
2. **http.Handler**
   - The Contract: This interface defines the behavior expected of any type that wants to handle HTTP requests. It has a single method:

     ServeHTTP(ResponseWriter, *Request)

   - Request Processing: Any type that implements this ServeHTTP method can act as an HTTP handler, receiving incoming requests and generating responses
3. **http.HandleFunc**
   - The Shortcut: This function provides a convenient way to register a handler function for a specific URL path (route). It internally creates an http.HandlerFunc that wraps your function and handles the request-response cycle.
4. **http.ListenAndServe**
   - The Engine: This function starts your HTTP server, making it listen for incoming requests on the specified address and port. It blocks the current goroutine, continuously accepting and handling requests until the server is shut down or encounters an error

Illustrative Analogy

Think of the net/http package as a toolbox equipped with everything you need to build a web server.

- The http.Server is the blueprint or foundation for your server.
- The http.Handler interface is the contract that defines how to handle incoming requests
- The http.HandleFunc function is a handy shortcut for registering simple handlers
- The http.ListenAndServe function is the engine that powers your server, bringing it to life and making it ready to accept requests.

With these core components in your grasp, you have the essential tools to create web servers in Go. In the upcoming sections, we'll demonstrate how to put these pieces together to build your first "Hello, World!" web server and explore more advanced concepts like handling HTTP requests and responses, serving static files, and implementing routing

The "Hello, World!" Web Server

Let's embark on our journey into Go web development by creating the quintessential "Hello, World!" web server. This simple yet powerful example will illuminate the core concepts of handling HTTP requests and generating responses using the net/http package.

1. Import net/http

We begin by importing the net/http package, which houses the essential tools for our web server.

```go
import (
    "fmt"
    "log"
    "net/http"
)
```

2. Define a Handler

A handler function acts as the bridge between incoming HTTP requests and your server's response. It receives the request details and crafts the appropriate response to send back to the client.

```go
func helloHandler(w http.ResponseWriter, r *http.Request) {
    fmt.Fprintln(w, "Hello, World!")
}
```

- `w http.ResponseWriter`: This interface provides methods for writing the HTTP response headers and body
- `r *http.Request`: This struct encapsulates information about the incoming request, such as the method, URL, headers, and body.

In this simple handler, we use `fmt.Fprintln` to write the "Hello, World!" message to the response body, followed by a newline character.

3. Register the Handler

We use `http.HandleFunc` to associate our `helloHandler` with the root path ("/"). This means that whenever a request is made to the root URL of our server, the `helloHandler` will be called to process the request and generate the response.

```go
http.HandleFunc("/", helloHandler)
```

4. Start the Server

The `http.ListenAndServe` function brings our web server to life. It listens for incoming requests on the specified address and port (in this case, `:8080`) and dispatches them to the appropriate handlers.

```go
fmt.Println("Server listening on :8080...")
err := http.ListenAndServe(":8080", nil)
if err != nil {
    log.Fatal(err)
}
```

- The `nil` argument indicates that we're using the default HTTP request multiplexer (we'll explore custom multiplexers later)
- The `log.Fatal` function is used to log the error and terminate the program if the server fails to start

5. Test in Browser

1. Save the code as a `.go` file (e.g., `main.go`).
2. Open your terminal, navigate to the directory where you saved the file, and run it using `go run main.go`.
3. You should see the message "Server listening on :8080..." printed in the terminal
4. Now, open your web browser and visit `http://localhost:8080`.

You should see the iconic "Hello, World!" message displayed in your browser, marking your successful foray into Go web development! This simple example demonstrates the core building blocks of a Go web server.

Handling HTTP Requests and Responses

In the dynamic world of web applications, the ability to process incoming HTTP requests and generate appropriate responses is fundamental. The *http.Request object in Go provides a gateway to access valuable information about the request, while the http.ResponseWriter interface empowers you to craft and send tailored responses back to the client.

Accessing Request Information

The *http.Request object, passed as an argument to your handler functions, encapsulates various details about the incoming request. Let's explore some key elements:

1. **Request Method: r.Method**
   - Reveals the HTTP method used for the request (e.g., GET, POST, PUT, DELETE).
   - This information is crucial for determining the intended action, such as retrieving data, submitting data, updating data, or deleting data
2. **URL Path: r.URL.Path**
   - Represents the path portion of the requested URL (e.g., /products, /users/123).
   - This is often used for routing requests to the appropriate handlers based on the URL structure.
3. **Query Parameters: r.URL.Query()**
   - Provides access to the query parameters included in the URL after the question mark (?).
   - Query parameters are typically key-value pairs used to pass additional data to the server (e.g., /search?query=golang&page=2).
4. **Headers: r.Header**
   - A map-like structure containing the HTTP headers sent with the request
   - Headers provide metadata about the request, such as the user agent, content type, and authentication information.

Constructing and Sending Responses

The http.ResponseWriter interface offers methods for building and sending HTTP responses back to the client.

1. **w.WriteHeader(statusCode)**
   - Sets the HTTP status code for the response.
   - Common status codes include:
     - http.StatusOK (200): Indicates a successful request
     - http.StatusNotFound (404): Resource not found
     - http.StatusBadRequest (400): Bad request from the client
     - http.StatusInternalServerError (500): Internal server error
2. **w.Write(data)**
   - Writes the provided byte slice (data) to the response body
   - You'll often need to convert your data (e.g., strings, JSON) to a byte slice before writing it
3. **fmt.Fprintln(w, ...)**
   - A convenience function that formats data and writes it to the response writer, followed by a newline character

Example: Time Handler

```go
func timeHandler(w http.ResponseWriter, r *http.Request) {
    currentTime := time.Now()
    fmt.Fprintf(w, "Current time: %s\n", currentTime.Format(time.RFC1123))
}
```

This handler function retrieves the current time and formats it according to RFC1123 before writing it to the response.

Key Points

- The `*http.Request` object provides access to request details.
- The `http.ResponseWriter` interface is used to construct and send responses
- Set the status code using `w.WriteHeader`
- Write data to the response body using `w.Write` or `fmt.Fprintln`

By understanding how to handle HTTP requests and responses, you're equipped to build dynamic web applications that can interact with clients, process their requests, and provide meaningful and informative responses.

Serving Static Files

Web applications rely on a variety of static files to create visually appealing and interactive user interfaces. These files include:

- **HTML (Hypertext Markup Language):** The backbone of web pages, defining the structure and content
- **CSS (Cascading Style Sheets):** Provides the styling and visual presentation of the HTML elements
- **JavaScript:** Adds interactivity, dynamic behavior, and client-side logic to web pages.
- **Images:** Enhance the visual appeal and provide context.
- **Other Assets:** Includes fonts, videos, and other resources that contribute to the user experience

Serving these static files directly from your Go web server simplifies deployment and eliminates the need for a separate web server or complex configuration.

The `http.FileServer` Handler

Go's `net/http` package makes serving static files a breeze with the `http.FileServer` handler. This specialized handler takes a directory path as input and serves files from that directory and its subdirectories, automatically mapping requested URLs to the corresponding files on disk

The `http.Handle` Function

To register the `http.FileServer` handler for a specific route or URL pattern, you utilize the `http.Handle` function.

- **Syntax:**

    ```go
    http.Handle(pattern string, handler http.Handler)
    ```

- **Parameters:**
    - `pattern`: The URL pattern to match (e.g., `/static/`, `/images/`)

- handler: The handler to be associated with the pattern (in this case, the http.FileServer instance)

http.StripPrefix: The Path Transformer

Often, you'll want to serve static files from a specific directory but avoid exposing the directory structure in the URL. The http.StripPrefix function comes in handy here. It removes a specified prefix from the URL path before searching for the file on disk.

Example: Serving Files from the "static" Directory

```go
package main

import (
    "fmt"
    "log"
    "net/http"
)

func main() {
    // Create a file server that serves files from the "static" directory
    fs := http.FileServer(http.Dir("static"))

    // Register the file server with the route "/static/" and strip the prefix
    http.Handle("/static/", http.StripPrefix("/static/", fs))

    fmt.Println("Server listening on :8080...")
    err := http.ListenAndServe(":8080", nil)
    if err != nil {
        log.Fatal(err)
    }
}
```

In this example

- We create a file server fs that serves files from the "static" directory.
- We register this file server with the route /static/ using http.Handle
- The http.StripPrefix function removes the /static/ prefix from the URL path before searching for the corresponding file within the "static" directory.

Now, if you have an index.html file within your "static" directory, you can access it in your browser at http://localhost:8080/static/index.html.

Key Takeaways

- http.FileServer creates a handler for serving static files from a directory
- http.Handle registers the file server with a specific route.
- http.StripPrefix removes a prefix from the URL path before serving the file

By leveraging these functionalities, you can seamlessly integrate static files into your Go web applications, providing the essential elements for creating visually appealing and interactive user interfaces.

Basic Routing

In the realm of web applications, where diverse URLs lead to various functionalities and content, routing emerges as the indispensable guide that directs incoming requests to their appropriate handlers. Think of routing as a map that associates specific URL paths or patterns with the corresponding functions within your Go web server, ensuring that each request is processed by the relevant logic.

The Essence of Routing

- **URL to Handler Mapping:** Routing establishes a clear connection between the URLs users access in their browsers and the handler functions responsible for processing those requests and generating responses.
- **Organized Structure:** It provides a structured and organized way to manage different functionalities within your application. This improves code maintainability and makes it easier to navigate and understand the relationship between URLs and their corresponding actions.
- **Dynamic Content:** Routing is fundamental for creating dynamic web applications. Different URL paths can lead to personalized content, user-specific data, or tailored responses based on request parameters, enhancing the user experience.

`http.HandleFunc`: The Simple Router

Go's net/http package provides a basic routing mechanism through the `http.HandleFunc` function. It allows you to register a handler function for a specific URL pattern, creating a simple yet effective way to route requests.

- **Syntax:**

    ```
    http.HandleFunc(pattern string, handler func(http.ResponseWriter, *http.Request))
    ```

- **Parameters:**
    - `pattern`: The URL pattern to match (e.g., /, /products, /users/{id}).
    - `handler`: The function that will handle requests matching the pattern.

Example

```
func homeHandler(w http.ResponseWriter, r *http.Request) {
    fmt.Fprintln(w, "Welcome to the homepage!")
}

func aboutHandler(w http.ResponseWriter, r *http.Request) {
    fmt.Fprintln(w, "This is the about page.")
}

func main() {
    http.HandleFunc("/", homeHandler)
    http.HandleFunc("/about", aboutHandler)

    // ... start the server
}
```

In this example, we register two handlers: homeHandler for the root path ("/") and aboutHandler for the "/about" path.

Third-Party Routers: Expanding Your Routing Capabilities

While `http.HandleFunc` is suitable for basic routing, more complex web applications often require advanced routing features, such as:

- **Path Parameters:** Extracting dynamic segments or variables from URL paths (e.g., /users/{id})

- **Custom Matching Logic:** Defining custom rules or conditions for matching URLs to handlers.
- **Middleware Integration:** Seamlessly incorporating middleware into the routing process.

For these scenarios, Go's ecosystem offers a plethora of third-party routing libraries, with `gorilla/mux` being a popular choice. These libraries provide a more flexible and expressive way to define routes, handle path parameters, and integrate middleware into your web applications.

Key Takeaways

- Routing is essential for mapping URLs to specific handler functions
- `http.HandleFunc` provides basic routing capabilities
- Third-party routers like `gorilla/mux` offer advanced features for complex routing scenarios

By understanding routing and its role in web applications, you can build Go web servers that respond intelligently to different URLs, delivering the appropriate content and functionality to users. As you progress in your web development journey, explore the capabilities of third-party routers to create even more sophisticated and dynamic routing mechanisms for your Go applications.

Going Beyond: Expanding Your Web Server

The simple web server we've built so far is just the tip of the iceberg in the vast ocean of Go web development possibilities. As you embark on more ambitious projects, you'll encounter scenarios where you need to generate dynamic content, handle user authentication, interact with databases, or consume external APIs. Let's briefly explore some of these exciting avenues for expanding your web server's capabilities.

Templates: Breathing Life into Static HTML

- **Dynamic Content Generation:** HTML templates empower you to infuse your web pages with dynamic content, tailoring the output based on data or user interactions.
- **Separation of Concerns:** Templates promote a clean separation between your presentation logic (the HTML structure) and your application logic (the Go code), making your code more maintainable and easier to update
- **The `html/template` Package:** Go's standard library provides the `html/template` package, which offers a robust templating engine for creating and parsing HTML templates.

Middleware: The Versatile Interceptors

- **Cross-Cutting Concerns:** Middleware functions act as interceptors in the request/response cycle, allowing you to add reusable functionality that applies to multiple routes or handlers
- **Common Use Cases:** Middleware is commonly used for tasks like:
    - Logging requests and responses
    - Authentication and authorization
    - Session management
    - Data validation and sanitization
    - Error handling and recovery
- **Modularity and Reusability:** Middleware promotes modularity by encapsulating common functionalities into separate functions that can be easily plugged into your web server's pipeline.

Databases and APIs: Connecting to the World

- **Data Persistence:** Databases provide a way to store and retrieve data persistently, enabling your web applications to manage user information, product catalogs, or any other type of structured data

- **External APIs:** Integrating with external APIs allows your web server to access a wealth of information and services, such as social media feeds, weather data, payment gateways, or machine learning models.
- **Go's Ecosystem:** Go offers a variety of database drivers and libraries for connecting to popular database systems like PostgreSQL, MySQL, and MongoDB. It also provides tools for interacting with web APIs, handling JSON data, and making HTTP requests.

The Journey Continues

As you continue to explore Go's web development capabilities, these advanced techniques and concepts will become invaluable tools in your arsenal. They will empower you to build sophisticated, data-driven, and interactive web applications that meet the demands of the modern digital landscape. Remember, the possibilities are endless, and Go provides the flexibility and performance to turn your web development aspirations into reality. So, keep learning, experimenting, and building, and let your creativity soar in the world of Go web development!

Chapter Summary

In this chapter, we took the first steps towards building web applications with Go, focusing on creating a simple yet functional web server using the powerful net/http package. We covered the following essential concepts:

- **Setting the Stage:** We began by understanding the role of web servers in serving web pages and handling client requests, emphasizing Go's suitability for web development due to its performance, concurrency support, and the net/http package.
- **The net/http Package**: We explored the key components of the net/http package, including http.Server, http.Handler, http.HandleFunc, and http.ListenAndServe, providing the foundation for building web servers in Go.
- **"Hello, World!" Web Server**: We guided you through creating a basic web server that responds with a "Hello, World!" message, demonstrating the core structure and functionality of a Go web server.
- **Handling HTTP Requests and Responses**: You learned how to access information from HTTP requests using the *http.Request object and how to construct and send responses using the http.ResponseWriter interface.
- **Serving Static Files**: We showed you how to serve static files like HTML, CSS, and JavaScript using the http.FileServer handler and the http.Handle function, enabling you to create visually appealing and interactive web pages.
- **Basic Routing**: We introduced the concept of routing, explaining how to map different URL paths to specific handler functions using http.HandleFunc. We also briefly mentioned third-party routers for more advanced routing scenarios.
- **Going Beyond**: We encouraged you to explore further possibilities for enhancing your web servers, such as using templates for dynamic content generation, middleware for adding reusable functionality, and integrating with databases and external APIs.

By mastering these fundamental concepts and techniques, you've built a solid foundation for web development with Go. You can now create simple web servers, handle HTTP requests and responses, serve static files, and implement basic routing.

Building a Chat Application with Go

Outline

- Introduction to Chat Applications
- Choosing the Right Approach
- Setting up the Project Structure
- Handling Client Connections: WebSockets
- Broadcasting Messages
- User Management and Authentication
- Data Persistence (Optional)
- Error Handling and Robustness
- Scaling and Deployment
- Further Exploration
- Chapter Summary

Introduction to Chat Applications

In today's fast-paced digital world, the need for instant and seamless communication has given rise to a plethora of chat applications. These applications facilitate real-time conversations between individuals or groups, transcending geographical boundaries and enabling instant exchange of messages, ideas, and information. From casual conversations with friends and family to collaborative discussions in professional settings, chat applications have become an integral part of our daily lives.

However, building a robust and scalable chat application is no simple feat. It presents several unique challenges that developers must overcome:

- **Concurrent Connections**: A chat application needs to handle a potentially large number of concurrent connections from users, each sending and receiving messages in real-time.
- **Message Broadcasting**: When a user sends a message, it needs to be efficiently broadcasted to all relevant recipients, ensuring that everyone stays in sync.
- **User Interactions**: Chat applications often involve various user interactions, such as joining and leaving chat rooms, sending private messages, or managing user profiles. These interactions need to be handled seamlessly and securely.
- **Scalability**: As the number of users and messages grows, the chat application needs to scale efficiently to maintain performance and responsiveness.

Go: A Natural Fit for Chat Applications

Go's unique blend of features makes it a natural fit for tackling these challenges and building high-performance chat applications.

- **Concurrency Model**: Go's built-in concurrency model, based on goroutines and channels, provides an elegant and efficient way to handle concurrent connections and manage the flow of messages between users.
- **Networking Capabilities**: The net/http package and its support for WebSockets enable real-time, bidirectional communication between the server and clients, essential for chat applications.
- **Performance**: Go's compiled nature and efficient memory management result in performant servers that can handle a large number of concurrent connections without sacrificing speed or responsiveness.

- **Simplicity**: Go's clean and concise syntax leads to code that is easy to read, understand, and maintain, even in complex chat application scenarios.

By leveraging Go's concurrency model, networking capabilities, performance, and simplicity, you can build chat applications that are not only functional but also scalable, reliable, and enjoyable to use. In the following sections, we will embark on a journey to create a simple chat application in Go, exploring the essential components and techniques involved in building such a real-time communication system.

Choosing the Right Approach

When embarking on the journey of building a chat application, the first crucial decision is choosing the underlying architecture that will govern the communication and interaction between users. Let's explore a few common approaches and their trade-offs.

Client-Server Architecture

- **Centralized Communication:** In the traditional client-server model, all communication flows through a central server. Clients (web browsers or other chat clients) establish connections to the server, and the server acts as the intermediary, relaying messages between users.
- **Advantages:**
  - **Simplicity:** Easier to implement and manage, especially for smaller applications or those with a limited number of users
  - **Centralized Control**: The server has full control over message routing, user management, and data persistence
- **Disadvantages**
  - **Single Point of Failure:** The server becomes a critical point of failure. If the server goes down, the entire chat application becomes unavailable.
  - **Scalability Challenges:** Scaling a client-server architecture to handle a large number of concurrent users can be challenging, requiring load balancing and other techniques

Peer-to-Peer (P2P) Architecture

- **Decentralized Communication**: In a P2P architecture, clients communicate directly with each other without relying on a central server. This can lead to improved performance and resilience, as the system is not dependent on a single point of failure
- **Advantages:**
  - **Resilience:** The system can continue to function even if some clients disconnect or become unavailable
  - **Reduced Server Load:** The server's role is minimized, potentially reducing infrastructure costs.
- **Disadvantages**
  - **Complexity:** Implementing a P2P architecture can be more complex, requiring peer discovery mechanisms, NAT traversal, and handling potential security concerns
  - **Message Routing Challenges:** Efficiently routing messages between peers can be challenging, especially in large networks.

Hybrid Approaches

- **Combining the Best of Both Worlds:** In some cases, a hybrid approach that combines elements of both client-server and P2P architectures might be beneficial. For example, you could use a central server for user authentication and presence management, while allowing direct peer-to-peer communication for message exchange in certain scenarios.

Focus for this Chapter: Client-Server Architecture

For the purpose of this chapter, we'll focus on building a simple chat application using the client-server architecture. This approach is relatively straightforward to implement and understand, making it a great starting point for learning how to build chat applications in Go.

In the upcoming sections, we will delve into the specifics of setting up the project structure, handling client connections using WebSockets, broadcasting messages, managing users, and addressing potential error scenarios. By the end of this chapter, you'll have a solid foundation for building real-time chat applications with Go and be equipped to explore more advanced architectures and features in the future.

Setting up the Project Structure

Before we dive into the code, let's lay a solid foundation by establishing a well-organized project structure for our chat application. This structure will help us keep our code modular, maintainable, and easy to navigate as we add more features and functionalities.

Core Files and Directories:

- `main.go`: This file will serve as the entry point for our server-side Go code. It will handle setting up the web server, establishing WebSocket connections, managing connected clients, and orchestrating the flow of messages.
- `client.html`: This HTML file will define the structure and layout of our chat client's user interface. It will include elements like the chat message display area, input field for typing messages, and any other UI components necessary for the chat experience.
- `client.js`: This JavaScript file will handle the client-side logic, including establishing the WebSocket connection to the server, sending and receiving messages, updating the chat display, and handling user interactions.

Additional Directories (Optional):

Depending on the complexity and features of your chat application, you might consider creating additional directories to organize your code and assets further:

- **static:** This directory can store static assets like CSS files, images, or other resources that your chat client needs to render the user interface.
- **templates:** If you plan to use HTML templates to generate dynamic content on the server-side, this directory can hold your template files

Example Project Structure:

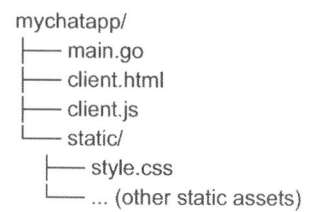

```
mychatapp/
├── main.go
├── client.html
├── client.js
└── static/
    ├── style.css
    └── ... (other static assets)
```

Key Points:

- Organize your project into logical files and directories
- `main.go` is the entry point for your server-side code
- `client.html` and `client.js` handle the client-side user interface and logic
- Consider additional directories like `static` and `templates` for organizing assets and templates

By setting up a well-organized project structure from the beginning, you lay the groundwork for a maintainable and scalable chat application. This structure will help you keep your code modular, making it easier to add new features, modify existing ones, and collaborate with other developers.

Handling Client Connections: WebSockets

In the dynamic realm of chat applications, where real-time, bidirectional communication is the essence, WebSockets emerge as the technological enabler. Unlike traditional HTTP, which follows a request-response cycle, WebSockets establish a persistent connection between the client (the user's browser) and the server, allowing for seamless and instantaneous exchange of messages in both directions.

This persistent connection eliminates the need for constant polling or long-polling techniques, reducing latency and enabling a truly interactive chat experience. In Go, the `gorilla/websocket` package provides a robust and user-friendly implementation for working with WebSockets, making it a popular choice for building chat applications and other real-time communication systems.

Upgrading HTTP Connections to WebSockets

The first step in establishing a WebSocket connection is to upgrade an existing HTTP connection. The `websocket.Upgrader` type from the `gorilla/websocket` package handles this upgrade process, ensuring that the client and server agree to switch from the traditional HTTP request-response model to a persistent WebSocket connection

- **Example:**

```go
var upgrader = websocket.Upgrader{
    ReadBufferSize:  1024,
    WriteBufferSize: 1024,
}

func upgradeHandler(w http.ResponseWriter, r *http.Request) {
    conn, err := upgrader.Upgrade(w, r, nil)
    if err != nil {
        log.Println("Upgrade error:", err)
        return
    }
    defer conn.Close()

    // ... handle WebSocket communication
}
```

In this example, we create an `upgrader` instance and use it within the `upgradeHandler` to upgrade an incoming HTTP request to a WebSocket connection. If the upgrade is successful, the conn variable holds a `*websocket.Conn` representing the WebSocket connection.

Establishing WebSocket Connections and Handling Messages

Once the WebSocket connection is established, you can use the conn object to send and receive messages.

- `conn.ReadMessage()`: Reads the next message from the connection. It returns the message type (e.g., text, binary), the message data as a byte slice and an error value.
- `conn.WriteMessage(messageType, data)`: Writes a message to the connection, specifying the message type and the data to be sent.

Example: Echo Server

```
for {
    messageType, p, err := conn.ReadMessage()
    if err != nil {
        log.Println("Read error:", err)
        break
    }
    fmt.Println("Received:", string(p))

    err = conn.WriteMessage(messageType, p)
    if err != nil {
        log.Println("Write error:", err)
        break
    }
}
```

This code snippet demonstrates a simple echo server that reads messages from the WebSocket connection and sends them back to the client.

Key Points

- WebSockets enable real-time, bidirectional communication in chat applications
- Use the `gorilla/websocket` package for WebSocket handling in Go
- Upgrade HTTP connections to WebSockets using `websocket.Upgrader`
- Use `conn.ReadMessage` and `conn.WriteMessage` to handle incoming and outgoing messages

By understanding how to establish WebSocket connections and handle messages, you've unlocked the capability to build real-time chat applications and other interactive systems in Go.

Broadcasting Messages

In the heart of a chat application lies the ability to broadcast messages, ensuring that every connected client receives real-time updates and stays in sync with the conversation. However, efficiently distributing messages to multiple clients presents a unique challenge in concurrent programming. Let's explore how Go's concurrency model and data structures can be leveraged to achieve seamless message broadcasting.

The Challenge

- **Multiple Clients:** A chat application might have numerous clients connected simultaneously, each represented by a separate WebSocket connection.
- **Efficient Distribution:** When a message is sent by one client, it needs to be efficiently distributed to all other relevant clients in real-time.
- **Synchronization and Concurrency:** The broadcasting mechanism must handle concurrent message sending and receiving from multiple clients while ensuring data integrity and avoiding race conditions

Managing Connected Clients

To facilitate message broadcasting, you need a way to keep track of all the connected clients.

- **Data Structures:** You can use various data structures to store and manage client connections, such as:
    - **Slices:** A simple slice can hold the WebSocket connections of all connected clients

- **Maps:** A map can store client connections using unique identifiers (e.g., usernames or session IDs) as keys

Broadcasting with Channels

Channels provide an elegant and efficient way to implement message broadcasting

- **Broadcast Channel:** Create a channel that all clients can send messages to.
- **Client Goroutines:** Each client connection is handled by a separate goroutine that:
  - **Receives messages from the client** and sends them to the broadcast channel
  - **Receives messages from the broadcast channel** and sends them to the client

Example:

```go
var clients = make(map[*websocket.Conn]bool) // Connected clients
var broadcast = make(chan []byte)            // Broadcast channel

func handleConnections(w http.ResponseWriter, r *http.Request) {
    // ... (upgrade HTTP connection to WebSocket)

    // Register client
    clients[conn] = true

    for {
        // Read message from client
        _, msg, err := conn.ReadMessage()
        if err != nil {
            // Handle error or client disconnection
            delete(clients, conn)
            break
        }
        broadcast <- msg // Send message to broadcast channel
    }
}

func handleMessages() {
    for {
        msg := <-broadcast
        // Send message to all connected clients
        for client := range clients {
            err := client.WriteMessage(websocket.TextMessage, msg)
            if err != nil {
                // Handle error or client disconnection
                delete(clients, client)
                client.Close()
            }
        }
    }
}

func main() {
    // ... (register handlers and start the server)
    go handleMessages()
}
```

In this example:

- The `clients` map stores connected clients.
- The `broadcast` channel is used for broadcasting messages

- The handleConnections function handles new client connections, registers them in the clients map and continuously reads messages from the client, sending them to the broadcast channel.
- The handleMessages goroutine continuously receives messages from the broadcast channel and sends them to all connected clients

Key Points

- Use data structures like slices or maps to manage connected clients
- Leverage channels for efficient message broadcasting
- Handle concurrent access to shared data structures using synchronization mechanisms if necessary

By implementing these techniques, you can create a robust and scalable broadcasting mechanism for your chat application, ensuring that messages are delivered to all relevant clients in real-time.

Remember that this is a simplified example. In a real-world chat application you'd likely need to handle more complex scenarios, such as private messaging, chat rooms, user presence, and message persistence. However, this foundation provides a solid starting point for building your own chat application in Go.

User Management and Authentication

In the realm of chat applications, where interactions between users are paramount, user management and authentication emerge as crucial components for ensuring security, privacy, and a personalized experience. User management involves handling tasks such as user registration, login, profile management, and presence tracking. Authentication, on the other hand, verifies the identity of users, ensuring that they are who they claim to be.

The Importance of User Management and Authentication

1. **Security and Privacy:** User management and authentication protect your chat application from unauthorized access and potential misuse. They help prevent malicious actors from impersonating users, sending spam messages, or accessing sensitive information.
2. **Personalized Experience:** By associating messages with specific users, you can create a more personalized and engaging chat experience. Users can see who sent each message, track online/offline status, and potentially customize their chat environment.
3. **Accountability:** User authentication provides a level of accountability, as actions within the chat application can be traced back to specific users. This can deter inappropriate behavior and facilitate moderation.

Potential Approaches

Several approaches can be employed for user management and authentication in your Go chat application:

1. **Simple Username-Based Authentication**
   - **Basic Implementation:** This involves storing usernames and passwords (hashed and salted for security) in a database or other storage mechanism. When a user logs in, the server verifies the provided credentials against the stored data.
   - **Suitable for Simple Scenarios:** This approach is relatively straightforward to implement and might be sufficient for small-scale or less sensitive chat applications.
   - **Security Considerations:** It's important to implement strong password hashing and salting techniques to protect against brute-force and dictionary attacks
2. **Integration with External Authentication Providers (OAuth)**

- **Leveraging Existing Platforms:** This approach allows users to authenticate using their existing accounts on platforms like Google, Facebook, or GitHub. It simplifies the login process for users and offloads the burden of user management and password security to the external provider.
- **Enhanced User Experience:** OAuth can provide a more seamless and convenient login experience for users, as they don't need to create and remember new credentials for your chat application
- **Security and Trust:** OAuth relies on established security protocols and can enhance the trustworthiness of your application by leveraging the security infrastructure of well-known platforms

Encouragement for Further Exploration

The implementation of user management and authentication can vary significantly depending on the specific requirements and security considerations of your chat application. We encourage you to explore these topics further and choose the approach that best suits your needs.

Key Points

- User management and authentication are essential for chat applications
- They ensure security, privacy, and a personalized experience
- Potential approaches include simple username-based authentication or integration with external providers like OAuth
- Choose the approach that best aligns with your application's requirements and security considerations

Remember that security is an ongoing concern, and it's crucial to stay informed about the latest best practices and potential vulnerabilities. By implementing robust user management and authentication mechanisms, you can create a chat application that is not only functional and engaging but also secure and trustworthy for your users.

Data Persistence (Optional)

While our basic chat application demonstrates the core concepts of real-time communication, it currently lacks the ability to persist chat messages beyond the server's runtime. If the server restarts, all messages are lost, creating a less than ideal user experience. To enhance the functionality and robustness of our chat application, we can introduce **data persistence**, allowing messages to be stored and retrieved even after the server restarts or crashes.

The Need for Persistence

- **Message History:** Data persistence enables users to access their chat history, even if they disconnect and reconnect later
- **Offline Messages:** It allows you to store messages sent while a user is offline and deliver them when they come back online.
- **Search and Retrieval:** With persisted data, you can implement search functionality, allowing users to find past messages or conversations

Potential Storage Options

Several options are available for storing chat messages persistently:

1. **Databases:** Databases, such as PostgreSQL, MySQL, or MongoDB, provide a structured and scalable way to store and retrieve data. They offer features like querying, indexing, and transactions, making them suitable for complex chat applications with large volumes of messages

2. **File Systems:** For simpler chat applications or prototypes, you might consider storing messages in files on the file system. This approach is less complex but might have limitations in terms of scalability and querying capabilities

Choosing the Right Storage Option

The choice of storage option depends on various factors, including:

- **Scalability Requirements:** If you anticipate a large number of users and messages, a database might be a better choice for its scalability and performance
- **Querying Needs:** If you need to perform complex queries or searches on chat data, a database with indexing and querying capabilities would be more suitable
- **Complexity and Development Time:** File-based storage might be quicker to implement for simpler scenarios, but databases offer more robust and scalable solutions for larger applications.

Integration with the Chat Application:

Once you've chosen a storage option, you'll need to integrate it into your chat application

- **Message Saving:** When a message is sent, store it in the chosen storage (database or file)
- **Message Retrieval:** When a user joins a chat or requests message history, retrieve the relevant messages from the storage and send them to the client

Key Takeaways

- Data persistence enables storing and retrieving chat messages beyond the server's runtime
- Potential storage options include databases or file systems.
- The choice of storage depends on scalability, querying needs, and complexity considerations

By adding data persistence to your chat application you can create a more robust and feature-rich experience for your users.

Remember: This section provides a brief overview of data persistence. The actual implementation will depend on your chosen storage option and the specific requirements of your chat application.

We encourage you to explore different storage mechanisms and experiment with integrating them into your chat application to enhance its functionality and provide a more complete user experience.

Error Handling and Robustness

In the dynamic and often unpredictable world of real-time chat applications, where connections can falter, messages can be malformed, and data inconsistencies might arise, robust error handling stands as the sentinel guarding against crashes, unexpected behavior, and a frustrating user experience. A chat application that gracefully handles errors not only maintains its stability but also provides informative feedback to users, fostering trust and confidence in its reliability.

Potential Error Scenarios

- **WebSocket Connection Errors:** Network issues, client disconnections, or server-side problems can disrupt WebSocket connections. It's crucial to handle these errors gracefully, notifying affected users and potentially attempting reconnection.
- **Message Parsing Errors:** If a client sends a malformed or invalid message, the server needs to detect and handle the error, preventing it from crashing the application or affecting other clients.
- **Data Inconsistencies:** Concurrent access to shared data structures or potential conflicts during message broadcasting can lead to data inconsistencies. Employ synchronization mechanisms and robust error handling to prevent and recover from such situations.

- **Authentication and Authorization Errors:** If your chat application implements authentication or authorization, handle potential errors like invalid credentials or insufficient permissions appropriately, providing clear feedback to the user.

Graceful Error Handling

When errors occur, strive to handle them gracefully, providing informative feedback to the user and taking appropriate corrective actions.

- **Error Logging:** Log errors to a file or a centralized logging system for later analysis and debugging. Include relevant context information like timestamps, user identifiers, and error details.
- **User Notifications:** Inform users about errors in a user-friendly manner. Use clear and concise messages that explain the problem and suggest possible solutions or workarounds.
- **Error Recovery:** In some cases, it might be possible to recover from errors gracefully. For example, if a WebSocket connection is lost, you could attempt to re-establish the connection or provide an option for the user to reconnect manually.
- **Fallback Mechanisms:** When critical errors occur or recovery is not possible, provide fallback mechanisms to gracefully degrade the user experience. For example, if message broadcasting fails, you might temporarily disable sending new messages while informing users about the issue.

Key Points:

- Error handling is essential for building robust and reliable chat applications
- Anticipate and handle potential errors related to WebSocket connections, message parsing, data inconsistencies, and authentication/authorization
- Log errors for debugging and analysis
- Provide informative and user-friendly error messages
- Implement error recovery or fallback mechanisms when possible

By embracing a proactive approach to error handling and providing clear feedback to users, you can create chat applications that are not only functional but also resilient and user-friendly. Your users will appreciate the seamless experience, and you'll gain the confidence to deploy and maintain your chat application knowing that it can gracefully handle unexpected challenges.

Scaling and Deployment

As your chat application gains popularity and attracts a growing number of users, ensuring its scalability and performance under heavy load becomes paramount. Scaling a chat application involves handling a large number of concurrent connections, efficiently broadcasting messages, and managing potential bottlenecks. Let's briefly explore some key considerations and approaches for scaling your Go chat application.

Scaling Challenges

- **Concurrent Connections:** Handling thousands or even millions of concurrent WebSocket connections can strain your server's resources.
- **Message Broadcasting:** Efficiently broadcasting messages to a large number of clients requires careful consideration of network bandwidth and server capacity
- **Data Persistence:** If your chat application stores messages persistently, the storage system needs to be able to handle a growing volume of data and provide fast read and write operations

Scaling Approaches

1. **Load Balancing:** Distribute incoming connections across multiple instances of your chat server using a load balancer. This helps spread the workload and ensures that no single server becomes overwhelmed
2. **Horizontal Scaling:** Increase the number of chat servers running in parallel to handle more concurrent connections and distribute the workload across multiple machines
3. **Distributed Messaging Systems:** For large-scale chat applications, consider using a distributed messaging system like Apache Kafka or RabbitMQ to handle message routing and broadcasting. These systems provide scalability, fault tolerance, and persistent message storage
4. **Caching:** Implement caching mechanisms to store frequently accessed data in memory, reducing the load on your database or other data sources
5. **Optimization:** Continuously profile and optimize your code to identify and address performance bottlenecks

Deployment Considerations

- **Cloud Platforms:** Consider deploying your chat application on cloud platforms like AWS, Google Cloud, or Azure, which provide scalable infrastructure and managed services for handling web applications.
- **Containerization:** Use containerization technologies like Docker to package your chat application and its dependencies into portable containers, simplifying deployment and ensuring consistency across different environments.
- **Orchestration:** For complex deployments with multiple servers and services, explore container orchestration platforms like Kubernetes to automate deployment, scaling, and management of your chat application.

Key Points:

- Scaling chat applications involves handling concurrent connections, message broadcasting, and data persistence at scale
- Potential approaches include load balancing, horizontal scaling, and using distributed messaging systems
- Consider cloud platforms, containerization, and orchestration for deployment and management

By understanding these scaling and deployment considerations, you can architect your Go chat application for growth and ensure that it can handle a large number of concurrent users while maintaining performance and reliability. Remember that scaling is an ongoing process, and it's crucial to monitor your application's performance, identify bottlenecks, and adapt your architecture as your user base and message volume increase.

Further Exploration

The simple chat application we've built together lays a solid foundation for exploring the vast and exciting world of real-time communication in Go. However, it merely scratches the surface of what's possible. As you embark on your own chat application development journey, we encourage you to unleash your creativity and expand upon this foundation to build more sophisticated and feature-rich experiences.

Here are some avenues for further exploration:

1. **Private Messaging:** Implement private messaging capabilities, allowing users to send messages directly to specific individuals or groups, fostering more intimate and focused conversations.
2. **Chat Rooms or Channels:** Introduce the concept of chat rooms or channels, where multiple users can gather and participate in group conversations centered around specific topics or interests.

3. **Message History:** Enhance the user experience by implementing message history persistence, allowing users to scroll back and view previous messages even after disconnections or server restarts
4. **File Sharing:** Enable users to share files with each other, adding another layer of richness and collaboration to your chat application.
5. **Rich Media Support:** Expand beyond text-based messages by incorporating support for images, videos, audio clips, or other forms of rich media.
6. **User Presence and Status:** Implement features to track user presence and display online/offline status, enhancing the real-time nature of the chat experience.
7. **Notifications:** Integrate push notifications or other mechanisms to alert users about new messages or events, even when they are not actively using the application.
8. **Moderation and Administration Tools:** For larger chat applications, consider adding moderation and administration tools to manage user behavior, enforce community guidelines, and ensure a safe and positive environment for all users.

The Path to Mastery

The journey to mastering Go programming and building powerful applications is paved with experimentation, exploration, and continuous learning. Don't be afraid to step outside your comfort zone, try new ideas, and push the boundaries of what you can create. The Go community is a vibrant and supportive resource, offering a wealth of knowledge, libraries, and frameworks to help you along the way.

Chapter Summary

In this chapter, we embarked on an exciting journey into the realm of real-time communication by building a simple chat application using Go's concurrency model and WebSocket capabilities. We covered the following key aspects:

- **Introduction to Chat Applications:** We started by understanding the role of chat applications in facilitating real-time communication and the challenges they present, such as handling concurrent connections, message broadcasting, and user interactions
- **Choosing the Right Approach:** We discussed different architectural approaches for building chat applications, focusing on the client-server model for our implementation
- **Setting Up the Project Structure:** We guided you through setting up a basic project structure for the chat application, organizing server-side and client-side code and potential directories for static assets and templates
- **Handling Client Connections with WebSockets:** We explored the importance of WebSockets for real-time communication and demonstrated how to use the `gorilla/websocket` package to upgrade HTTP connections to WebSockets and handle incoming and outgoing messages
- **Broadcasting Messages:** We tackled the challenge of efficiently distributing messages to multiple connected clients, using channels and data structures to manage connections and broadcast messages
- **User Management and Authentication**: We briefly touched upon the importance of user management and authentication in chat applications, suggesting potential approaches like simple username-based authentication or integration with external providers like OAuth
- **Data Persistence (Optional):** We discussed the possibility of adding data persistence to store chat messages and enable features like message history and offline messaging
- **Error Handling and Robustness:** We emphasized the importance of error handling in chat applications, particularly when dealing with WebSocket connections, message parsing, and potential data inconsistencies
- **Scaling and Deployment:** We briefly discussed considerations for scaling chat applications to handle a large number of concurrent users, mentioning approaches like load balancing, horizontal scaling, and distributed messaging systems.

- **Further Exploration**: We encouraged you to experiment, expand upon the basic chat application, and explore more advanced features like private messaging, chat rooms, message history, file sharing, and rich media support

By completing this chapter, you've gained valuable insights into the fundamental concepts and techniques for building chat applications in Go. You've learned how to leverage Go's concurrency model and WebSocket capabilities to create real-time communication systems that can handle multiple connections, broadcast messages efficiently, and manage user interactions.

Remember that this is just a starting point. The world of chat applications is vast and offers endless opportunities for innovation and creativity. We encourage you to continue exploring, experimenting, and building upon the foundation you've established here. With dedication and perseverance, you can create chat applications that connect people, foster communities, and make a positive impact on the digital world.

As we conclude this chapter, we invite you to reflect on the knowledge you've gained and the possibilities that lie ahead. We hope that this journey into building a chat application with Go has sparked your imagination and inspired you to create even more ambitious and impactful projects in the future. Keep coding, keep learning, and keep pushing the boundaries of what you can achieve with Go!

Appendices

Appendix A: Go Syntax Quick Reference

This appendix serves as a concise reference for essential Go syntax elements, providing a quick lookup for common language constructs and patterns. It is not an exhaustive list of all Go syntax but rather a handy cheat sheet for frequently used elements.

Basic Syntax

- **Comments:**
  - Single-line: `// This is a comment`
  - Multi-line: `/* This is a multi-line comment */`
- **Packages:**
  - Declaration: `package packageName`
  - Import: `import "packageImportPath"`
  - Import with alias: `import alias "packageImportPath"`
- **Functions:**
  - Definition: `func functionName(parameters...) returnType { ... }`
  - Call: `functionName(arguments...)`
- **Variables:**
  - Declaration: `var variableName dataType`
  - Declaration with initialization: `var variableName dataType = initialValue`
  - Short declaration: `variableName := initialValue`
- **Constants:**
  - Declaration: `const constantName dataType = value`
  - Short declaration: `const constantName = value`
- **Control Flow**
  - `if` statement:

    ```
    if condition {
        // ...
    } else if condition {
        // ...
    } else {
        // ...
    }
    ```

  - `for` loop:

    ```
    for initialization; condition; post {
        // ...
    }
    ```

  - `for-range` loop:

    ```
    for index, value := range collection {
        // ...
    }
    ```

- switch statement:

```
switch expression {
case value1:
    // ...
case value2:
    // ...
default:
    // ...
}
```

Data Types

- **Basic Types:**
    - Numeric: `int, int8, int16, int32, int64, uint, uint8, uint16, uint32, uint64, float32, float64, complex64, complex128`
    - String: `string`
    - Boolean: `bool`
- **Composite Types:**
    - Array: `[size]dataType`
    - Slice: `[]dataType`
    - Map: `map[keyType]valueType`
    - Struct:

    ```
    type structName struct {
        fieldName1 dataType1
        fieldName2 dataType2
        // ...
    }
    ```

Operators

- **Arithmetic:** +, -, *, /, %
- **Comparison:** ==, !=, >, <, >=, <=
- **Logical:** &&, ||, !
- **Bitwise:** &, |, ^, <<, >>
- **Assignment:** =, +=, -=, *=, /=, %=, &=, |=, ^=, <<=, >>=
- **Others:** & (address-of), * (dereference)

Concurrency

- **Goroutines:** `go functionName(arguments...)`
- **Channels:**
    - Declaration: `make(chan dataType)` or `make(chan dataType, bufferSize)`
    - Send: `channel <- value`
    - Receive: `value := <-channel`
    - Close: `close(channel)`

Additional Notes

- This quick reference is not exhaustive; refer to Go's official documentation for comprehensive details
- Go's syntax is designed for clarity and simplicity; prioritize readability in your code

- Use comments and documentation to explain the purpose and intent of your code
- Adhere to Go's naming conventions and best practices for clean and idiomatic code

This quick reference serves as a handy companion as you navigate the world of Go programming. Keep it close at hand to refresh your memory on essential syntax elements and conventions, empowering you to write efficient, readable, and maintainable Go code.

Appendix B: Go Toolchain Reference

This appendix serves as a quick reference for the essential tools and commands within the Go toolchain. These tools are instrumental in building, testing, documenting, and managing your Go projects. Familiarize yourself with these commands to streamline your development workflow and leverage the full power of Go's ecosystem.

Core Commands

- `go build`
    - Purpose: Compiles Go source code into executable binaries.
    - Usage: `go build [package]`
    - Common Flags:
        - `-o <output>`: Specify the output file name.
        - `-v`: Print the names of packages as they are compiled.
        - `-x`: Print the commands executed during the build process.
- `go run`
    - Purpose: Compiles and runs Go programs directly, without creating a separate executable.
    - Usage: `go run [file.go | package]`
- `go test`
    - Purpose: Automates the execution of test functions within a package.
    - Usage: `go test [package]`
    - Common Flags:
        - `-v`: Enable verbose output.
        - `-run <pattern>`: Run only tests whose names match the specified pattern.
        - `-cover`: Generate a test coverage report.
        - `-bench`: Run benchmarks.
- `go get`
    - Purpose: Downloads and installs Go packages from remote repositories.
    - Usage: `go get <importPath>`
    - Common Flags:
        - `-u`: Update an existing package to its latest version
        - `-d`: Download the package without installing it
- `go doc`
    - Purpose: Provides access to Go documentation from the command line
    - Usage: `go doc <package | symbol>`
    - Common Flags:
        - `-all`: Show all documentation, including unexported identifiers
        - `-u`: Include documentation from packages that are not directly imported

Additional Commands

- `go install`: Compiles and installs a package or command
- `go clean`: Removes object files and cached data
- `go fmt`: Formats Go source code according to the official style guidelines
- `go vet`: Performs static analysis to identify potential errors and suspicious constructs
- `go mod`: Manages Go modules (dependency management)
- `go env`: Prints Go environment information

Go Toolchain Ecosystem

Beyond the core commands, the Go toolchain offers a rich ecosystem of tools and subcommands for various purposes, including:

- `go tool pprof`: The Go profiler for performance analysis
- `go tool cover`: Tool for working with test coverage data
- `go build -race`: Enables the race detector to identify potential data races in concurrent programs
- `go generate`: Automates code generation based on special comments in your source code

Further Exploration

This appendix provides a brief overview of the essential Go toolchain commands. We encourage you to consult the official Go documentation and explore online resources for a more comprehensive understanding of the available tools and their capabilities. As you gain more experience with Go, you'll discover how these tools can streamline your development workflow, enhance code quality, and empower you to build powerful and efficient Go applications.

Remember that the Go toolchain is constantly evolving, with new tools and features being added regularly. Stay curious, explore the documentation, and embrace the power of the Go toolchain to unleash your full potential as a Go developer.

Appendix C: Further Learning Resources

As you continue your Go programming journey beyond the confines of this book, a vast landscape of knowledge and resources awaits exploration. The Go community is vibrant and active, offering a wealth of materials to deepen your understanding, expand your skills, and stay abreast of the latest developments in the Go ecosystem. This appendix serves as a compass, pointing you towards valuable resources that can fuel your continued growth as a Go programmer.

Official Go Resources

- **The Go Website (golang.org):** The official Go website is your primary source of information. It offers comprehensive documentation, tutorials, blog posts, and the latest news about the language and its ecosystem.
- **The Go Blog (blog.golang.org):** The official Go blog features articles, updates, and insights from the Go team and the community, keeping you informed about new developments, best practices, and upcoming features.
- **The Go Language Specification:** For a deep dive into the formal language specification, refer to the official documentation: https://golang.org/ref/spec

Online Courses and Tutorials

- **A Tour of Go:** This interactive tour provides a hands-on introduction to Go's syntax and features, allowing you to experiment with code directly in your browser. (https://tour.golang.org/)
- **Go by Example:** A collection of annotated Go code examples that demonstrate various language features and common programming patterns. (https://gobyexample.com/)
- **Effective Go:** This official guide offers insights into writing idiomatic and effective Go code, covering topics like naming conventions, error handling, concurrency, and more. (https://golang.org/doc/effective_go.html)
- **Online Platforms**: Numerous online platforms like Coursera, Udemy, and Pluralsight offer Go courses and tutorials, catering to different learning styles and skill levels

Books

- **"The Go Programming Language" by Alan A. A. Donovan and Brian W. Kernighan**: This comprehensive book provides a deep dive into Go, covering its syntax, standard library, concurrency model, and best practices.
- **"Concurrency in Go" by Katherine Cox-Buday**: This book focuses specifically on Go's concurrency model, exploring goroutines, channels, and synchronization techniques in detail
- **"Go Web Programming" by Sau Sheong Chang**: This book guides you through building web applications and APIs with Go, covering topics like HTTP handling, routing, templates, and database interactions.

Community and Forums

- **Go Forum (forum.golangbridge.org):** The official Go forum is a great place to ask questions, share knowledge, and connect with other Go enthusiasts.
- **Gophers Slack (invite.slack.golangbridge.org):** The Gophers Slack community offers real-time chat channels for discussing Go-related topics, getting help, and collaborating with other developers
- **Reddit (r/golang):** The Go subreddit is a vibrant community where you can find news, articles, discussions, and helpful resources

Open Source Projects

- **Explore GitHub**: GitHub is a treasure trove of open-source Go projects. Studying the code of popular projects can provide valuable insights into real-world Go usage, design patterns, and best practices.
- **Contribute to Open Source**: Consider contributing to open-source Go projects to deepen your understanding, gain experience, and give back to the community.

Staying Up-to-Date

- **Go Newsletters:** Subscribe to Go newsletters like "Go Time" or "Gopher Academy Blog" to stay informed about the latest news, releases, and events in the Go world.
- **Conferences and Meetups:** Attend Go conferences or local meetups to connect with other Go developers, learn from experts, and share your knowledge.

Remember, learning is a continuous journey. By actively engaging with these resources, participating in the Go community, and continuously challenging yourself with new projects and ideas, you'll continue to grow as a Go programmer and unlock the full potential of this powerful and versatile language.

Conclusion

Throughout the pages of "Go Programming Mastery," we've embarked on an enriching journey, delving into the intricacies of the Go language, from its fundamental building blocks to advanced techniques and real-world applications.

We began by laying a solid foundation, exploring Go's origins, syntax, data types, and control flow mechanisms. We then ventured into the world of functions, data structures, and custom types, equipping you with the tools to organize and manipulate data effectively.

As we progressed, we uncovered the power of pointers and memory management, enabling you to interact directly with memory and build dynamic data structures. We also learned how to handle errors gracefully and ensure the robustness of your Go programs.

The exploration of packages and interfaces revealed Go's emphasis on modularity, reusability, and code flexibility. You discovered how to organize your code into packages, leverage the standard library, and achieve polymorphism through interfaces.

Concurrency, a hallmark of Go, took center stage as we explored goroutines, channels, and synchronization techniques, empowering you to build high-performance and scalable applications that harness the full potential of modern hardware. We also delved into advanced concurrency patterns, providing you with the tools to tackle complex synchronization and coordination challenges.

The world of file I/O and web development unfolded as we learned how to read from and write to files, interact with web APIs, handle JSON data, and build web applications using Go's `net/http` package. You gained the skills to create command-line tools, simple web servers, and even real-time chat applications, showcasing the versatility and practicality of Go.

Finally, we explored advanced techniques like generics, testing, benchmarking, and best practices, enabling you to write reusable, efficient, and maintainable Go code that adheres to the language's philosophy of simplicity and clarity.

As you close this book, remember that the journey of Go programming mastery doesn't end here. The Go ecosystem is constantly evolving, with new libraries, frameworks, and tools emerging regularly. Embrace the spirit of continuous learning, explore new horizons, and challenge yourself to build even more ambitious and impactful projects.

We hope that this book has ignited your passion for Go and equipped you with the knowledge and skills to create exceptional software. Now, go forth and unleash your creativity, build amazing applications, and contribute to the vibrant Go community. The world of Go programming awaits your mastery!

Printed in Great Britain
by Amazon